Outrageous Invasions

Outrageous Invasions

Celebrities' Private Lives, Media, and the Law

ROBIN D. BARNES

OXFORD
UNIVERSITY PRESS

Oxford University Press, Inc., publishes works that further Oxford University's objective of excellence in research, scholarship, and education.

Oxford   New York
Auckland   Cape Town   Dar es Salaam   Hong Kong   Karachi   Kuala Lumpur   Madrid   Melbourne
Mexico City   Nairobi   New Delhi   Shanghai   Taipei   Toronto

With offices in
Argentina   Austria   Brazil   Chile   Czech Republic   France   Greece   Guatemala   Hungary   Italy
Japan   Poland   Portugal   Singapore   South Korea   Switzerland   Thailand   Turkey   Ukraine
Vietnam

Published by Oxford University Press, Inc.
198 Madison Avenue, New York, New York 10016

Oxford is a registered trademark of Oxford University Press
Oxford University Press is a registered trademark of Oxford University Press, Inc.

Library of Congress Cataloging-in-Publication Data

Barnes, Robin D.
   Outrageous invasions : celebrities' private lives, media, and the law / Robin D. Barnes.
      p. cm.
   Includes bibliographical references and index.
   ISBN 978-0-19-539276-0 ((hardback) : alk. paper)
1. Freedom of the press—United States. 2. Freedom of the press—Europe. 3. Privacy, Right of—United States. 4. Privacy, Right of—Europe. 5. Celebrities—Legal status, laws, etc.—United States.
6. Celebrities—Legal status, laws, etc.—Europe. I. Title.
   K3255.B37 2010
   342.08'58—dc22   2009044855

1 2 3 4 5 6 7 8 9

Printed in the United States of America on acid-free paper

Note to Readers
This publication is designed to provide accurate and authoritative information in regard to the subject matter covered. It is based upon sources believed to be accurate and reliable and is intended to be current as of the time it was written. It is sold with the understanding that the publisher is not engaged in rendering legal, accounting, or other professional services. If legal advice or other expert assistance is required, the services of a competent professional person should be sought. Also, to confirm that the information has not been affected or changed by recent developments, traditional legal research techniques should be used, including checking primary sources where appropriate.

(Based on the Declaration of Principles jointly adopted by a Committee of the American Bar Association and a Committee of Publishers and Associations.)

You may order this or any other Oxford University Press publication by visiting the Oxford University Press website at www.oup.com

Caroline Louise Margaret Grimaldi

*With appreciation for your strong sense of familial honor,
dignity and respect for the bonds of sisterly devotion*

Contents

Acknowledgments

I WISH TO ACKNOWLEDGE my research assistants Dan Estes and Lucinda Jacobs for their research, editorial comments and willingness to explore prescriptive elements throughout this project.

Howard Klemme, Professor Emeritus at the University of Colorado provided ongoing inspiration, and Chris Collins at Oxford University Press encouraged development of the project as it moved from a scholarly paper toward a concrete proposal for the manuscript.

Dean Nell Jessup Newton provided funding for sabbatic leave through the University of Connecticut Research Foundation. Dean Kevin Cole, at the University of San Diego Law School, provided generous summer research support for completion of the final stages and production of the teaching supplement used in a seminar titled *Privacy and Defamation in the U.S. and European Union.*

Introduction

CAUSE CELEBRE, THE FRENCH APHORISM for famous lawsuit or surprising legal victory, is the best way to describe the June 2004 ruling of one of the world's most respected courts.

As a matter of tremendous social and political importance, the international community owes a great debt to Caroline von Hannover, Princess of Monaco. Her longstanding determination prompted Europe's highest Court, in *Case of Von Hannover v. Germany*,[1] to radically alter the extent to which the media can arbitrarily disrupt the private lives of the rich and famous. The European Court of Human Rights' ruling in her favor signals a return to those universally recognized values that serve to distinguish the public and private realm, thereby sustaining the conditions which democracies rely upon to flourish.

Growing concerns about widespread immunity from liability enjoyed by tabloid publishers in the United States today prompted me to explore this topic. The book chronicles the experiences and the legal battles waged by celebrities both in the United States and European Union against an unrepentant press corps that continuously invades their private lives. Celebrities are routinely subjected to stalking, harassment, invasion of privacy, and defamation, in clear violation of their constitutional rights as citizens of this nation.

---

1. *Von Hannover v. Germany*, 2004-III Eur. Ct. H.R. 294.

This book offers analyses of the doctrinal developments in cases coming out of the United States Supreme Court and the High Courts of Europe to demonstrate that American celebrities are entitled to, but not receiving, the same protections as their European counterparts.

Citizens of the United States & European Union are guaranteed constitutionally protected rights to safety, privacy and freedom of self-expression. We outlaw the behaviors commonly attributed to journalists, editors and photographers under guidelines intended for cultivation of civilian life. The rules of social engagement foster the sense of community, mutuality and responsibility that are the hallmark of free societies. Specific cases are introduced for analyzing the avowed purpose of a free press, and the nature of privacy in a democracy. The evolution of the entertainment press and the emergence of "infotainment" as a news format led to expansion of concepts like "public figures" and "matters of public concern" in ways that all but eviscerate meaningful standards of protection for many individuals harmed by defamatory publications.

The book is designed to assist readers in and beyond the United States in identifying the universally recognized values that serve to distinguish public from private realms of authority, and the enduring commitments to the rules of civic engagement that tend to bolster democratic governance. The process of erecting institutional democracies requires legal enforcement of certain prerequisites, especially as they pertain to the social and psychological conditions secured by individual rights. As a matter of human right, every individual is entitled to protection for that sphere of privacy that guards familial dignity and shelters development of personal and political consciousness. This level of protection is a counter-force to socio-legal trends that disproportionately elevate such loosely-defined concepts as the "public's right to know." Legal developments in the European Union effectively secure personal power to shape the public images that represent who we are as free individuals. This work engages the debate about the historic and future role of the press, alongside the importance of preserving cherished rights of privacy in Western-style democracies.) The European Court of Human Rights has risen in international stature for its lucid articulation of important speech-related principles while setting rational boundaries when that freedom is abused by members of the press.

As the United States intensified its efforts to promote democracy world-wide, the quality of its own democratic institutions has come under closer scrutiny. Most significantly, freedom of the press as a core value has undergone significant change since the American Revolution. The changes wrought by the Civil Rights and Global Peace Movements included a series of cases starting in the mid-1960s, that granted the press consistently greater freedom. These developments enabled tabloid publishers to expand their cottage industry of disseminating the intimate details of the lives of the rich and famous. In the new millennium, there is disturbing evidence that the extension of protection to the tabloids led to a significant distortion of the public debate. This book explores the potential long-term effects of that expansion.

Chapter One examines *Case of Von Hannover v. Germany* as an introduction to successive themes in the international debates over media rights in relation to celebrities throughout the world. While highlighting the fundamental claims of Von Hannover in the European Courts, the chapter demonstrates how she became an internationally known figure. It draws attention to the artificial nature of legal classifications that casually combine those born into royalty, and those who actively promote their artistic or athletic talent with general public figures and government officials. As a member of Monaco's Royal Family, Von Hannover became a lucrative target for the tabloid press. The photos displayed and information revealed in the German publications that culminated in a ten-year struggle in that nation's courts provide an interesting contrast to the photos and information that first prompted heightened constitutional protection for the press. *Case of Von Hannover* balances the competing constitutional interests in ways that underscore why privacy is pre-requisite in constitutional democracies.

Analyzing the basis for the ultimate ruling in her favor is an important starting point for the book.

Chapter Two, *Celebrities of the World Unauthorized,* illustrates the nature of media invasion. The vast array of law suits evince a clear pattern in which the tabloid press has made sport of humiliating and disparaging celebrities without any regard for their safety, privacy or familial dignity. Entertainment media, and the photographers they employ increasingly engage in stalking, harassment, unlawful detention, and infliction of emotional distress. There appear to be virtually no boundaries to what they can print, in a nation where *tell-all* bloggers are outnumbered only by Americans all-too-willing to hit the talk-show circuit, exposing family secrets and showcasing deviant behaviors, all in exchange for 15 minutes of sympathy, fame, or revenge. Tabloid publishers freely manufacture factoids from unnamed sources, and use paparazzi to create "news" by provoking confrontations that force celebrities to defend themselves. Thus, today's celebrities are caught in a morality-free zone, even as *truth* has become the rallying cry and primary defense offered by the "entertainment press".

Chapter Three, *Public Media, the Quintessential Role of a Free Press,* chronicles the history of free speech, expression and association in the United States and the rationale for guaranteeing freedom to the press in a democratic society, alongside rules governing malicious, scandalous and defamatory publications. The special protections afforded to the press are explored through its characterization as a "Fourth Estate," owing its existence to the desire for a mechanism outside of governmental control as an additional check on the three official branches.

Chapter Four, *Nature of Privacy in the Hierarchy of Fundamental Rights,* provides a fascinating look at historical conceptions of privacy and the primary basis for its protection. Those who fought for and defended the U.S. Constitution linked these concepts to the dignity and honor of the individual, as a key component of a functioning and sustainable democracy. This chapter highlights traditional arguments for allowing an individual to determine the extent to which their thoughts, sentiments and emotions would be communicated to others. Links between privacy, choice, reputation and democracy have been explicitly acknowledged and protected by the European Court of Human Rights in the post-modern era. European law protects reputation and privacy surrounding the development of one's personal and political consciousness in order to "safeguard the essential dignity and worth of every human being."[2]

Chapter Five, *Emergence of Infotainment*, analyzes the rise of sensationalism in public media and the influence of tabloid media on public discourse. Courts have taken judicial notice of the fact that dissemination of information in an entertainment format might be more effective for alerting an audience to information they consider to be important or interesting. The fact that comedic entertainment has played a crucial role in the dissemination of information and formation of opinions in the political realm is certainly noteworthy. The unanswered question is whether blanket protection for opinion, parody and political satire serves the public interest and how we might fashion an appropriate means of judicial inquiry in relation to such material. A jurists' obligation to examine which of the essentially private matters seized upon by the entertainment press are essential to the public welfare may be the only check upon profiteering machinations of an info-taining press corps.

Chapters Six, *Public Figures or Public Property*, illustrates the sources of difficulty in articulating a legally cognizable "public interest" in the lives of those whose natural, artistic, and athletic talent, or circumstances of birth or lineage have thrust them into the lime light. By juxtaposing our conception of public figures in the United States with our treatment of and rules surrounding access

---

2. European Union, *Charter of Fundamental Rights of the European Union*, Article 1, Human Dignity, 7 December 2000. Official Journal of the European Communities, 18 December 2000 (2000/C 364/01).

to public property, we recognize that the category of public figure is ill-defined. Treating every celebrity as a general public figure, has given way to a remorseless brand of media invasion into their personal lives and the lives of ordinary citizens that are supposedly involved in "matters of public concern."

Chapter Seven, *U.S. Supreme Court's Normative View of Media Invasion,* explores the doctrines established by the Court from the 1960s, when courts began excluding large numbers of individuals from the reach of legitimate constitutional and statutory protections through the widespread imposition of the "actual malice" standard, first articulated in the landmark case of *New York Times v. Sullivan.*[3] There the Court expressed the need for constitutionally mandated breathing space to make way for the practical elements involved in securing freedom for the press. The *Sullivan* ruling voided a huge damage award that was designed to bankrupt the nation's major news organizations for only slightly erroneous reports that were critical of official abuse of power in the discharge of public duties. Contrary to the obvious jurisprudential purpose highlighted by the unique facts of that case, the wholesale extension of the doctrine to nearly every subsequent defamation case has attenuated individual rights in the realms of both privacy and defamation, contrary to the equal protection mandate of the Fourteenth Amendment to the U.S. Constitution. Undue protection for media broadcasters against legitimate claims of false reporting, defamation, and disclosure of true information in a false light, invites rather than punishes such invasions, even as it erodes our larger commitment to the goals of democratic processes.

Chapter Eight, *European Courts' Balanced Response to Media Invasion,* examines the clear and prudent departure of Europe's Highest Court from American media-privacy law norms. Relevant provisions of European Law relate human dignity and rights not only to the free development of personality, but also to respect for

---

3. *New York Times Co. v. Sullivan,* 376 U.S. 254 (1964).

private and family life. The balancing of interests undertaken by European Justices to resolve tension between privacy and free speech in a democratic nation, represent significant and welcomed developments that recognize the high importance of free media and communication in a democracy, without giving the press presumptive priority. This approach is more comprehensive insofar as it provides judicial recognition of the injuries that stem from the interaction between distinct kinds of intrusions upon privacy, and because it affirms appropriate measures proposed by the Assembly in calling upon the governments of the member States to meet with national organizations of journalists. Thus, a combined focus on the regulatory apparatus and insuring simplified legal processes for dealing with press offenses to ensure that victims' rights are better protected, guards familial dignity, shelters development of personal and political consciousness, and secures personal power to shape the public images that represent who we are as free individuals.

Chapter Nine, *Undue Burden on Celebrity Speech and Association*, explores the roles of celebrity citizens in shaping civic norms. Many celebrities have paid a heavy price for their political activism. Their support of change in cultural norms has often produced a fierce battleground over control and distribution of their private information. This chapter explores the possible chilling effect of this development on the willingness of others to speak out on political issues, and the impact on the American public.

Chapter Ten, *John Lennon and Michael Jackson*, offers insight into governmental fears around the influence of superstars. This chapter analyzes the social and political messages of these mega stars, and the threat that each posed to government's ability to influence public opinion.

Chapter Eleven, *Nascent Influence on American Democracy*, highlights basic trends arising from our current state of affairs, noting how extension of First Amendments freedoms coupled with corporate monopolies have supported gradual erosion in the effectiveness of news media, the only institution that enables meaningful public participation for purposes of influencing government actors.

The book concludes by demonstrating the nexus between disintegration of privacy rights and the weakening of democratic institutions. This work represents the first comprehensive attempt by a scholar of constitutional democracy to address problems in the laws of defamation and invasion of privacy by the entertainment press from a comparative law perspective.

The supplement to this book, titled *Privacy and Defamation in the U.S. and European Union,* contain cases, statutory materials, codes, legal articles, and popular news stories for use along with the book as the core reading in related courses, and an electronic teaching manual for planning and preparation.

ONE

Case of Von Hannover v. Germany

※ The Royal House of Monaco

Princess Caroline of Monaco has been the subject of enormous media attention since the moment of her birth. There are many ways to describe the public's interest in her story. An objective observer would recognize its idyllic origins in a genre that initiates an intertextual play on the phrase *Once Upon a Time* . . . "Europe's oldest dynasty was founded in 1215, when wealthy Genoese merchant Rainier Grimaldi established a fortress on the rock that was to become the heart of the principality."[1]

Like an artistic creation, Caroline's life has been framed by the media as a mere sequel to one of "Hollywood's Greatest Love Stories." She is, after all, the daughter of the late Prince Rainier III of Monaco and the late American actress Grace Kelly. Media accounts of the romance between her parents are nothing short of a "real-life" fairy tale. Indeed, ask anyone over 70 what it was like to have an American Princess on the international stage.

As an absolute monarch, the Sovereign Prince Rainier III was among the world's most eligible bachelors when he married Grace Kelly. Kelly, already a beloved Hollywood actress spawned by Philadelphia's elite, became Princess of Monaco when she joined Europe's longest reigning monarchy. The Grimaldi Family has ruled the tiny nation for over 700 years. The fiercely independent

---

1. Anne Edwards, The Grimaldis of Monaco (1992).

principality of Monaco gleams like a diamond above the Mediterranean and has been characterized "as the jewel in the crown of Europe's lush Cote D'Azure."[2] Prince Rainier reportedly declared that Grace Kelly was "the manifestation of all that we hope for and dream about Monaco."[3]

Kelly was born in Philadelphia in 1929. She attended the American Academy of Dramatic Arts before her Broadway debut in 1949. She then moved to film and won the highly coveted Academy Award for Best Actress in 1954. On a trip to the Cannes Film Festival in France, she was invited to dine with Prince Rainier of Monaco. By 1956, the couple became engaged. The world watched in awe at what the media billed as "the Wedding of the Century!" MGM filmed the ceremony, which was highlighted with a 10-karat diamond. It was attended by Hollywood's elite and guests from every corner of the globe who showered the couple with cars and jewels. They then set sail for their honeymoon on Rainier's yacht, as His and Her Serene Highness, Prince Rainier and Princess Grace of Monaco.

The couple later celebrated the birth of three children: Princess Caroline in 1957, Prince Albert in 1958, and Princess Stephanie in 1965. Kelly lived with great style and influential presence, which proved useful in founding various charitable organizations that provided exceptional inspiration to the citizens of France and Europe. Her charismatic beauty, generosity, and fame made her a legend in her own time.

She died in an automobile accident during September of 1982. Prince Rainier passed away during spring 2005.

The imprint Grace Kelly left upon the citizens of Monaco and on the world dais will never be forgotten. The adoration far surpassed

2. John Glatt, The Royal House of Monaco: Dynasty of Glamour, Tragedy and Scandal (1998).

3. J. Randy Taraborrelli, Once Upon a Time: Behind the Fairy Tale of Princess Grace and Prince Rainier (2003).

anything that Diana, Princess of Wales experienced, partly because Kelly would not have discussed her private life with members of the press and was not subjected to the same level of criticism or intense media scrutiny.

However, Kelly's daughters have had to live within the legend, abiding in the shadows, subject to the unique pressures and pains of 20th century media law that is quite unlike the golden era of worldwide adoration of their mother. "Back in the day," early media moguls, though interested in the "human side" of Monaco's royal couple, were forced to show restraint in what they reported. But Kelly's children came of age in an era where media restraint was indeed a thing of the past.

Photographed in France/Published in Germany

Caroline von Hannover's court battles with media defendants lasted more than a decade. The layouts and headlines over the course of her life are evidence of the facts of her case. The wholesale intrusion upon her privacy rights was wrought by persistent stalking by various photographers in search of grist for the gossip mill. Eventually, the controversy came before the European Court of Human Rights [ECtHR] which viewed the resulting publications and the methods used to secure the offending photographs from a holistic constitutional prospective. In *Case of Von Hannover v. Germany*, the ECtHR analyzed the specific context in which the following incidents occurred.[4]

---

4. The case originated in Application No. 59320/00 against the Federal Republic of Germany lodged with the European Court of Human Rights under Art. 34 of the Convention for the Protection of Human Rights and Fundamental Freedoms by Caroline von Hannover, a national of Monaco, on June 6, 2000.

🕮 Stipulated Facts

The subject of von Hannover's legal complaint was an exposé published in German magazines of her private life, coupled with as many as 43 photographs displayed over a lengthy period on front covers with various headlines and captions. The publications contained photos accompanied by the following story lines.

1993

"I Don't Think I Can Be the Ideal Wife for a Man"[5]

"Caroline and Melancholy"

"Her life is a novel with countless disasters"[6]

"Caroline with _____ & _____, her children"[7]

"Simple Happiness"

"It is a hot day this summer"

"Princess Caroline is canoeing with her daughter _____ on the Sorgues"

"This is a small river not far from _____, the village in _____ where Caroline lives"[8]

"From New York to London the rich and beautiful whisper about Le Style Caroline"

"A canoe instead of a yacht"

"A sandwich instead of caviar"

"Housewife Caroline Casiraghi"

"She loves to go shopping herself"

"Wednesday is market day"

---

5. Roig, *Ich glaube nicht, dass ich die ideale Frau für einen Mann sein kann*, BUNTE, Aug. 5, 1993.

6. This caption appears under a photo of Caroline von Hannover on horseback with the original caption reading, "*Caroline und die Melacholie. Ihr Leben ist ein Roman mit unzähligen Unglücken*" in *Ich glaube nicht, dass ich die ideale Frau für einen Mann sein kann*, BUNTE, Aug. 5, 1993.

7. *Vom einfachen Glück*, BUNTE, Aug. 19, 1993.

8. *Id.*

"Le Style Caroline is copied worldwide"
"Her strappy sandals in which she goes to the flower
market"
"Her pareo that she wears as a dress"
"Every Saturday evening table no. 3 (right of the entrance)
is reserved for Caroline"
"In the evenings, people sit in Sous les Micoculiers
& drink light red summer wine, Caroline and Vincent
are guests like the baker, the olive grower
or parish priest"
"Caroline cycles home"
"Her [house] lies at the end of the bumpy country
lane _____"
"The end of loneliness approaches"
"Le Style Caroline attracts the rich and beautiful"
"Lady Di is said to have authorised an estate agent to find a
plot of land . . . Julio Iglesias is searching too"
"Caroline's youngest, _____, 6 has bumped himself"
"Vincent and Caroline comfort him"
"Caroline's bodyguard is a woman"
"She even looks like the Princess"
"Mostly they go to the market together"
1997
"Caroline . . . a woman returns to life"
"THE KISS"
"They are not hiding anymore"
"Out and about with Princess Caroline in Paris"
"Prince Ernst August played fisticuffs"
"Princess Caroline fell flat on her face"

ℳ Motion to Enjoin Publication

Von Hannover first sought an injunction in the Hamburg Regional
Court against any further publication of the articles and photos by

German defendant Burda Publishing.[9] Her claim rested on the assertion that she has the right to protect her personality, access to her private life, and use and control of her image.

Invariably, the tabloid press has sought to document her every move in order to trade upon her name and image to increase sales of their product. The defendant publisher argued that Caroline von Hannover was a figure of contemporary society, and as such, her rights to protection of private life *stopped at her front door*. However, the defendant's failure to explain how the distinction between ordinary citizens and "figures of contemporary society" relates to the values sustained by a free press rendered its constitutional arguments vague, offering little more than a defense to an ordinary trespass charge.

In interpreting the Convention Articles as a whole, the ECtHR identified Article 8 of the European Human Rights Convention (which insures the right of the individual to be left alone) as the doctrine governing the facts of this case. This provision was balanced against Article 10, which protects free expression. Ruling in von Hannover's favor, the European Court drew a necessary distinction between reporting facts that are capable of contributing to public debate in a democratic society (particularly as they relate to politicians and the exercise of their functions) and reporting details of the private life of someone who exercises no official function. Where no contribution was made to any debate of general interest, the court held that free expression had to be given a "narrow interpretation." One judge warned that under American influence, it is all too easy to "make a fetish of freedom of the press."[10]

---

9. On Aug. 13, 1993, von Hannover sought an injunction in the Hamburg Regional Court (Langericht) against any further publication by the Burda publishing company of the first series of photos (1993) on the ground that they (1) infringed her right to protection of her personality rights guaranteed by Art. 2 § 1 and 1 § 1 of the Basic Law, and (2) infringed her right to protection of her private life and to the control of the use of her image, guaranteed by §§ 22 et seq. of the Copyright Act.

10. *Von Hannover v. Germany*, 2004-III Eur. Ct. H.R. 284 (Zupančič, J., concurring).

The applicable law in the United States is found in the First Amendment to the U.S. Constitution:

> Congress shall make no law respecting the establishment of religion, or prohibiting the free exercise thereof; or abridging the freedom of speech, or of the press; or the right of the people peaceably to assemble, and to petition the Government for redress of grievances.[11]

⁓ Coverage of the Verdict by U.S. Journalists

The sparse media coverage of *Case of Von Hannover* in the United States supports the fetish assessment and exposes what could be dubbed a "mindset of infringement."[12] It consists of blatant disregard for basic elements of personal privacy and individual autonomy, which are widening media trends in the United States and abroad. *USA Today* reported legal minutiae, such as publisher reaction, procedural history, cabinet decisions concerning appeals, and potential consequences if Germany fails to comply with the ruling—but nothing at all about the merits of the case.[13] Efforts to discount the significance of the constitutional issues raised were evident in the *New York Times'* characterization of the facts, namely, that the case was about "the publication of five photographs."[14] Articles about the case appearing in the European press also tended

---

11. U.S. CONST. amend. I.

12. Robin D. Barnes, *The Caroline Verdict: Protecting Individual Privacy Against Media Invasion as a Matter of Human Rights*, 110 PENN ST. L. REV. 599, 600 (2005–06).

13. Pascal Le Segretain, *Princess Caroline Photos Won't Be Published*, USA TODAY, Sept. 1, 2004.

14. Doreen Carvajal, *For the Famous, "Privacy" Even in Plain Sight*, N.Y. TIMES, Oct. 10, 2004, § 4, at 12.

to emphasize that they showed Caroline going about her daily routines.

Without discussing the nature of von Hannover's claim, most news sources promoted a one-dimensional view supporting the legitimacy of the original publications. According to the *New York Times* article "For the Famous, Privacy Even in Plain Sight," the photos were: "benign enough to fill a staid family scrapbook," "a pensive Caroline on horseback," "a blurry portrait of her in a swim suit"—in short, "a mundane collection of paparazzi photographs." [15] These characterizations are intended to alert the reader that the case was *much ado about nothing*. From the perspective of journalists in the United States, it was as if the European Court of Human Rights had overstepped some universally accepted boundary that separates true democratic institutions (i.e., those who enforce an elevated role for free speech in society) from those lacking in political will (i.e., those content to rely upon a pseudo-democratic façade).

This particular story's headline was calculated to draw attention away from the central arguments. Invoking the old class-struggle rhetoric, it emphasizes that "For the Famous" we find yet another set of unearned privileges. Summarizing the issues as being one of "privacy," "Even in Plain Sight?" reveals the media's general disposition toward entitlement. Even when assessing those who are merely capitalizing upon or engineering awkward and embarrassing moments purely for financial gain, the general tendency is to circle the wagons and demand constitutional cover for the publishing license. This treats all publications as a monolith and falsely presumes that litigation concerning the probative value of this issue is prohibited because every challenge could only reflect differences in personal tastes, beliefs, or opinion. Paraphrasing the late U.S. Chief Justice Roger Tanney: public figures have no rights which the press are bound to respect.

---

15. Jonathan Coad, *Europe: Public Image*, LAWYER, Aug. 2, 2004 at 17.

Without offering a single significant detail, the *Times* article concluded that "the so-called 'Caroline Verdict' is really about protecting the famed and fabled so that privacy, in theory, now exists in public spaces for high-watt stars who want to block publication of unauthorized photographs."[16] The article goes on to say:

> In the United States the press is much more clearly protected by the constitutional right to freedom of expression . . . But in Europe, the Court of Human Rights concluded that there are limits to how the press can meet the public's fascination with the daily lives of the rich and famous.[17]

Favoring unqualified intrusion without discussion of the merits of the case, America's premier outlet for printed news "informed" the public that it has a right to know and to be concerned that the rich are once again being given special privileges. It went on to suggest that, for now, it is really only a concern in Europe, because in U.S. courts, the very fact the public wants to know intimate details of celebrities' private lives offers enough justification under our Constitution to provide it to them. Thus we now have a cottage industry of daily radio programming with upbeat ditties inviting listeners to tune in for a daily dose of celebrity smack (down).

Long-Term Impact of the European Court of Human Rights Decision

Contrary to blithely ignoring the importance of a free press, the ECtHR concluded that although rights of free expression extend to the publication of photographs, this is precisely the area in which

---

16. Carvajal, *supra* note 14.

17. *Id.*

the protection of privacy rights and reputation takes on particular importance. Burda could hardly claim to be disseminating *ideas*—neither those of Caroline von Hannover nor anyone else. The defendant published images accompanied by narratives containing very personal information about an individual without her consent. These facts remain, even if the pictures were not shot in the hostile climate of the automobile chase where most tabloid photos are taken; the difference is a matter of degree rather than kind. Stalking is still characteristically defined as obsessive and predatory in nature, and celebrities are endlessly stalked by papparazzi.[18]

Caroline von Hannover spent years in unsuccessful litigation in the German courts trying to establish the right to protect her private life. She was hounded by photographers as soon as she left her house. The deprivation of privacy stemmed from her family's inability to move about freely without continuous observation by agents of the media. She was even unable to benefit from her choice to live in France, where her consent is required prior to lawful publication of any photographs taken outside of official events,[19] as the photos in question were shot in France, then sold and published in Germany. Thus, the protection of private life from which she benefited in France was methodically circumvented by virtue of the decisions of the German courts.

Although supportive of the essential role played by the press in a democratic society, von Hannover challenged the abuses of tabloid

---

18. *See generally* BLACK'S LAW DICTIONARY 1440 (8th ed. 2004).

19. *See* CODE CIVILE., art. 9 which provides "*Chacun a droit au respect de sa vie privée.Les juges peuvent, sans préjudice de la réparation du dommage subi, prescrire toutes mesures, telles que séquestre, saisie et autres, propres à empêcher ou faire cesser une atteinte à l'intimité de la vie privée: ces mesures peuvent, s'il y a urgence, être ordonnées en référé*" (Everyone has the right to respect for his private life. Without prejudice to compensation for injury suffered, the court may prescribe any measures, such as sequestration, seizure, and others, appropriate to prevent or put an end to an invasion of personal privacy; in case of emergency those measures may be provided for by interim order.)

publishers who unscrupulously sought huge profits from tracking her every move. It may make sense to describe the shots taken as mere photographs, which are mostly benign or downright mundane when arranged in the center of a conference table. Yet the contexts in which they were actually published render such descriptions less like naive distortions and more like *misinformation*.

Publication of a random group of photographs without narrative rarely satisfies curiosity, voyeurism, or the entertainment wishes of the public at large. Without the narrative, the overwhelming majority of the public may not even recognize those portrayed. When coupled with a derisive story line, the "mundane collection" leaves the press free to mix fact with conjecture; exaggerate comments from disgruntled associates, ex-lovers, or former employees; and offer comparisons out of context. The statements are defamatory in nature insofar as they diminish the esteem, respect, or confidence in which the subjects are held, thus inciting adverse and derogatory opinions about them. The relative gamble for the publisher surrounds the willingness of the target to fight in court to prove that the stories are false, thereby risking wider dissemination of the information that caused the original humiliation.

The articles that sparked the lawsuit against Burda did not prompt recognition of von Hannover's role in a matter of public concern. In *Case of Von Hannover*, the ECtHR declared that because the photos were not used to genuinely inform people but merely to entertain, use of another's image derived from scenes relating to private life requires prior consent.[20] There is a lawful exception allowing publication of photos taken of figures of contemporary society in the exercise of any official function. Europe's highest court properly recognized this distinction. In the United States, federal courts follow an altogether different standard in which voyeurism and curiosity about celebrities without much regard for intrusiveness or reputation is rewarded and protected under the

---

20. *Hannover v. Germany* [2004] ECtHR.

superficial genre of reporting known as "infotainment,"[21] a concept analyzed more extensively in Chapter Five.

It is relevant to note that some legal skirmishes reflect isolated instances of power struggles between celebrities and the press that include naked power plays, attempts at controlling a damaged public image, double standards for the wealthy, and/or jurisdiction over what is arguably part of the public domain. *Case of Von Hannover* is about something much deeper.

Caroline von Hannover was entitled, as a citizen of the free world, to a final word on basic questions of civil and human rights. These rights are universal in scope, belonging to those whom German courts characterize as "figures of absolute general interest"[22] as much as anyone else.[23] The general interest characterization is more precise than its U.S. counterpart ("public figures")[24], because the term implies a state of ownership and domain of the collective. The badges and incidents of popularity and notoriety that move individuals beyond the rank of mere citizens in the United States and toward lower standards of immunity from defamation and invasion of privacy are covered more extensively in Chapter Six.

Europe's figures of absolute general interest are defined as those "individuals who, by birth, professional position, or personal

---

21. *Infotainment* is the portmanteau of information and entertainment and refers collectively to electronic, print, and visual media.

22. *See* BverfG, Apr. 26, 2001, Order of the 1st Chamber of the First Senate: Photographic Reporting and Protection of Privacy, 1BvR 758/97, http://www.bundesverfassungsgericht.de/en/ decisions/rk20010426_1bvr075897en.html.

23. "[F]igure of contemporary society 'par excellence'" ("'absolute' Person der Zeitgeshichte") (*Von Hannover* at § II (c)(aa)). Alternatively, the word *Zeitgeshichte* may be translated as "contemporary history," thus making the phrase "absolute person of contemporary history" (*see* the Federal Constitutional Court, Order of the 1st Chamber of the First Senate on Photographic Reporting and Protection of Privacy, http://www.bverfg.de/ entscheidungen/rk20010426_1bvr075897en.html).

24. *See generally* Gertz v. Robert Welch, Inc., 418 U.S. 323, 331–35 (1974).

achievements, are exposed to increased public interest over a long period of time."[25] The ECtHR offered a salient analysis, consistent with the mandates of the European Convention, balancing the "public's right to know" with the question of jurisdiction over the details of von Hannover's private life. The American constitutional debate dances about issues of currency and relevance regarding the "public's right to know." The traditional association is steeped in procedures designed to insure government accountability. For example, the Freedom of Information Act "allows ordinary citizens to hold the government accountable by requesting and scrutinizing public documents and records. Without it, journalists, newspapers, historians and watchdog groups would [have difficulty maintaining government accountability]."[26] In logical sequence, the plaintiffs in *Case of Von Hannover* and similar suits question how "the public's right know" serves as sufficient justification for converting celebrity lives into ongoing reality shows.

There is no reasonable justification for giving the press free reign to broadcast von Hannover's daily schedules and habits. To announce to the world that she may be found here and there at particular days and times invites scrutiny and judgment about her personal choices. Offering digital images and directions to her home while displaying photographs of her children jeopardizes their growth and development and places them at serious risk for kidnapping. Illustrating the neighborhoods and roads on which she cycles alone effectively forecloses future opportunities for healthy exercise and peaceful reverie. Publishing photographs and descriptions of her bodyguard(s) presents a material danger.

The ECtHR correctly noted that Burda manufactured a series of articles without contribution to a debate of general interest.

---

25. Daniel Kaboth, *Germany: The Publicity of Privacy*, LEGAL WEEK, July 29, 2004, http://www.legalweek.com/Articles/120822/Germany+The+publicity+of+privacy.html.

26. Editorial, *The Day Ashcroft Censored Freedom of Information*, S.F. CHRON., Jan. 6, 2002, at D4.

The publisher defendant in *Case of Von Hannover* had urged the Court to consider that since the death of her mother in 1982, von Hannover had officially became first lady of the reigning family in Monaco and was as such an example for the public. As a member of the royal family, Caroline von Hanover is the president of certain humanitarian and cultural foundations (e.g., the "Princess Grace" foundation and the "Prince Pierre de Monaco" foundation). She also represents the royal family at events such as the Red Cross Ball. She does not, however, perform any function within or on behalf of the State of Monaco or any of its institutions.

Burda also attempted to lay blame on the Grimaldi Family, whom it claimed always sought media attention and was therefore responsible for the public's interest. However, this fact when coupled with her official functions would hardly convert Caroline von Hannover into a commodity for the press. She exercised no official function in need of public scrutiny, and every story related solely to her personal choices and private life. The publisher conceded that its articles and photos were published in order to satisfy the curiosity of its readership. As such, they could not be deemed relevant to a dialog of general societal interest, despite the fact that their subject is well-known to the public.

The ECtHR reasoned that the extent of von Hannover's "victimization" was not at issue, but rather her constitutional right to privacy under Article 8 of the European Convention on Human Rights. The right to "live one's own life with a minimum of interference" is enforceable against public and private actors and entities.[27] Media intrusion cannot be justified for an individual who excites the interest of the general public and the press based solely on her membership in a royal family when she is not exercising any official functions.

The ECtHR unanimously held in von Hannover's favor, ruling that the publications violated Article 8 of the Human Rights

---

27. *Von Hannover*, 2004-III Eur. Ct. H.R. 284 (Zupančič, J., concurring).

Convention by arbitrarily invading her privacy. The Convention is protective of a host of individual rights that reach far beyond the U.S. Bill of Rights, adopted shortly after ratification of the U.S. Constitution in 1788. Granting the plaintiff injunctive relief by preventing further publication of unauthorized material was an excellent place for the ECtHR to begin. The court also artfully avoided the circular debates about the circumstances leading to publication and the undiscoverable aspects of publisher motive. Instead, it clearly delineates what is rightfully part of the public's legitimate interest while forcing publishers to seriously consider potential penalties for further incursions.

Jeff Rosen has remarked that Americans see privacy as a protection of liberty, while Europeans see it as a protection of dignity. He then posed the question of "whether one conception trumps the other—or are both destined to perish?"[28] Those fortunate enough to live in Europe have a European Convention of Human Rights that avoids the categorical elevation of one set of rights deemed fundamental over another. The preamble of the Charter of Fundamental Rights states that its purpose is to reaffirm: "the rights as they result, in particular, from the constitutional traditions and international obligations common to the Member States, the European Convention for the Protection of Human Rights and Fundamental Freedoms, the Social Charters adopted by the Union and by the Council of Europe and the case law of the Court of Justice of the European Union and of the European Court of Human Rights."[29] Neither the Charter nor Conventions, traditions nor obligations, Council nor Courts treat civil and human rights as mutually exclusive categories. Stanford University Scholar Lawrence Friedman doubts that Caroline von Hannover would have prevailed

---

28. Jeffrey Rosen, *Judicial Decisionmaking: The Case of Life, Liberty & Property in the Modern Technological Age*, 3 ENGAGE 6 (2002).

29. Convention for the Protection of Human Rights and Fundamental Freedoms, 213 U.N.T.S. 221, E.T.S. 5.

had she brought a similar claim against the National Enquirer in the U.S. because celebrities are virtually exempt from privacy law.

The interesting thing about Case of von Hannover is that as a citizen of the European Union, the plaintiff continued through the legal system in search of a resolution of a jurisdictional dilemma. Von Hanover lived in France, a country that has enacted specific legislation protecting individual privacy. However, photographers stalked her around France then sold the photos to a German publisher who distributed them worldwide.

European courts have taken proper notice that criticizing the personal choices of the rich and famous has become a highly lucrative commodity for certain sectors of the media. Its victims are essentially celebrities whose private lives serve as a stimulus to sales. In seeking peaceful resolution, courts all over the world admonish celebrities to accept that the "special position they occupy in society—in many cases by choice—automatically entails increased pressure on their privacy."[30] However, unless existing anti-defamation laws are adequately enforced everywhere in the world, we cannot justify the current state of affairs unless we are also being asked to assume that celebrities *choose* and volunteer for the false imprisonment, stalking, and harassment that has become all too prevalent.

Celebrities remain aware of the inspiration they provide and just how star-struck fans can actually become as they boldly interrupt their target's breakfast, lunch, dinner, shopping, jogging, and everything else to seek that highly coveted autograph. Most celebrities provide periodic interviews in an effort to share those parts of their lives that are secluded from public view. They know the average fan wants to know, see, hear, and touch.

However, a court declaring that the public has a right to know everything because of public desire to know is operating

---

30. Res. 1165 of the Parliamentary Assembly of the Council of Europe on the Right to Privacy, § 6 (1998).

outside of its jurisdiction. It is not the province of the courts or leg-islatures to make knowing possible and no constitutional authority exists to tell those who have been raked over the coals with lies and unfounded accusations that they must grin and bear it. Every individual when acting outside of public or official duty is a private citizen and entitled to an equal measure of respect for that status.

TWO

Celebrities of the World *Unauthorized*

✹ Glamour, Glitz, and Stardom

Average citizens have long stood in awe of the fortunes and lifestyles of the world's most talented artists, athletes, and humanitarians. But few can fathom the rage of the storm preceding the rainbow leading to that coveted pot of gold. The subjects of this book are among the most famous of those in the post-modern era.

Fame has traditionally been associated with individual demonstrations of superior skill or striking deeds as displayed by a select few, then chronicled by contemporary authors and historians. Celebrity, on the other hand, is more transient, relying on marketing, timing, and instant appeal. As it requires less skill and more luck, the dynamic and transitory nature of entertainment television studios is where it all begins. Hollywood rewards striking glamour, and flashy persona outranks talent or extraordinary displays of character. The fleeting glow of today's pop icons adds to the angst of budding stars who value their privacy. For many, it poses a Hobson's choice: they desire fame and achieve celebrity, but risk obscurity if they reject the pseudo-standards of today's entertainment culture. According to Andy Warhol, beyond Hollywood Boulevard everyone can count on receiving 15 minutes of fame. Conventional wisdom dictates the making of hay while the sun shines.

Television programming featuring *Lifestyles of the Rich and Famous* (which preceded *MTV Cribs*) transport youthful minds into the world of celebrity for the cost of a monthly cable bill. It is a lot like Christmas—it feeds the "me first" credo that developed in recent decades of generational allegiance to a ruthless brand of individualism, baptized in the cult of private pursuit. In the 1970s, when students were asked to reveal their deepest concerns, they overwhelmingly worried about their capacity to develop a meaningful life philosophy. Conversely, today's undergraduates are preoccupied with making their first million dollars. The philosophy of marketing and mining one's own network has swept an entire generation.

When time will not permit proper acknowledgment of a birthday or anniversary, it becomes a case of "benign neglect" easily remedied with a gift card for a high-tech toy guaranteed to be obsolete in six months. Today's youth seem convinced they are one lucky break away from becoming the next Michael Jordan, Beyonce Knowles, or Paris Hilton, as if years of Xbox and an *awesome* physical trainer will allow them to extend their 15 to at least 22 minutes of "well deserved" fame. In the 2007 report *Jaded*, the Learning Skills Council announced that one in seven teenagers in the United Kingdom hoped to achieve fame by appearing on reality TV.[1]

※ The Price of Fame?

The natural impulse of today's celebrities to garner recognition for their hard work and contributions is severely frustrated when the rewards of Hollywood appear commensurate with their level of willingness to reveal salacious tidbits about their private lives in television and magazine interviews. Even the more respected television journalists invite them to share personal information about their individual strengths and weaknesses. A brief moment of candid reflection with a reputable interviewer is subject to distortion just moments later on the front pages of the tabloid press. Tabloid publishers that cannot procure actual celebrity interviews freely manufacture factoids from the embellished remarks of

---

1. *Jaded*, THE ECONOMIST, 57, Jan. 27, 2007.

unnamed sources (or former lovers) that go on to become part of a "bulging clippings file," as characterized by one European judge—and the drama lives on.

The United States outlaws stalking and harassment to protect the safety and well-being of individuals, but falls short of enforcing these standards on behalf of our nation's artists and musicians. Equality under the Fourteenth Amendment requires protection for all citizens even when the invasions are not universally experienced. American celebrities are certainly entitled to, but do not receive, the same privacy protections under law as their European counterparts. If there were a United Brotherhood for the Merchants of Sleaze, the *National Enquirer* in the United States would give Germany's Burda publishers a run for the leadership post.

For example, Cuban actress Cameron Diaz sued the *National Enquirer* for $10 million for falsely reporting that she was "caught cheating."[2] The paper claimed to have discovered her kissing an MTV producer outside a Los Angeles studio. The mother-in-law of the producer is a named plaintiff because of the harm that arose when the Connecticut teacher was pulled out of her classroom by an *Enquirer* reporter and asked for her response to the news that this producer was "leaving her daughter for Diaz." Likewise, actress Brooke Shields and her former husband, tennis champion Andre Agassi, filed suit against the paper for false and fabricated statements that "her therapy ended a nightmare of pill-popping, binge-eating and tears," as well as false stories about fights between in-laws at their wedding over a prenuptial agreement.[3] Christie Brinkley sued the paper for claiming she had "cracked up": appearing delusional in public and displaying an irrational fear of cows.[4]

---

2. *See Diaz Sues Over Pictures*, THE INDEPENDENT, June 3, 2005, at 35.

3. *See* the Internet Movie Database, *Biography for Brooke Shields*, http://www.imdb.com/name/nm0000222/bio.

4. The Smoking Gun Archive, http://www.thesmokinggun.com/archive/brinkley1.html.

Starlet Pamela Anderson and her former husband, musician Tommy Lee, sued the *Enquirer* for falsely reporting they had entered into a secret deal to sell rights to their honeymoon sex tape for $8 million.[5] Media mogul Martha Stewart sued the paper for running headlines accusing her of being mentally ill, with quotes from a doctor[6] it billed as a "nationally renowned expert of the condition of border-line personality disorder," who claimed that Stewart had all the textbook symptoms.[7] Actor Bill Cosby threatened a $250 million lawsuit and demanded a retraction and apology for false, vicious, and defamatory accusations when the paper reported that a former co-star told New York City police he had fondled her.[8] Singer Celine Dion sued the *Enquirer* for intentional infliction of emotional distress when it falsely reported she was pregnant with twins from her husband's frozen sperm.[9] The *Enquirer* may also have weakened Eddie Murphy's nuclear family when it published tales from drug-addicted transsexuals about alleged trysts with the actor.[10] The German publisher that lost in Case of *Von Hannover* was also sued for falsely reporting that Tom Cruise had sex with a gay porn star.[11]

---

5. MTV News, *Tommy Lee and Pamela Anderson Settle Libel Suit with National Enquirer*, May 6, 1998, http://www.mtv.com/news/articles/1432386/19980506/lee_tommy.jhtml.

6. The *National Enquirer* published a 1997 story subtly headlined "Martha Stewart Is Mentally Ill," which quoted "nationally renowned expert" Dr. Leland Heller as calling Stewart a "textbook example [of] borderline personality disorder" with a proclivity for "self-mutilation and suicidal threats."

7. *See* JOHN G. GUNDERSON, BORDERLINE PERSONALITY DISORDER: A CLINICAL GUIDE 52–53 (2001).

8. *See* MICHAEL ERIC DYSON, IS BILL COSBY RIGHT? (OR HAS THE BLACK MIDDLE CLASS LOST ITS MIND?) 147–48 (2006).

9. *See* BBC News, *Celine Sues US Tabloid for $20m*, http://news.bbc.co.uk/2/hi/entertainment/661089.stm.

10. *See Eddie Murphy's Secret Sex Life: His Transvestite Hooker Tells All*, NAT. ENQUIRER, May 20, 1997, at 1.

11. *See* Marianne Goldstein, *Cruise Files 2nd 100m Gay Rumor Suit*, N.Y. DAILY NEWS, June 5, 2001, at 4.

Young female celebrities bear the brunt of the exploitation. The work of legitimate photographers has been digitally altered by pornographers guilty of copyright infringement and trademark dilution. Violations of the statutory right of publicity are skyrocketing with malicious misappropriation of the images of models and actresses being advertised as "celeb-porn" sites. Actresses of all ages have been objectified regardless of their willingness to be filmed in the nude. For example, Jennifer Aniston sought an injunction against *Man's World* Publications after "stalkerazzi" scaled her neighbor's eight-foot wall and shot pictures of her sunbathing topless in her own backyard.[12]

Laws in New York and California where most celebrities live and work offers virtually no protection for the rich and famous in public space. A law known as the California Paparazzi statute reads:[13]

(a) A person is liable for physical invasion of privacy when the defendant knowingly enters onto the land of another person without permission or otherwise committed a trespass in order to physically invade the privacy of the plaintiff with the intent to capture any type of visual image, sound recording, or other physical impression of the plaintiff engaging in a personal or familial activity and the physical invasion occurs in a manner that is offensive to a reasonable person.

(b) A person is liable for constructive invasion of privacy when the defendant attempts to capture, in a manner that is offensive to a reasonable person, any type of visual image, sound recording, or other physical impression of the plaintiff engaging in a personal or familial activity under circumstances in which the plaintiff had a reasonable expectation of privacy, through the use

---

12. *See* Stephen M. Silverman, *Aniston Sues Photographer Over Topless Pics*, PEOPLE MAG., Dec. 5, 2005.

13. CAL. CIV. CODE § 1708–1728.

of a visual or auditory enhancing device, regardless of whether there is a physical trespass, if this image, sound recording, or other physical impression could not have been achieved without a trespass unless the visual or auditory enhancing device was used.[14] Thus, covert monitoring of celebrities in public has become a multi-million dollar industry.

Sometimes invasions take the form of insulting "offers." The reported price tag for the round-the-clock support team needed to care for Nadya Suleman's 14 children when the birth of octuplets added eight to the six she had at home (all under the age of eight) is $135,000 per month. Suleman was propositioned by Vivid Adult Entertainment Company[15] and told that if she agreed to perform sex acts in eight scenes with eight different men, the company would pay her $1 million dollars and provide free medical insurance for her entire family. The head of the company stated: "She's struggling financially and this is a woman who wants to provide for her kids. This way she can hold her head high and not be using taxpayer money to support her family."[16]

Some have asked whether this kind of autonomy is really just another form of SEXploitation. Others view this as consistent with the social norms that produce countless sexually graphic scenes in film and on stage, along with the many celebrities who have posed for *Playboy* magazine such as Drew Barrymore, Mariah Carey, and Dolly Parton. Is this any more "scandalous" than celebs featured in guest appearances with the scantily clad, burlesque-style singing sensations Pussycat Dolls, including Victoria Beckam, Eva Longoria, Christina Applegate, and Charlize Theron?[17]

---

14. CAL. CIV. CODE § 1708.8.

15. Chris Hogg, *Octo-Mom Nadya Suleman Offered $1 Million to Star in Porn*, Feb. 25, 2009, http://www.digitaljournal.com/article/268010.

16. McKay, *Porn Plot:* Vivid's *Sordid Plans for Nadya "Octomom" Suleman* Feb. 26, 2009, http://www.foxnews.com/story/0,2933,500688,00.html.

17. http://top40.about.com/od/artistsls/p/pussycatdolls.htm.

Coincidentally, *trading on sexual appeal in lieu of talent* simply reflects human nature. Proctor & Gamble owns dozens of brands, including Herbal Essences. Its televised ads for the shampoo feature women faking orgasm while washing their hair with the tag line: *A totally organic experience.* The product's profit margin reportedly shot from zero to $700 million in just seven years.[18] The debate here is not what the public responds to, but why? From whence cometh the severe judgment of Suleman over her decision to have 14 children, but only limited discussion of whether she should "work" for Vivid? Public empathy or outrage over the wider implications of these bare-all choices was notably absent. Yet when a photo of Billy Ray Cyrus's 15-year-old daughter Destiny Hope that some perceived as racy was taken and published in *Vanity Fair* magazine, he was characterized as being a second-rate country musician whose only talent is exploiting his daughter.

▓ Stalkerazzi Undeterred

Tabloid photo hounds in California trapped Arnold Schwarzenegger and Maria Shriver as they dropped their kids off at school. At the time, the former actor/now-governor was recovering from heart surgery and Shriver was healing from pregnancy-related complications. As one photographer smashed into the front of their Mercedes, the other pulled up behind them, then jumped out shooting pictures, prompting the Santa Monica City Attorney's office to file charges of false imprisonment and battery.[19] The high risk of getting nabbed in a tabloid feeding frenzy where cash is king, nothing is sacred, and a lawsuit is looming just round the bend have driven a

18. Sex Sells? Oh Really? Feb. 5, 2008, http://entrepreneurs.about.com/b/2008/02/05/sex-sells-oh-really.htm

19. *See* Bernard Weinraub, *2 Paparazzi Convicted of Stalking Celebrities*, N.Y. TIMES, Feb. 4, 1998, at E8.

few stars over the edge. There are surely those days and times in every celeb's life when enough is just *enough*!

In one instance, Alec Baldwin confronted paparazzi staking out his Los Angeles home. The intruder was waiting to videotape the actor's wife and newborn baby's arrival home from the hospital. The evidence in the suit brought against the actor shows Baldwin approached the vehicle with a can of shaving cream, then spread the contents all over the car window to obscure the camera's view. The photographer claimed he was hit in the face, but as the window was rolled up, it was more likely his nervousness and fumbling with the camera caused any relevant impact. In any event, Baldwin was acquitted of battery charges in criminal court. However, fast-forwarding to civil court, a jury awarded the same photographer $4500 in damages after finding that Baldwin acted with malice.[20] When? While slathering shaving cream across the driver's window? Perhaps, but even so, under the totality of the circumstances, the photographer was probably entitled to no more than $11.62 (the cost of a basic car wash at Sunset and Vine, plus tax).

Actresses Denise Richards and Pamela Anderson were also named in a lawsuit filed by two photographers, Scott Cosman and Rick Fedyck, who allege the actresses verbally and physically assaulted them on a movie set at the River Rock Casino Resort in Vancouver, Canada.[21] They also claim the pair issued false statements to the Royal Canadian Mounted Police that led to their arrest and subsequent detainment for nearly three days.

Former first lady Jacqueline Kennedy Onassis complained in court about the constant surveillance that made one summer vacation intolerable for her children. Photographer Ron Galella risked contempt of court for violating an order requiring him to stay a

---

20. *See* Harold Kurtz, *Pictures at a High Price: Paparazzi Take More Than Celebrities' Photos*, WASH. POST, Sept. 1, 1997, at A1.

21. *See* Access Hollywood, *Photographers Sue Denise Richards & Pamela Anderson*, http://www.accesshollywood.com/news/ah4601.shtml.

minimum of 25 feet from Onassis and 30 feet from her children, Caroline and John. Gallela, who violated the order as Onassis left Manhattan theaters and again on her residential property at Martha's Vineyard claimed he was just doing his job.

Author Charles Sykes warns that privacy has indeed come to an end. He asks readers to "think about the most painful episodes of your life: the time you were fired, got divorced, when your child failed at school or ran afoul of the law, or when you wrestled with what seemed unsolvable dilemmas about the medical care of an aged parent. Now imagine that any of those events had played out on the public stage, or been the subject of gossip columns, exposes, or the fodder for talk shows."[22] Sykes aptly describes the everyday life of the modern celebrity.

🕊 Abuse of the Telephoto Lens

International fashion model Naomi Campbell was photographed by the London-based *Mirror* when leaving a Narcotics Anonymous meeting. The photographs were covertly taken by a freelance photographer employed by the paper using a telephoto lens from inside a parked car.[23] The United Kingdom's premier tabloid then published the photos in a series of back-to-back articles with an undertone of smugness that the model had been caught lying.

Monte Carlo is one of Europe's leading tourist resorts; it is located in Monaco, a region known as a hub of wealthy gamblers, glitzy yachts, glamour, and celebrity sightings. The Monte Carlo Beach Club is an exclusive establishment where guests routinely arrive by private jet, take a helicopter to the resort, board private yachts for recreation, and pay approximately $1000 per night for a standard

---

22. CHARLES J. SYKES, THE END OF PRIVACY 18 (1999).

23. *See* Louise A. Barile, *Naomi Campbell Wins Tabloid Case*, PEOPLE, Mar. 27, 2002.

room. Access is strictly controlled, and journalists are barred without express permission from the owner. Nonetheless, this is another venue where Princess Caroline's problems with photographers occurred. While at the club, photos of von Hanover in a bathing suit taken at a distance of several hundred meters from the window or roof of a neighboring house were later published by a German tabloid. One showed her tripping over an obstacle and falling under the caption: "Princess Caroline fell flat on her face." As her visit to the club was not a matter of public concern, we can easily conclude the photos and story were meant to demean her in the eyes of the public. As detailed in Chapter One, von Hannover's legal battle was based upon her conviction that such actions violated important constitutional boundaries.

From a societal standpoint, the crux of the matter is only tangentially related to rampant commercialization. The freelance photographer who positions himself a hundred feet away from an individual whom he shoots with a telephoto lens, then sells the product for use by the tabloid press without regard for the likelihood of his subject's humiliation, mental anguish, or suffering, is a pawn in a game where the legitimacy of the rules of civility are under attack. We outlaw stalking because "these rules represent the special claims which members [of a community] have on each other, as distinct from others, and hence they embody the very substance and boundaries of community life."[24] Their continued violation strikes at the heart of constitutional democracy.

🎞 Lies, Malice, and Forethought

When business is slow, paparazzo create stories by provoking confrontations that force celebrities to defend themselves, while

---

24. Robert C. Post, *The Constitutional Concept of Public Discourse: Outrageous Opinion, Democratic Deliberation, and Hustler Magazine v. Falwell*, 103 HARV. L. REV. 601, 618 (1990).

another "captures the moment"—all so that a tabloid can manufacture "late-breaking news," reporting how so-and-so is "*Out of Control!*" Sydney University Professor Marc Brennan concluded that tabloids are telling more lies "due to competition and the need to build stories around photos they buy."[25] Thus, today's celebrities are caught in a morality-free zone where all bets are off. They are constantly measured and compared to those who live to reveal it all in what often looks like a national free-for-all. To cope with this madness, celebrities write autobiographies where they reveal more than they would like, in part to either explain the criticism or to preempt predatory journalism. The need to defend is the very antithesis of the muck-raking tradition that undergirds our commitment to a free press. Celebrity biographies can be lucrative for both writers and publishers. An authorized biography, written with the consent and approval of its subject, includes materials, sources, and live interviews with the artist alongside some measure of pre- or post-publication marketing support.

When consent is withheld for whatever reason, valuable time and energy is diverted with attempts to counteract those who trade on the word *unauthorized*. These publications promise to reveal secrets its readers "won't want to miss," and claim to have finally uncovered *the* truth behind the façade to lure susceptible consumers. Unauthorized biographies are written for monetary gain, with some being penned by a former spouse, relative, or employee in search of revenge and "just compensation." Andrew Morton easily qualifies as a writer solely motivated by pecuniary gain. He is best known for his ability to package all prior sordid rumors about a celebrity into a one-stop source of ready revenue. The following description of his unauthorized biography about actor Tom Cruise is paradigmatic of his ilk:

---

25. Lleyton complains about tabloid lies, http://au.lifestyle.yahoo.com/b/sunrise/10207/lleyton-complains-about-tabloid-lies/.

For two years, award-winning biographer Andrew Morton has been tirelessly seeking out everyone from former teachers and girlfriends to Scientology insiders to friends who have watched a once-bullied, "nothing special" outsider transform himself into an icon *Forbes* has called the most powerful celebrity in the world. Here, with never-seen photos and never-heard revelations, is a riveting, sometimes shocking portrait of the real Tom Cruise—his work, his love life, his marriages, his religion—from a master at uncovering the true story behind the public face of celebrity.[26]

The adoration of Grace Kelly was unrelenting during her 26-year reign as sovereign of Monaco. As described in Chapter 1, now that the rules have substantially changed regarding privacy, defamation, and propriety, her daughter Caroline has been forced to defend the family from those promising a moment-to-moment account of her lifestyle and personal choices. In what looks like an international free-for-all, one expose threatens to diminish the esteem in which Kelly was held during life. Post-mortem reviewers dug deep for an opportunity to ride the wave. A biography Web site is cashing in with pieced-together footage from various scenes of Kelly's life; as a dvd marketed worldwide with the following promotional clip:

Grace Kelly grew up on the Philadelphia Mainline, and her high-society roots served her well when she became Princess Grace. But despite the fairytale romance with Monaco's Prince Rainier, in later years her marriage became just another performance. This illuminating BIOGRAPHY® goes behind the public facade to tell the real story of the woman whose entire life was lived in the public eye. Insiders tell of the comfort she took in her children, the slow disintegration of her relationship with the Prince, and

---

26. http://www.amazon.com/Tom-Cruise-Unauthorized-Andrew-Morton/dp/0312359861.

her battle to maintain some semblance of privacy in the face of the relentless pursuit of paparazzi. And clips from her most memorable performances capture the young star at the height of her fame.

Similar promotions are available for *behind the façade* tales of other stars such as: "Sex, Sinatra and the Women Who Fell For Him"; "The Secret Life of Humphrey Bogart"; and "The Dark Side of Genius, the Life of Alfred Hitchcock."

Celebrities and/or their families have responded in a variety of ways. Some give press conferences, as did Prince William upon release of *Shadows of a Princess*. He was asked about "press coverage of [his] late mother" in the wake of the new tell-all book written by her one-time most senior aide, Patrick Jephson. William stated publicly for the first time since her death that he and his brother were quite upset that their "mother's trust has been betrayed and that even now she is still being exploited three years after her death."

The celebrities and families (who often rely upon handlers and advisors with mixed motives) have predictably stepped into the morass. Celebrities are pushed and pulled in several directions by loyalties to their art and to their fans, a need to pay the bills, and the crushing sounds of the steady stream of 30-minute entertainment news shows popping up in syndication, saturating the airwaves with footage of every embarrassing or careless moment. Thus, not only must they face the fact that almost nothing is truly private, they must confront the reality that the very details of their existence will be brought forward for judgment and criticism—and most assuredly for comparison to the new face in the crowd.

⅍ Defending Privacy against Demands for Disclosure

Many well-intentioned people struggle with issues of fairness on the celebrity privacy question. For one, there is simply no denying that we live in a "tell-all" society. Next, equitable concerns are unavoidable when examining the social utility of allowing those who enjoy the benefits and power attached to fame to retain substantial control of their public image. For example, it seems odd to concede that Tom Cruise should be allowed in spring 2005 to jump up and down on a talk show sofa in front of 50 million viewers of *The Oprah Winfrey Show*, raving about his love for his intended, only to find himself married and divorced by the winter of 2012 and asking the media machine to "please respect his privacy during this very difficult time." No one appears willing to question the inalienable right everyone has to reveal all: to expose the bloody, idiotic, and pathological nature of their lives and relationships. But if that also means that the media should have the power to uncover what the individual deems private, then we have given way to the madness. Would an outcry on behalf of the public's interest in the right to conceal be a logical corollary? How about the individual choice to reveal today, yet conceal tomorrow? Individual willingness to tell all and media clamor to reveal all is prime evidence of a dysfunctional society.

🎞 American Social Dysfunction

A July 1992 *Psychology Today* article warned that the U.S. had become a culture of self-diagnosers.[27] The article failed to mention that this condition might just be the tip of the iceberg. Cultural preferences for experts who pathologized rather than explained behaviors, fed a brand of social discourse that failed to promote understanding of the nuances of building a productive life. The value of life-long learning and the elements of various developmental stages through which we all stumble on the sometimes rocky

---

27. *Whimperers Anonymous: Have We Become a Culture of Self-Diagnosers?* PSYCHOL. TODAY, July 1992, at 8.

road of character building have all but disappeared from public dialogue. The end product of the therapeutic movement's demand for close examination of codependent tendencies is *less* engagement. Rather than embracing the skills required to undertake a meaningful process of self-transformation, we travel along the frontiers of victimhood. Atlanta psychiatrist Frank Pittman describes the phenomena as a subculture of "Whimperers Anonymous."[28] Its fellow travelers minimize the mutuality and reciprocity of our interactions, holding instead they are all victims of someone else—usually their parents. As psychologists point to early childhood trauma as the beginning of most dysfunction, the natural tendency is to look outside ourselves for explanations of life experiences.

The famous among us are often caught in the interpretive void. This is most visible when celebrities publish autobiographies for hefty advances, then expect commanders of the same media brigade that routinely chase them down the freeway to sympathize with revelations of familial dysfunction or histories of abuse or neglect. For example, MTV's biographical sketch of musician Melissa Etheridge aptly describes her as "one of the most popular recording artists of the '90s due to her mixture of confessional lyrics; pop-based folk-rock; and raspy, Janis Joplin/Rod Stewart-esque vocals."[29] Nevertheless, the autobiography by Etheridge, *The Truth Is: My Life in Love And Music* was greeted with a long list of criticisms. She was chided for inconsistency with earlier stories about her years growing up in Kansas, for placing too much of the blame on her ex for the breakup of their 12-year relationship, and for harping on the emotional trauma in her life while giving short shrift to the highlights of her music career. One reviewer ultimately concluded that Etheridge suffered from "tarnished celebrity syndrome", which leads a celebrity to "conjure up a sob story that engenders

---

28. *Id.*

29. MTV.com, Melissa Etheridge, http://www.mtv.com/music/artist/melissa_etheridge/artist.jhtml#bio.

sympathy to acquit them from blame" after "weathering some public calamity."[30] Etheridge's cathartic offering of her life experience, wherein she explained the problems in her long-term spousal relationship from her own perspective, was dubbed an indulgent attempt to alleviate public humiliation.

We may never recover the sense of propriety and proportionality that governed the journalism profession years ago. It is difficult to first understand what motivates individuals to reveal intimate details of their private lives in the pages of a book, especially one over which they have editorial control. That difficulty is quickly surpassed by the daunting task of accounting for the unabashed sense of entitlement among journalists. In Etheridge's case, it led to a stinging rebuke of a life story, despite the reviewer's lack of firsthand knowledge of the singer's life. Presumptions related to individual privacy, propriety, and proportionality seem dated, as if they come from a Jane Austen novel citing a rule book in which privacy, civility, and polite conversation still matter (never mind virtue). Lack of training in social decorum and the discarding of the notion of a guarded personal life have rendered these concepts all but obsolete.

As a society, we have lost all semblance of respect for personal narrative and the right of the individual to enjoy the *freedom*, in the words of Justice Sandra Day O'Connor, that stands at the heart of liberty—the right to define one's own concept of existence, of meaning, of the universe, and of the mystery of human life. There we have one U.S. Supreme Court justice's attempt to define privacy in the age of exposure and disclosure, and thanks to the Internet, worldwide dissemination at the speed of light. Before we became a tell-all society, celebrities were entitled to a private life. These days the mere mention of celebrity privacy invasion invokes the old standby reasoning: it is the price one must pay to be rich and famous.

---

30. Review of *The Truth Is . . . My Life in Love and Music*, http://www.epinions.com/content_174897532548.

𝒲 Shameless Self-Promotion

An article "Decline and Fall of the Private Self" explains what tendencies toward overexposure have done to the modern psyche.[31] In discussing a $20 million lawsuit against Jessica Cutler, who after posting her sexual exploits on Capitol Hill on an Internet diary was dubbed the *leading lady of tell-all bloggers*, the author concludes that "waves of revelation are fast eroding our notions of private identity."[32] Mass electronic communication eliminates the self-censorship that normally occurs when dealing with an individual or communicating face-to-face. Psychologist Jefferson Singer notes that "in the larger theater of society: even if you're playing the role of the loser—blogging about being unhappy and unattractive—at least you're part of the show."[33] Certain kinds of publicity are not without their rewards.

As an offshoot of daytime talk shows, reality TV shows debuting in prime time allow Americans to fantasize about gaining status through instant celebrity. Millions are watching; it is all about being in the right place at the right time and being willing to do whatever is required to turn on the spotlight. Jessica Cutler's sex-blog disclosures netted her a *Playboy* centerfold, a book deal, and a contract with the Home Box Office cable television network. However, Cutler was also sued by a former Capitol Hill attorney who claimed her publication of their sexcapades subjected him to a level of "humiliation and anguish beyond that which any reasonable person should be expected to bear in decent, civilized society."[34] Obviously she

---

31. Carlin Flora, *Decline and Fall of the Public Self: Once Upon a Time, People Kept Secrets. Today's Tell-All Bloggers and MySpace Denizens Have Made the Notion of a Guarded Personal Life Feel Obsolete. What Effect Does Such Exposure Have on the Psyche?*, PSYCHOL. TODAY 82–87 (May/June 2007).

32. *Id.* at 84.

33. *Id.* at 86.

34. Flora, *supra* note 32.

would not trade the perks she received from the revelations to restore his dignity, but the public is also left wondering: was he truly humiliated, or just hoping to cash in on her celebrity?

ℳ The Impact of Daytime Talk Shows

According to Dr. Stuart Fischoff, talk shows exist to entertain the masses while exploiting the exhibitionism of the walking wounded. From Phil McGraw to Oprah, Jerry, Tyra, Montel, and their progeny, we have witnessed an entire generation of people willing to expose long-held family secrets, to showcase deviant or taboo desires, or behave in as asinine and antisocial way as possible—all for a fleeting moment of glory, pity, or revenge. Ambushing guests with humiliating and titillating drama is the rule on the talk show circuit rather than the exception. A public besieged by scandals, radio shock jocks, "combat conservatives", and political talk show "journalists" with their obscenities and insults are now weary of the polarizing fray. Left with a conflation of yellow, pink, and white journalism, Fischoff believes that extreme exploitation will not end until our culture stops its free fall from civility and shame and privacy reassert themselves in the pantheon of social values.[35]

Not since Norma Jean Mortenson, aka Marilyn Monroe (of whom writer Paul Rudnick once asked: "how much deconstruction can one blond bear?") has the "media-drenched image of a tragic dumb blond" become so celebrated as an American archetype.[36] Monroe suffered through reports that she was "an increasing nightmare to work with" before dying from an overdose of drugs at age 36. Her personal history was laid bare for decades to come. What Rudnick surmised was that there is an endless adoration for the on-screen

---

35. Stuart Fischoff, *Confessions of a TV Talk Show Shrink*, Psychol. Today 38–45 (Sept/Oct. 1995).

36. www.im.ntu.edu.tw/~b91041/TIME100/time-092.doc

image of Monroe that must be reconciled with the image emerging from the countless biographies chronicling tales of abusive foster homes, predatory Hollywood scum, failed marriages, trysts with other stars and politicians, and "miscarriages, abortions, rest cures and frenzied press conferences." Most of the reconciliation of the public and private images of Marilyn Monroe was done by those who were interested and who voluntarily embraced that process. In retrospect, this at least spared an entire nation of the daily barrage of news produced by the tabloid hunt that drove Britney Spears to the brink of her sanity.

According to one report, during 2006 reports of Spears's transgressions escalated in an 18-month period "beyond almost any in pop history."[37] The stories alleged she:

> Flashed her vagina, shaved her head, physically attacked paparazzi and [entered] rehab (twice). She has been charged with hit-and-run, effectively declared an unfit mother by the state of California and been fired by her lawyers (again, twice). She turned in the most disastrous performance of her career at MTV's Video Music Awards show, got dumped by her management firm and has cleaned her hands of almost everyone who played any significant role in her first 25 years of life.[38]

Paparazzo first tracked, then filmed, and later televised Spears' every move, exploiting the circumstances of her life with the most damaging headlines. In real time, the public was treated to an account of every twist and turn of an unfolding tragedy that included excerpts from every publicly filed document and court hearing related to her divorce and custody of her two young boys.

---

37. Britney Spears Blender Magazine Cover and Article Road to Ruin, http://thestarblogger.com/2008/01/28/britney-spears-blender-magazine-cover-and-article-road-to-ruin.aspx.

38. *Id.*

Reports surfaced as fiction mixed with fact with virtually no efforts being made to distinguish between the two. Spears and her children were targets of an extreme pursuit, including relentless tracking and reporting, that never resulted in any major reform or high-level demand for enforcement of celebrity rights to be left alone. The masses merely stood by and watched. "When it looked like things could not possibly get worse, police were called to Britney's home when she refused to relinquish her two children after their scheduled visit. . . . After a three-hour standoff, she was strapped to a gurney and taken by ambulance to Cedars-Sinai Medical Center. The next day, she lost all visitation and custody rights to her kids."[39]

Tabloids then announced their considered opinion that Britney Spears had collapsed after ruining her career and marriage and losing custody of her kids. Without official acknowledgement of the role played by the tabloids in driving her to the brink, concern for ratings and magazine sales was quickly displaced with fears around liability. Daytime television talk show host Phil McGraw "showed up at Cedars-Sinai Medical Center to help Spears 'get real' with her 'issues'—supposedly with her family's blessing." This invasion provided a convenient opportunity to direct public outrage at a specific target because McGraw was perceived as having taken the feeding frenzy to a whole new level.[40] "He's crossed the line," mental health pros wailed after he appeared before Spears and then turned the private meeting into a very public plea to "treat" the troubled star on a special *Dr. Phil* show. After facing intense criticism for such predatory behavior, McGraw reported that Spears' troubles were just "too intense" for him to go on with the idea. One reporter believes that he calculated that "using this girl's current madness to build a ratings juggernaut might seem a little iffy." Even if so, it did not stop McGraw from pursuing Nadya Suleman, the California mother of octuplets born just three years later.

---

39. *Id.*

40. http://showbizblog.ctv.ca/blog/_archives/2008/1/10/3458120.html.

The role played by television talk shows in today's freewheeling real-time destruction of those who enter public life cannot be underestimated. Psychologist Stuart Fischoff explains why in his 1995 article with an analysis of the process that is more relevant today than it was 15 years ago.[41]

⁇ Emotion, Conflict, and Revenge

Three women are seated next to me on stage, ready to talk, their chests nervously heaving, faces frozen in polite smiles. They listen as Geraldo details their shocking biographies to the audience. My pulse accelerates as Geraldo moves beside me, his hype escalating: "Dr. Stuart Fischoff, a clinical psychologist from Los Angeles, is here to help answer the $64,000 question: *Why would a woman marry her rapist?*"[42]

In "Confession of a TV Talk Show Shrink," Fischoff acknowledges that he knew nothing about the women on stage except "bits and pieces of their self-justifying explanations." No one can speak authoritatively to that question. "People are authorities on women, on marriage, on rape. But no one is an authority on why women marry their rapists." Thus, Fischoff was forced to rely upon generalizations: low self-esteem and the illusory bonds between rape and the romantic myth of being taken because one is so needed, so desirable. "It's not about love and desire" . . . "It's about anger and dominance." The three women did not and could not hear the doctor because they had agreed to appear on national television to be validated. Fischoff writes: "In the show's last segment, Geraldo stands on stage, points to me, and says, 'In thirty second or less, Dr. Fischoff, give us your impression of these women.'

---

41. *Id.*
42. *Id.*

My mind gulps. 'Thirty seconds? Is he kidding?' No, he's not. My thoughts run wild. 'What the hell am I doing here?'"

Fischoff believes talk shows "exist to entertain and exploit the exhibitionism of the walking wounded." People who need to attack or humiliate a spouse or exact revenge seek out TV talk shows. The proliferation and appeal are causally linked to the endless opportunities they provide to "compare one's own life with those on the screen and breathe a superior sigh of relief . . ., [uplifted] to see people make fools of themselves on talk shows." They offer "vicarious revenge" soothing the seething inside of those who have also been betrayed or deeply disappointed in relationships. No host, in Fischoff's experience, is interested in calm intellectual discourse because it is the emotions and conflict that make the show addictive for the viewing audience. But what people fail to grasp is that the "conflicts provoked on stage by hosts and studio audiences are not the scripted fictions of a made-for-TV movie. The tumultuous dramas talk show guests enact are their lives, their wounds, the crimes of their hearts and their loins. Unlike actors, talk show guests must ultimately answer for their on-camera confessions when they return to their everyday lives." Moreover, according to Fischoff, the spectacle itself demands increased levels of crudeness and degradation:

> Guests will say the most intimate things precisely because they have watched others do it before them. If guests discuss their sex lives, other guests will do the same. If guests attack their spouses, other guests will do the same. And if guests admit to incest, incredibly, other guests will go on to do the same. Like some revivalist tent show, once guests have fallen to the ground, touched by the spirit, speaking in tongues, others will follow, tongues wagging, shame and privacy shunted aside.

He continues:

> As an expert, you sit on stage and feel the negative charges of electricity hurtling out of the audience, enveloping the guests.

> But your expert status is by no means a safe-house. The audience's opinions are deliberately placed on even footing with those of the expert. The expert may have the training, the clinical experience, or other bona fides to offer an educated opinion about a topic under discussion. But the audience members come armed with their personal experiences, the equalizing power of the studio mike, and the encouragement of the host to "let it rip." A meeting of the minds it isn't. If you go against the audience's strident opinions, they go against you.

Fischoff hardly expected that television "producers [will] be brought to their senses and pull back from the class warfare of the haves exploiting the have not exhibitionists for the amusement of voyeuristic audiences." Little did he suspect that what began as simple amusement might later feed a different appetite altogether.

Exploring the Mob Mentality

When we became a culture of self-diagnosers, talk show therapy became the new religion. This was only the beginning of far more disturbing trends in public media and the collective psyche. As discussed above, today's tell-all blogs and round-the-clock reality TV were preceded by daytime talk shows that in the twinkling of an eye produced an entire generation of people willing to expose their darkest secrets, aberrant behaviors, and perverse yearnings before millions of viewers. "It's one thing to recount your troubles and misdeeds to a stranger in a bar. It's quite another to do it in front of 20 million people." Psychologist Jeff Singer laments the "way in which our lives seem valid only if they obtain some veneer of media recognition." If a blog is necessary to convert our mundane lives into an "electronic saga," and if the social milieu now requires extensive exposure to increase the value of our existence, then the natural corollary would include a public demand for pervasive humiliation in order to diminish another. This clearly relates to how easily

Britney Spears' private life was made into a public spectacle without corresponding public outrage.

In the late 1960s, cognitive, behavioral, and biological models of the mind/brain and mental illness began replacing psychoanalytic theories. In North America, the prevailing viewpoint in the 1980s was that psychic unrest was a disorder essentially separate from the self. The belief that "mood, and later anxiety, disorders could be managed by cognitive training and medication, meant that failure to take responsibility for one's difficult personality" or a "pathological unconscious mind was no longer stigmatized." The end product of therapeutic movements was the demand for explanations beyond the individual and for medicinal relief that pharmaceutical companies all too happily supplied. The other end product of this movement was a form of backlash leading to hypervigilance in scrutinizing the choices of others.

Along with public media's ratings-based delivery of jarring and up-to-the-minute news, conflict has now become an indispensable element of storytelling. It resembles ancient Rome,[43] where most citizens preferred to watch "gladiators locked in mortal combat, [where they must] kill or be killed in order to satisfy the bloodlust of spectators"; we are ever more desirous of catching our opponents—and catching them unaware. Whether the motive is a social or political cause, according to one Web site a new breed of citizen called the video vigilante has chosen "to arm himself with a video camera in an effort to expose a wrong, motivate justice, and positively impact the community."[44] According to one writer, this brand of infotainment has produced conditions where "the nation is thrown into a paroxysm of indignation" over reports of a 30-year-old drunk driving conviction of former President Bush "while his views on abortion or the military go largely un-debated."

---

43. Stephen R. Munzer, *Moral, Political, and Legal Philosophy: Intuition and Security in Moral Philosophy*, 82 MICH. L. REV. 740, 750 (1984).

44. http://www.videovigilante.com/.

In short, this brand of displaced outrage and hyper-condemnation has spiraled out of control.

✺ The Internet Fury Machine

Writer Kim Zetter explores the exigency and judgments surrounding cyberstalking through the story of Sarah Wells, a middle-aged mother in Virginia who used her blog to unleash her fury before becoming a victim of rage herself.[45] The facts are simple: 13-year-old Megan Meier was driven to suicide by insidious online attacks. The torment was engineered by Lori Drew, a middle-aged woman who set up a phony MySpace account and fabricated the identity of a 16-year-old named Josh Evans to woo Megan to learn what the girl was saying about Drew's teenage daughter. Once Megan divulged that information, "Josh" turned on her, heaping verbal abuse that eventually drove the emotionally vulnerable teen over the edge.[46]

News accounts of Megan's death failed to "identify the perpetrator of the deadly hoax by name, but included enough detail to track her down through online property-tax records." SarahWells, although hundreds of miles away, felt that lack of remorse for the teens death was bad enough, but dragging the dead girl's father into courts and pressing charges for his act of vandalism, further hurt the family whose daughter had suffered a great deal because of her. . . . "The fact that it involved an adult targeting a child, and that Megan's father—and not Lori Drew—was facing criminal charges, made it a clear-cut cause for cybermob outrage."[47] Prime ingredients for Wells' fixation upon Drew were present: a trusted

---

45. http://www.wired.com/print/politics/onlinerights/news/2007/11/vigilante_justice.

46. *Id.*

47. *Id.*

adult preying on the emotions of a vulnerable child coupled with the Internet "where people instigate mobs in ways they wouldn't do offline."[48]

With a few minutes of sleuthing, Wells identified the woman as Lori Drew of O'Fallon, Missouri. After confirming it with someone in the O'Fallon area, she posted Drew's name to her blog as the perpetrator. Her readers and other bloggers joined and posted Drew's husband's name, their home address, phone number, cell number, information about their advertising company, and the names and phone numbers of their clients.[49] As the matter took on a life of its own, Drew's advertising clients were urged to fire her, death threats were made against her, windows were broken, and calls were made to set the Drew house on fire. There were also increased police patrols and a peaceful protest on their street.

Wells has stated that she feels no regret: "I think this should follow her wherever she goes," adding "there should be pressure on her to be sorry and to do something to make it better." Ironically, "Wells herself felt the capricious hand of internet justice . . . when another blogger condemned her as a 'vigilante' and posted her address and phone number online."[50]

℀ The Devolving American Psyche

According to psychology professor Sharon Lamb, current studies of emotion fail to integrate the cumulative responses of groups of emotions in their analyses. Isolating specific physiological traits in conjunction with the cultural practices that differentiate typical responses from both a normative and psychoanalytic perspective would be a significant development for advancing understanding of

---

48. *Id.*

49. *Id.*

50. *Id.*

emotional triggers. Collective ambivalence around our own personal deficiencies discourages a wider recognition that all individuals continuously experience simultaneous emotions. As a culture, we exhibit many signs of deep ambivalence around our urges to condemn others. Whenever needs or desires are uncertain or contradictory and situated outside of conscious awareness, those needs will conflict with what we consciously believe and express about ourselves. If we take that bit of psychoanalytic theory as truth, what is the hidden side of condemnation? Where is the ambivalence? What are the uncertain, contradictory, and unacceptable feelings? Disgust, fear, anger, and outrage factor into expressions of condemnation. Yet, those who condemn find it relatively easy to admit their experience of disgust, outrage, and indignation, but not their fear.[51]

> In Western society, anger and outrage are more acceptable emotions to individuals than fear because as one experiences anger and outrage, and one has the option to act on these feelings, one often feels powerful. For Westerners, anger and outrage are associated with strength rather than weakness; but this is not true in all Western cultures.

> [I]n the United States, . . . anger is action. It is force. Social constructionists argue that it overwhelms us.

As a passionate force of energy, the anger we feel allows us to act and target others without taking responsibility for the damage we might inflict. Contrary to weakening our sense of authority, superiority, and strength, anger is rarely the response of those who consider themselves a "victim." Our fears, on the other hand, are primal insofar as they relate to safety, security, and a sense of helplessness.

---

51. Sharon Lamb, *Responsibility and Blame: Psychological and Legal Perspectives: The Psychology of Condemnation: Underlying Emotions and Their Symbolic Expression in Condemning and Shaming*, 68 BROOK. L. REV. 929, 936–39 (2003).

As part of the basic early-surfacing set of emotions upon which all social relations are built, in an adult fear is often "dressed up to make it acceptable in two important ways":

> First, the individual psyche transforms less acceptable emotions into more acceptable or empowering ones, e.g., fear into anger.

> Second, we use the defense of projective identification, denying parts of ourselves and finding unconscious ways to project them onto another. When we feel fear, through projective identification we find a way to make someone else afraid so that we no longer have to own and experience that uncomfortable emotion. Condemnation serves this function by allowing us to deny our own fears, making those condemned quake at their punishment.

This phenomenon has proliferated through the international psyche with alarming effect. According to the author of *MOBBING: Emotional Abuse in the American Workplace*, mobbing involves the deployment of rumor, innuendo, intimidation, humiliation, discrediting information, and isolation—in short, a malicious, nonsexual and nonracial, general harassment. A CNN report on the phenomenon notes that vigilantes are geared well beyond the shame of exposure, reprimand, and debate. Public shaming before thousands while exposing their identities, photographic images, and personal contact information that subject the target to fraud, identity theft, and threats of violence toward them and their families have all been vigorously and gleefully pursued. According to law professor Daniel Solove, permanent records of norm violations is "upping the sanction to a whole new level . . . allowing bloggers to act as a cyber-posse, tracking down violators and branding them with digital scarlet letters."[52]

---

52. DANIEL SOLOVE, THE FUTURE OF REPUTATION: GOSSIP, RUMOR, AND PRIVACY ON THE INTERNET 6 (2007).

✻ Celebrity Gurus and Backlash Scandals

Few modern celebrities have provided as much grist for the scandal mill as morals maven Laura Schlessinger, a radio talk show host known to most as "Dr. Laura." Schlessinger's incessant moralizing from the quintessential bully pulpit features vitriolic responses to listener questions and presents an interesting line of questions in the debate over where her privacy begins and the public interest in having her exposed her as a "fraud" actually ends. The emergence of Dr. Laura and Dr. Phil onto the national stage epitomizes the lightning rod effects of privacy invasion in the new slash-and-burn talk television and radio formats. These fuel even more questions around professional authenticity and the effectiveness of quasi-therapeutic settings, which have been ignored by the media in an era where the public yearns for validation by means of another's submission to the whip or scourge.

Dr. Robert Epstein, in the article "Physiologist Laura" reports that after monitoring Schlessinger's radio show, he was "both sickened and saddened by what we've found." "Schlessinger's doctorate is in physiology, not psychology, but calling herself 'Dr.' while dispensing psychological advice suggests otherwise. In a survey we conducted recently in New York, of 50 people who said they knew who Schlessinger was, 44% said she was either a psychologist or a psychiatrist." Epstein concludes "if she's really talking to an audience of 18 million admirers every day, we're a nation in deep trouble, and here's why":

First, her advice is often divisive, potentially driving apart spouse from spouse, lover from lover, even parent from child.

Second—and this is doubly ironic given both her checkered personal history and her image as a mental health professional—she often conveys the message that people can't change:

In one poignant call, a young woman said that she had married a prisoner who had "drastically changed" in order to give him a "second chance." Laura's reply? "You're lying . . . You don't know that he changed." To a woman concerned about her fiancé's behavior, Laura advised against counseling, because "there's no counseling for character." As a young woman, Schlessinger herself dated and "shacked up" with a married man, posed for nude pictures, and committed other indiscretions of a sort that she now condemns daily. She has changed; can't others do so too? If people can't change, what's the point of psychotherapy or, for that matter, of advice shows?

Third, she not only models intolerance and abusive behavior but also advocates such behavior—even violence. She cuts people off—people calling for help, people trusting her with their problems. She calls people names: "he's evil," "you're a whore," "they're crappy people," "you're a doormat," "they're both sickos." No legitimate mental health professional would ever give the kind of hateful, divisive advice that Schlessinger doles out daily. Real therapists try to heal wounds and bring people together, not instigate conflict.[53]

Schlessinger's role as a national media figure poisons the well of discourse.

Democratic nations operate under a social compact whose boundaries promote civility, community, and civic responsibility. These boundaries work in tandem with a host of interactive rules that are the hallmark of a well-ordered society, because the rules incorporate those limits. Although social conceptualizations of order, propriety, and respect are fluid, changing, and subject to rationally imposed time, place, and manner restrictions, most people are becoming less adept at understanding when a line has

---

53. *Id.*

been crossed. When operating in the public interest the media should highlight rather than blur those boundaries.

Freedom of the Press in Democratic Societies

The European Court of Human Rights in *Case of Von Hannover* emphasized the context in which the offending photos and articles were published, noting the atmosphere of ongoing harassment that the European Human Rights Convention specifically forbids. The original role of the press is to inform the public of those matters that affect social, political, and economic change. Neutral reporting rather than celebrity stalking is the mandate under which freedom was granted to the press. Thus, it is important to know why a free press is essential and why some regulation of the press is desirable, which is analogous to legitimate curtailment of any other abusive power.

THREE

Public Media
The Quintessential Role of a Free Press

A free press is not a privilege, but an organic necessity in a great society. One sign of the importance of a free press is that when antidemocratic forces take over a country, their first act is often to muzzle the press.[1]

In American civil jurisprudence, the free trade in ideas has historically enjoyed a heightened level of constitutional protection. Two centuries of rhetoric surrounding the First Amendment to the U.S. Constitution demonstrate that even ideas repeatedly shown to be antithetical to truth and the most damaging to individuals and society still receive protection without regard to the extent of their dissemination. Conversely, ideas deemed valuable based upon near-universal consensus around matters of general welfare are often suppressed. These "market conditions" have attenuated constitutional protections for individual reputations against powerful entities. That such protection is mandated by the Constitution and consistent with the goals of a free press is not entirely clear from examining its evolutionary path.

---

1. WALTER LIPPMAN, A PREFACE TO MORALS (1929).

𝕸 Historical Backdrop

Among U.S. constitutional law scholars, there is substantial agreement that the First Amendment is indeed the holy ground upon which critical legal scholars must remove their shoes before stepping. The Bill of Rights refers to the first 10 amendments to the Constitution. The First Amendment is typically cited as the most important in the Bill of Rights, as evidenced by its primacy in the constitutional order. However, it was actually the third among the original amendments presented to the Continental Congress. The celebrated clauses (five in all) guaranteeing liberty of conscience in the realms of religion, speech, press, assembly, and petition, along with academic freedom and freedom of association as inherent liberties, became the first of many presented for ratification only after the two preceding amendments failed to gain the requisite number of votes.

The nation's founders enacted the First Amendment in response to censorship and prosecution for criticism of the British Crown. English libel law was invoked to punish statements damaging to another's reputation or impugned the integrity of officials acting on behalf of church and state, whether true or false. Monarchies reigned throughout Europe where national allegiance to a single established church was the rule rather than the exception. Government, like the church, was perceived as an agent of divine law.

The historic concern of the First Amendment related to official suppression of dissent through seditious libel laws.[2] Criticism of politicians in matters related to their official conduct was deemed an important component of a functioning democracy. Truth or falsity of the alleged infraction as the basis for liability was the first battleground.

---

2. *See* EDWIN G. BURROWS & MIKE WALLACE, GOTHAM: A HISTORY OF NEW YORK CITY TO 1898 153–55 (1998).

Public sentiment in 1735 favored protection for true statements (against the trial judge's express instructions concerning its lack of relevance under common law) when a jury acquitted a man who had merely printed statements critical of New York's governor. The report alleged that a local judge was only removed from office in retaliation for a ruling that went against the governor's interests. Retaliatory behavior by public officials is still grounds for removal. A report found that former Alaska Governor Sarah Palin, the first female G.O.P. VIP candidate, abused her official power when she removed a high-ranking official in apparent retaliation for his refusal to fire a state police officer involved in a nasty divorce from Palin's sister.

The plain text of the First Amendment, authored by James Madison and ratified by Congress in 1791, is simple:

Congress shall make no law respecting an establishment of religion, or prohibiting the free exercise thereof; or abridging the freedom of speech, or of the press; or the right of the people peaceably to assemble, and to petition the Government for a redress of grievances.[3]

Madison championed liberty of conscience as a necessary component of civic engagement in pursuit of representative governments. A number of state governments included mirror clauses in their state constitutions for the same purposes. Our national ethos represents a straightforward general theory of superpower superiority: the United States has the oldest living constitution and a thriving democracy as a direct result of these safeguards. This theory is subject to relatively little scrutiny. We take as an article of faith that strong support for free expression means the electorate is (or at least may one day be) comprised of model citizens who speak

---

3. U.S. CONST. amend. I.

out, vote, and give consent to those who govern as those fully and purposefully engaged in civic culture.

Toward the end of the French Revolution, Edmund Burke, an 18th-century British politician, is credited with declaring that although there are three Estates in Parliament, the Reporters Gallery constituted a Fourth Estate more important by far than the others.[4] Overnight, the term *Fourth Estate* became synonymous with the press. Its popularity is a testament to the notion that the avowed purpose of the press clause in the Constitution was to create a mechanism outside of governmental control as an additional check on the three official branches.

However, during the same period, Federalists claimed that threats to national security arising from those sympathetic to French revolutionaries required the immediate passage of the Sedition Act of 1798. Thus, it became a federal crime to publish false, scandalous, and malicious writing against the U.S. president or members of Congress with the intent to defame, to bring them into contempt or disrepute, or to excite hatred against them. The Sedition Act was passed and set to expire just prior to the presidential election of 1800, with the only men prosecuted under the law being editors and proprietors of newspapers sympathetic to rivals of the ruling political party.

Despite the Bill of Rights being designed to prohibit such laws, and their only being applicable to national government, a lively debate ensued with the 1868 passage of the Fourteenth Amendment concerning the logic and necessity of extending key provisions in the Bill of Rights to individuals against infringement by state authorities. Under an ad hoc approach, the prohibitions of the First Amendment were first initially applied to state and local governments through the doctrine of incorporation 128 years after its passage.

---

4. THOMAS CARLYLE, HEROES AND HERO WORSHIP IN HISTORY 228 (John Chester Adams ed., 1907).

The U.S. Supreme Court's 1919 ruling in *Near v. Minnesota* was the first to invalidate a state law that targeted the press.[5] The state statute punishing malicious, scandalous, or defamatory publications as a public nuisance was specifically designed to close down a single newspaper, the *Saturday Press*, which published anti-Semitic rants and included details of corrupt practices by prominent business and government figures. On appeal to the Supreme Court, the paper claimed the law violated the free press clause. With exceptions for wartime emergencies, a narrow majority held the newspaper had a constitutional right—nay duty—to publish its views without threat of government censorship. The four dissenting justices rejected this broad view as they read the First Amendment as insuring the liberty to publish truth in good faith and for justifiable ends. The disagreement over who is qualified to enforce such norms has yet to subside. Subsequent cases invalidating taxes on newspapers and all forms of prior restraint became the rule rather than the exception.

As the debate about necessary limits on free expression raged on, enlightenment scholars searched for a means of justifying its protection. Scholars of constitutional history have debated endlessly about the three main justifications for freedom of conscience, reaching a general consensus around three concepts: (1) the search for truth to aid the task of self-governance, (2) the ability to freely access information for evaluating candidates for public office, and (3) the freedom of general inquiry essential to notions of self-actualization.

The primary champion of the ideological free-for-all was the late Justice Oliver Wendell Holmes, who declared: "[the] Constitution was made for people of fundamentally differing views and the accident of our finding certain opinions natural, familiar, novel or even shocking ought not to conclude our judgment upon the question whether statutes embodying them conflict with the Constitution of

---

5. Near v. Minnesota, 283 U.S. 697 (1931).

the United States."[6] Therefore, the main goal is the freedom to search for truth.

Holmes declared that speech operates in a competitive realm where a consumer's natural selection of true ideas and authentic representations are certain. However, this theory ignores the possibility that average citizens may deny the truth when they hear it, and that persistent challenges to an objective truth may not propel us toward "verification" of the offered claim.

Failure of markets, financial or otherwise, is worthy of constitutional notice in the context of free speech. On one hand, we justify elevating protection for nearly every kind of speech as a means of discovering something important about the world, but on the other, we fail to incorporate general knowledge of the psychological processes embraced by most people. Thus, the notion rings hollow that all viewpoints are entitled to representation in the Millsian marketplace of ideas[7] without a corresponding entitlement or access to a shared market space and resources, reproducing all the traditional problems of the economic market without addressing core First Amendment issues.

The Power of Persuasion against the Fortress of Belief

Research has shown that understanding is chosen or created rather than discovered. People rarely embrace ideas because they ring true; instead, they do so based upon how closely those ideas align with their own core beliefs. Emotional and irrational appeals have great impact and subconscious repressions, phobias, and desires all influence individual capacity to assimilate messages. Stimulus response (*I too fell flat on my face once while wearing a bathing suit*)

---

6. Lochner v. New York, 198 U.S. 45, 65 (1905).

7. JOHN STUART MILL, ON LIBERTY (1859).

and selective attention and retention processes (*I conveniently forgot those crazy promiscuous college years as I think how awful it is that she's been with so many men*) influence daily understanding and perspectives.

Rather than treat truth as the cream that rises to the top of a frothy refreshing debate, a more lucid approach to First Amendment jurisprudence might take into account that individuals tend to affirm as truth only the information that confirms their own long-held beliefs. Opportunities to influence opinion by so-called rational means are possible largely only in those areas where an individual has not already formed an opinion. As we move toward areas in which public opinion is up for grabs, we quickly encounter the twin obstacles of credibility and access.

✍ Credibility and Access to Public Debate

As a matter of political expediency, a host of labels were created to discount the message of particular speakers. For example, we imbue Harvard graduates with near-instant credibility, assuming they are among the best and the brightest and therefore likely to be individuals with whom we could meaningfully engage. Yet when the Harvard graduate is a woman who has something important to say about what she sees as systemic affronts to women's rights, she is labeled a radical feminist to discount the message. As with the emergency broadcast system, we are forewarned that if the messenger is a "radical feminist" or prone to playing the "race card," we are likely to be dragged into a meaningless debate, or worse yet, engaged by an individual who "has their own agenda." The labeling effectively guarantees that freedom of inquiry, debate, and access to the marketplace of ideas do not rise to the level of established rights that members of the ruling elite at either the micro or macro level are bound to respect.

Few critiques of public media focus on whose interests are served by giving the Associated Press (or any other news producer) unqualified rights to present only one side of major political debates while ignoring issues of credibility and the unequal distribution of power. As we shall note throughout, the *New York Times, Boston Globe, Wall Street Journal*, and other major newspapers are large-scale corporations. If the authors of the Constitution could have envisioned the modern news organization, would they have provided greater or lesser protection for the rights of the individual? There is an absence of credible proof that we can *discover* an objective truth, coupled with ample evidence that those in power go to great lengths to thwart its discovery. Hence, the critical inquiry becomes: how does truth seeking continues to serve as a justification for heightened speech protection if we discount the claim that the justification itself has become the very orthodoxy against which the freedom provides a necessary hedge?

𝍌 Truth v. Dead Dogma

Conceptualizing liberty of conscience as a precursor for the exercise of political rights has converted a now famous philosophical refrain into judicial mantra: a living truth is preferable to a dead dogma.[8] Justice Learned Hand stated:

> The interest, which [the First Amendment] guards, and which gives it its importance, presupposes that there are no orthodoxies—religious, political, economic, or scientific—which are immune from debate and dispute. Back of that is the assumption—itself an orthodoxy, and the one permissible exception – that truth will be most likely to emerge, if no limitations are imposed upon utterances that can with any plausibility be regarded as efforts to present grounds for accepting or rejecting propositions whose truth the utterer asserts, or denies.[9]

---

8. *Id.*

9. Int'l Bhd. of Elec. Workers v. NLRB, 181 F.2d 34, 40 (2d Cir. 1950).

Some scholars deny the power to discover an objective truth or reach an optimal level of self-governance by implication. However, they do agree with Justice Jackson's assessment: "If there is any fixed star in our constitutional constellation, it is that no official, high or petty, can prescribe what shall be orthodox in politics, nationalism, religion, or other matters of opinion, or force citizens to confess by word or act their faith therein."[10] One scholar has argued that the only consistent justification for the First Amendment relates to the value of *self-actualization*.[11] Those who lay claim to the liberty extolled by debates surrounding the U.S. Constitution and certain articles of the European Convention reference the inviolable nature of human dignity that must be respected and protected both for (and especially during) the development of one's personality. A comprehensive doctrinal analysis of the ostensible role of free speech in modern civic culture reveals a certain preoccupation (some would say lip service) to the ideals of authenticity and autonomy. Authenticity implies a duty to reach one's "full potential," and autonomy suggests that only those possessing the courage it takes to "live your own life or be your own person" reap the rewards of enlightened self-expression or actualization. The search for truth in substantiation of theories grounded in open markets, self-governance, and self-realization (and as hedge against orthodoxy) has led to a necessary extension of protections for academic freedom.

Enlightenment philosophers believed it was the duty of government and citizens to work together toward discovering the truth while exposing false and misleading ideas.[12] The court in *Sweezy v.*

---

10. West Virginia State Board of Education v. Barnette, 319 U.S. 624, 642 (1943).

11. Martin H. Redish, Money talks: speech, economic power, and the values of democracy, 72, 2001 NYU Press.

12. Johann Gottlieb Fichte, *Zurückforderung der Denkfreiheit von der Fürsten Europens die sie bisher unterdrückten. Eine Rede* (1793); *see also*, Lindsey Armstrong Smith, *Johann Gottlieb Fichte's Free Speech Theory*, 4 AM. COMM. J. 1, 3 (2001).

New Hampshire concurred with these views toward collaboration as part of the government's obligation to educate the public: "No one should underestimate the vital role in a democracy that is played by those who guide and train our youth. To impose any strait jacket upon the intellectual leaders in our colleges and universities would imperil the future of our Nation."[13]

Academic freedom is a constitutionally protected means to a constitutionally desired end, wherein freedom from orthodoxy in teaching and learning is the customary method of exploring truth without fear as the core of the pedagogical enterprise. Freedom of association is the end result of that exploration. Outside of the need to protect lawful political organizing, inquiry, and affiliation, the power of mass movements to render significant and lasting changes in the political landscape holds significant First Amendment implications. Contrary to the received wisdom, courts have provided far less protection for groups and individuals facing government repression, than have members of Congress in responding to the manifest will of the people.[14] Yet, from a constitutional perspective, the guarantees afforded to the press were ushered in by the courts on the coattails of associational freedom and the political reforms demanded during the early civil rights and peace movements.

⅍ Freedom of Association in the United States

The early labor and civil rights cases provided the impetus toward a strong statement of principle governing associational freedom in the United States. The conditions preceding the declarations are well-known by those who have studied that history. Works such as the *Price of Dissent* provide ample analysis of the conditions that led

---

13. Sweezy v. New Hampshire, 354 U.S. 234, 250 (1957).

14. David Kairys, *Introduction* to THE POLITICS OF LAW: A PROGRESSIVE CRITIQUE 1, 10–11 (David Kairys ed., 3d ed. 1998).

to political repression in the United States.[15] Many of its contributors lived to actually talk about the crimes against those involved in demand for human rights for Black America from the post-slavery era: from apartheid in American employment, housing, and education and the concept of the minstrel in its various forms as a weapon in the fight over imagery in popular culture to Klan violence, lynching, and the mob violence that ravaged the all-black town of Rosewood, Florida. Throughout the 1950s and '60s, when the American South was still a hotbed of terrorism, killing a Negro or a civil rights worker was simply not punished as a crime. Concerted efforts by numerous civil rights organizations to register Black voters southerners in 1964 became known as Mississippi Freedom Summer. Racial terrorism resulted in six murders, 35 shootings, 30 bombings of homes, 35 church burnings, and 80 beatings. Citizens from every part of the nation began to march in protest against the scandalous misuse of police power. Those marching in Selma, Alabama made national headlines:

> The news from Selma, Alabama, where police beat and mauled and gassed unarmed, helpless and unoffending citizens will shock and alarm the whole nation. It is simply inconceivable that in this day and age, the police who have sworn to uphold the law and protect the citizenry could resort, instead, to violent attacks upon them. Decent citizens will weep for the wronged and persecuted demonstrators, for the decent citizens of Alabama who must recoil in horror from the spectacle of sadism, for the good name of the nation before the world. This brutality is the inevitable result of the intolerance fostered by an infamous state government that is without conscience or morals.[16]

---

15. BUD SCHULTZ, THE PRICE OF DISSENT: TESTIMONIES TO POLITICAL REPRESSION IN AMERICA (2001).

16. Editorial, *Outrage at Selma*, WASH. POST, March 9, 1965, at A-16, *in* DAVID J. GARROW, PROTEST AT SELMA: MARTIN LUTHER KING, JR., AND THE VOTING RIGHTS ACT OF 1965 87 (1980).

In the face of brutal repression, the National Association for the Advancement of Colored People [NAACP] continued the fight for racial justice the abolitionists began in 1909.[17] When the national office of the NAACP opened offices in a southern state, the jurisdiction's official machinery went into operation.

The organization became the bane of existence for southern leadership and a natural target for anti-Black legislation. Southern state strategies included attempts to have civil rights organizations classified as subversive and widely imposed severe economic reprisals for Blacks who became involved in civil rights.[18] Federal troops were required to uphold court-ordered desegregation in the high schools.[19]

It was in *NAACP v. Alabama* when the U.S. Supreme Court first protected freedom of association. State officials had demanded a

---

17. The NAACP was formed in response to the 1908 race riot in Springfield, capital of Illinois and birthplace of President Abraham Lincoln. Appalled at the violence committed against blacks, a group of white liberals that included Mary White Ovington and Oswald Garrison Villard (both the descendants of abolitionists) issued a call for a meeting to discuss racial justice. Some 60 people, only seven of whom were African American (including W. E. B. Du Bois, Ida B. Wells-Barnett, and Mary Church Terrell) signed the call, which was released on the centennial of Lincoln's birth. Echoing the focus of Du Bois' militant all-black Niagara Movement, the NAACP's stated goal was to secure for all people the rights guaranteed in the 13th, 14th, and 15th Amendments to the U.S. Constitution; these rights promised an end to slavery, equal protection of the law, and universal adult male suffrage, respectively. (*See* Kate Tuttle, *NAACP, National Association for the Advancement of Colored People: An Interracial Membership Organization, Founded in 1909, that is Devoted to Civil Rights and Racial Justice, in* AFRICANA: THE ENCYCLOPEDIA OF THE AFRICAN AND AFRICAN AMERICAN EXPERIENCE 388 (Kwame A. Appiah & Henry L. Gates, Jr. eds., 2003).

18. *See* Robin D. Barnes, *The Reality and Ideology of First Amendment Jurisprudence: Giving Aid and Comfort to Racial Terrorists, in* FREEING THE FIRST AMENDMENT: CRITICAL PERSPECTIVES ON FREEDOM OF EXPRESSION (Robert Jensen & David Allen eds., 1995).

19. *See* Constance Baker Motley, *The Historical Setting of* Brown *and Its Impact on the Supreme Court's Decision*, 61 FORDHAM L. REV. 9 (1992).

list of all NAACP members, which the organization refused to give.[20] The Court found that state officers wanted the list to expose NAACP members to community reprisals (such as loss of employment, calling or denial of bank loans, mortgage foreclosures, and KKK violence). The court found an interplay between governmental and private action: "only after the initial exertion of state power represented by the production order, did the private action take hold."[21]

Students protests at the University of California at Berkeley from 1963–67, at Columbia University in 1967 and 1968, at Kent State University in 1970, and Jackson State University in 1970 are among the most memorable worldwide for the participants' determination to eliminate racism, halt the draft, and end the Vietnam War. Contemporaneous statements of principle were developed about citizen support for the role of a free press. The post–1960s' era ushered in a period of excitement and sense of purpose for the national press.

The Supreme Court's ruling in the landmark case of *New York Times Co. v. Sullivan* also grew out of calls for enforcement of civil rights against government repression. Brutality against civil rights advocates in Montgomery, Alabama, prompted a group of civil and human rights organizations along with prominent individuals to take out a full-page advertisement in the *New York Times* entitled "Heed Their Rising Voices."[22] The ad reported details of the violent responses to peaceful protests that civil rights workers faced and solicited donations for legal fees and the like. Although police

---

20. NAACP v. Alabama, 357 U.S. 449 (1958).

21. Robin D. Barnes, *Blue by Day and White by [K]night: Regulating the Political Affiliations of Law Enforcement and Military Personnel*, 81 IOWA L. REV. 1079, 1141 (1996).

22. New York Times Co. v. Sullivan, 376 U.S. 254 (1964) (per curiam), establishing constitutional protection for libel of public figures and indirectly establishing the informational function of some forms of advertising. The ad appeared on March 29, 1960. (*See* Susan Dente Ross,*"Their Rising Voices:"A Study of Civil Rights, Social Movements, and Advertising in the New York Times*, 75 JOURNALISM & MASS COMMC'N. Q. 518 (1998).)

commissioner I.B. Sullivan was not mentioned by name, he still sued the *Times*, alleging that its factual errors defamed his reputation concerning performance of his official duties. A local jury found in Sullivan's favor and awarded him a $500,000 in damages.

Justice William Brennan, Jr. wrote for the majority:

> [W]e consider this case against the background of a profound national commitment to the principle that debate on public issues should be uninhibited, robust, and wide-open, and that it may well include vehement, caustic, and sometimes unpleasantly sharp attacks on government and public officials. The present advertisement, as an expression of grievance and protest on one of the major public issues of our time, would seem clearly to qualify for the constitutional protection. The question is whether it forfeits that protection by the falsity of some of its factual statements and by its alleged defamation of respondent.[23]

The case was hailed as a victory for proponents of a free press as it pertains to important matters of national debates. Just seven years later, following an intense battle with the Justice Department the *New York Times* secured a second complete victory in the Supreme Court as well as the most prestigious honor in the publishing industry, the highly coveted Pulitzer Prize, in a case involving the Pentagon.

The Pentagon Papers

In June 1971, a reporter for the *New York Times* obtained a leaked copy of government documents that were classified at the time and known to contain details of the U.S. government's decision-making process regarding the war in Vietnam. The *New York Times* published

---

23. *New York Times*, 376 U.S. at 270.

a series of articles with details of how the government misled the American people about the war. The newspaper published its first report on June 13, 1971; on June 14th it received a telegram from U.S. Attorney General John Mitchell warning that publication of classified information was a violation of the Espionage Act and that further publication would cause "irreparable injury to the defense interests of the United States."[24]

The most interesting part of the case is the shared sense, among news editors, of a unifying mission regarding the responsibilities of a free press in a democracy. Just as the *New York Times* began publication of the Pentagon Papers, the Justice Department secured a temporary injunction against it. The next day, the *Washington Post* began publishing information from its copy of the Pentagon Papers. As the government sought to enjoin the *Post*, the *Boston Globe* published its take on the documents. Unsurprisingly, the lower courts were busy illustrating key elements of chaos theory. The underlying order in apparently random views on the applicability of the press clause is that when data surfaces that is damaging to the government (without threatening national security), the burden of proof shifts to the government to justify restraint.[25]

However, the underlying order was not viewed unanimously by the lower courts, and the government claimed that publication threatened national security interests. Thus, the Supreme Court agreed to an expedited hearing. In a 6–3 decision, the Court ruled in *New York Times Co. v. United States* that publication of the series could continue because prior restraint on publication "bears[s] a heavy presumption against its constitutional validity."[26]

---

24. Telegram from John Mitchell, Attorney General, to the N.Y. Times, *in* Margaret A. Blanchard, Revolutionary Sparks: Freedom of Expression in Modern America 370 (1992).

25. *See, e.g.*, Org. for a Better Austin v. Keefe, 402 U.S. 415, 419–20 (1971).

26. *New York Times*, 403 U.S. at 714 (per curiam) (*quoting* Bantam Books, Inc. v. Sullivan, 372 U.S. 58, 70 (1963)).

The Court based its decision on a number of different concepts. Justice Brandeis viewed participation in public discussion as part of a person's civic duty and a fundamental principle of American governance.[27] The ability to enter that discussion to carry out the person's responsibilities as a citizen required complete and timely information from independent sources. Justice Potter Stewart also saw the role of an independent press as essential in exposing governmental corruption.[28] Justice William O. Douglas concluded that the press facilitates the public's "right to know,"[29] which includes knowing that which is crucial to the governing process. Despite the risk that some disclosures may have a serious impact, the dominant intent behind the press clause was to prohibit the practice of governmental suppression.[30] Thus, in the midst of an important national debate over U.S. involvement in the war in Vietnam, the Supreme Court made it clear that citizens were entitled to the information that allowed for their intelligent participation.

🎞 Freedom of Information Act

The concept of participatory governance originated from the theory that the people, from whom all power is derived, must be secured in their right to obtain government documents and to have guaranteed access to information through publicly held meetings. Thus, statutory rights to obtain desired information and to observe decision makers in action (such as judicial proceedings) have all been justified as part of the public's right to observe and to critique the

---

27. *See* Whitney v. California, 274 U.S. 357, 375 (1927) (Brandeis, J., concurring).

28. *See* Houchins v. KQED, Inc., 438 U.S. 1, 17 (1978) (Powell, J., concurring) (quoting Estes v. Texas, 381 U.S. 532, 539 (1965)).

29. *New York Times Co.*, 403 U.S. at 721.

30. *Id.* at 723–24.

efficacy of governmental operations. In responding to growing demands for transparency and cooperation, federal and state versions of public access to information laws were proposed.

Congress passed the Freedom of Information Act [FOIA] in 1967.[31] Members of the press, political organizers, and consumer organizations along with leaders of public interest and advocacy groups made it clear they expected both thorough and timely responses to requests for government information. This is key to obtaining the knowledge necessary for casting an "intelligent ballot, to sign a petition for or against some proposal, write letters to the legislature, and in general fulfill the obligations of a citizen. And it would be impossible without the presence of a free press."[32]

%% Editorial Discretion, Confidential Sources, and Fair Reporting

During this period, the U.S. Supreme Court also extended protection for editorial discretion. A Florida statute granting political candidates the right to equal space to reply to a newspaper's criticism and attacks on their record was struck down by the Court in *Miami Herald Publishing Co. v. Tornillo.*[33] The Court ruled that forced or compelled publications would place an undue burden on the press by diverting resources away from other priorities and impermissibly intruding on editorial prerogative.[34] Statutory discrimination through imposition of special taxes or selective taxes upon members of the press has also been struck by the Court.[35] In a twist on

---

31. 5 U.S.C. § 552 (1967).

32. USINFO.state.gov, *Rights of the People: Individual Freedom and the Bill of Rights*, http://usinfo.state.gov/products/pubs/rightsof/press.htm.

33. Miami Herald Publ'g. Co. v. Tornillo, 418 U.S. 241 (1974).

34. *Id.*

35. Minneapolis Star & Tribune Co. v. Minnesota Comm'r of Revenue, 460 U.S. 575 (1983).

the traditional framework of accountability in libel cases, false or defamatory third party statements made in public proceedings and part of public records that are fairly and accurately reported will not result in publisher liability.[36]

Fair Public Trials

The 1980 case *Richmond Newspapers, Inc. v. Virginia* dealt with decisions to summarily close the courtroom doors.[37] Following three mistrials of a defendant charged with murder, the judge and both attorneys agreed to close the courtroom to spectators at the start of a fourth trial. This was a matter of grave concern to the U.S. Supreme Court as it affected the rights of those accused to have a jury of their peers, a speedy public trial, effective assistance of counsel, and impartial judicial proceedings, especially in capital cases. It also impacted the public's interest in the fair administration of justice. The judicial use of gag orders, sealing of court documents, changes in venue, sequestering of jurors, and a host of other procedural mechanisms have long been utilized keeping those interests in mind. As the Court found the right of the public and press to attend criminal trials is guaranteed under the First and Fourteenth Amendments, it overturned the trial court's decision.[38]

Balancing the Public's Right to Know

Offering special protections to the press as a matter of general importance is consistent with the goals of democracy. However,

---

36. *See* Jonathan Donnellan & Justin Peacock, *Truth and Consequences: First Amendment Protection for Accurate Reporting on Government Investigations*, 50 N.Y.U. L. Rev. 237, 239–43 (2006).

37. Richmond Newspapers Inc., v. Virginia, 488 U.S. 555 (1980).

38. *Id.*

ascertaining the appropriate balance when confronted with equally legitimate areas of societal concern has been more difficult than it needs to be and has been handled quite poorly in some instances. For example, as a part of the investigative process, journalists must occasionally rely on confidential sources to gather important information that they might not otherwise be able to lawfully obtain. The First Amendment provides journalists with a limited privilege not to disclose their sources or information.[39] Yet reporters who observed and then wrote about matters directly relating to criminal conduct could not exercise such privileges when called to testify before a grand jury.[40] Shield laws now protect news gathering by providing a qualified privilege in less compelling circumstances by shifting the burden of proof so that those seeking disclosure must prove relevance, necessity, and inability to obtain the information from other available sources.[41]

As state laws shielding the use of unnamed sources have increased, so have the number of stories utilizing them, thereby prompting an increase in prosecutorial attempts to subpoena journalists' work product. Journalists have been called to identify confidential sources and/or to produce items used to record information, such as notes, documents, and photographs. Invariably, government officials seem to assert interests that involve public safety, morality in relation to minors, or national security as a compelling justification when seeking confidential information.

At other times, retaliatory actions by government officials who have attempted to utilize the journalist's privilege have been duly noted. The most recent and shocking case dealt with the claim that high level government officials leaked the name of a Central

---

39. *See* Associated Press v. United States, 326 U.S. 1, 20 (1945*)*; Branzburg v. Hayes, 408 U.S. 665, 681 (1972).

40. *Branzburg*, 408 U.S. at 671.

41. *See, e.g.*, Daniel Joyce, *The Judith Miller Case and the Relationship Between Reporter and Source: Competing Visions of the Media's Role and Function*, 17 Fordham Intell. Prop. Media & Ent. L.J. 555, 564–68 (2007).

Intelligence Agency [CIA] operative in retaliation for her husband's exercise of free speech. He revealed that the Bush Administration presented fake evidence to the American public to justify the invasion of Iraq. In June 2003, a conversation among reporters and Bush administration officials revealed the employment of a classified, covert CIA officer. Her husband had previously stated in various interviews and subsequent writings his belief that the administration knowingly revealed her identity realizing it would place her life in danger as retribution for his op-ed entitled "What I Didn't Find in Africa," published in the *New York Times* on July 6, 2003, where he charged that the administration's claim that Iraq had weapons of mass destruction was only a pretext for going to war.[42] The retaliatory acts threatening the life of CIA operative Valerie Plame stand out from the rest. Former President Bush's top aides were accused of facilitating and covering up some of the most egregious violations of rights in modern history.

Historically, the courts have been reluctant to extend unqualified protection to confidential sources. However, journalists claim that without the promise of confidentiality, reluctant sources remain silent, thereby chilling the free flow of information. Publishers warn that the burden on news gathering that results from compelled disclosure outweighs the public interest in obtaining the information as future sources with legitimate fears of retribution will decline to speak without anonymity. Compelled disclosure tends to hinder investigative reporting into high level corruption, such as was found in the Enron case. Thus, the only sustained public interest appears to relate to law enforcement, held to outweigh the "uncertain burden on news gathering."[43]

---

42. Joseph C. Wilson, *What I Didn't Find in Africa*, N.Y. TIMES, July 6, 2003.

43. *Branzburg*, 408 U.S. at 689.

𝕎 The Decline of Investigative Journalism Meets a Change in Journalistic Standards

The burdens on news gathering appear to be substantial, but rarely openly challenged as part of a wave of political repression or an attempt to affect a quid pro quo. We would have to concede in every principled discussion of the First Amendment guarantee of a free press that investigative journalism focused upon government officials and powerful corporate actors is the closest we will ever get to the heart of what the guarantee was designed to protect. Ask any serious journalist about necessary safeguards and very different accounts of the reality on the ground begin to emerge, as the so-called protective surface adopts a mercurial nature.

Investigative reporting is designed to uncover information about wide-scale corruption and injury to large segments of the public. There are reporters for whom serious news is the only news, and they have indeed paid a price for revealing information that powerful corporate and government actors have fought to keep secret. As reporter Judith Miller herself has said, "A case like mine is a warning to people not to talk because the government will come after you."[44]

David Walker of the UK's *Guardian* believes that today's journalists and editors undertake deliberate political activism in their writing, demonstrating a dangerous trend toward mixing commentary and factual reporting and thereby increasing public distrust of political discourse.[45] The business of trading off-the-record or leaked information for favorable coverage and the phenomenal growth of stories based upon unsubstantiated information weakens representative politics. If the press is to play a constitutionally protected role in providing checks and balances against the State's

---

44. Katharine Q. Seelye, *2 Reporters Express Dismay But Say They're Resolute*, N.Y. Times, Feb. 16, 2005.

45. Nicholas Jones & David Walker, Invisible Political Actors: The Press as Agents of Anti Politics (2004).

abuse of power, then setting of adequate priorities is required. The courts have near exclusive jurisdiction over enforcement as natural guardians of the constitutional order. Today, the United States operates:

> [U]nder a system that guarantees heightened deference to individual and institutional advocates, despite irreconcilable differences in their nature and origins, as well as enormous inequities in their capital resources and overall means of influence. The long-term implications of maintaining a free press under corporate domination, and in light of evolving technologies that impact public media generally, are ripe for constitutional analysis.[46]

If constitutionally guaranteed liberties includes the right to live as we wish without intruding upon the rights of others or jeopardizing public health and safety, from whence cometh the great debate? In two words: *tabloid publishers* and the support they receive from conventional media channels. Tabloid publishing, as with yellow journalism, has always been at odds with the desire for high levels of civility and other-regarding norms. Beyond civility, issues of tangible harm in the realm of individual reputation and dignity have not always been easy to redress. However, at the intersection of the invasion of an individual's privacy, the making of defamatory statements, and blatant profiteering, the Constitution stands as a reminder of the higher order values and primary evidence of our social and political contract. Nothing about the general circumstances of individuals with celebrity status justifies denying them the protections available to average citizens. Instead of offering celebrities the average citizen protection to which they are entitled,

---

46. Robin D. Barnes, *How Civil Rights and Pro-Peace Demonstrations Transformed the Press Clause Through Surrogacy*, 34 WM. MITCHELL L. REV. 1021, 1025 (2008).

we have consistently provided them with less protections, thereby inducing the very free-for-all whose political consequences are now evident.

In short, detailed coverage of Wall Street's corporate scandals and their impact on global economic markets is far closer to what the public has a right to know than whether Angelina Jolie is planning to have more children. We have allowed lofty statements of principle to devolve into massive deregulation of public media giants so that information widely disseminated in the public sphere has been manipulated in all the ways and by all the means useful for converting us into a tell-all society with only vague notions of the role of public media.

FOUR

Fundamental Nature of Privacy

The essence of democracy is its assurance that every human being should so respect himself and should be so respected in his own personality that he should have opportunity equal to that of every other human being to show what he was meant to become.

—Anna Garlin Spencer

※ Historical Foundations in the United States

In the late 1800s, more than a century after America's declaration of independence from the tyranny of King George III, Justice Louis Brandeis coauthored a famous essay declaring that the law must afford a remedy "for the unauthorized circulation of portraits of private persons; and the evil of invasion of privacy by the newspapers."[1] Arguably, the view that privacy was a necessary means for preservation of dignity and reputation was less complex in the late 19th century. Concepts related to sacred duties and the inalienable interests in life, liberty, and autonomy meant that familial honor was an important element of civic life.

---

1. Samuel Warren & Louis Brandeis, *The Right to Privacy*, 4 HARV. L. REV. 193, 195 (1890).

Today, as Richard Epstein observes, accounting for a rule of privacy that answers all of the practical and theoretical questions posed by today's cadre of Ivy League scholars could take another century. In the late 1960s, psychologist and sociologists joined the debate as legal scholars began to look almost exclusively at the growing need to regulate governmental use of private information. Professor Paul Schwartz provides a comprehensive review of the history of data protection from a comparative law perspective.[2]

In the United States, the debate has expanded to include the social and personal dimensions of privacy. Privacy is recognized as significant for autonomous feats and essential for relaxation, solitude, and shared intimacy. Moreover, privacy is a prerequisite for the adequate formation of personal, political, and spiritual identities. Despite confirmation of these observation through sociological studies, scholars have mostly examined privacy in relation to its practical implications than to an underlying psychological and constitutional primacy.

As a result, there is tangible neglect regarding the formation of adequate legal remedies in those cases where dissemination of private matters creates or maintains feelings of shame, injures wholeness, and diminishes familial integrity. The contours of the dialogue regarding long-standing methods of influencing or protecting identity and behaviors as they relate to issues of guilt, disgust, reconciliation, and redemption have shifted as the courts grapple with litigation about the rightful ownership of information traditionally reserved for personal diaries, letters, or unpublished biographies.

Professor Anita Allen supports legal protection of private behaviors and information in ways consistent with elements of societal accountability: actions taken as a "matter of actual and felt imperatives, including obligations, duties, and responsibilities."[3] She notes

---

2. Paul Schwartz, *Premption and Privacy*, 118 YALE L.J. 902 (2009).

3. Anita Allen, WHY PRIVACY ISN'T EVERYTHING: FEMINIST REFLECTIONS ON PERSONAL ACCOUNTABILITY 17 (2003).

that we all have some obligation to report, explain, and justify certain acts or omissions, then submit ourselves to appropriate sanctions upon grounds of our voluntary obligations arising out of consent, reliance, dependency, and, at times, public need.[4]

✺ Rules of Deference and Demeanor

Our collective tendencies toward overexposure and diminishing capacities for self-evaluation have led to widespread intrusion upon and trivialization of breaches involving confidential communications. Emotional release is subject to such severe ridicule that the social utility of privacy is now openly questioned as a possible nuisance. American philosopher Martha Nussbaum notes that the desire to stigmatize others grows out of individual insecurity. Without actual control over our social standing, we define a dominant group as lacking in nothing (and seek to establish our own proximity thereto) while projecting inadequacy onto outsiders. "[Only] to the extent that societies can teach people that the desired condition is one of interdependence, rather than control and self-sufficiency, [can] such pernicious tendencies . . . be minimized."[5]

Growing disdain for privacy as a normative feature of American society has spawned a shared crisis of identity. The development of identity in relation to what others think of us is a process that automatically responds to institutionalized values, everyday norms, and the example set by the clan. Social philosopher George Mead describes the organized self as merely reflective of the attitudes that are common to the group. Sociologist Erving Goffman notes how rules of "deference and demeanor" are routinely violated in institutions such as prisons and military installations as a means of

---

4. *Id.*

5. Martha C. Nussbaum, *Danger to Human Dignity: The Revival of Disgust and Shame in the Law*, 50 THE CHRON. HIGHER EDUC. B6 (2004).

separating and unhinging the identity of new initiates.[6] As a matter of great constitutional importance, interdisciplinary scholars primarily need to address from a constitutional perspective how privacy operates as a critical facet in the formation of identity.

Revisiting the premise of the Warren–Brandeis essay (as one of the better illustrations of our historical conception of individual and familial privacy) is equally important. Participation in the forms of mutual respect to which an individual has been socialized to expect secures their sense of dignity. Our ability to develop familial-style relations in an atmosphere protected from unwanted public scrutiny was singled out by Justice Brandeis as a defining characteristic of personal liberty. Interestingly, Brandeis favored extending the common law rights to the individual to determine the extent to which his or her thoughts, sentiments, and emotions would be communicated to others.[7] A century later, Justice Sandra Day O'Conner observed that under our Constitution, privacy is a liberty interest based upon individual sovereignty that shields our most intimate and personal choices.[8]

The core legal conception is simple: a meaningful *life* animated by the *liberty* to *pursue* individual *happiness* is found in the exercise of autonomy and its implications for the self-worth of the individual, because personhood and beliefs about the meaning of life cannot be defined under the coercive thumb of a state or the members of its society. The American Bill of Rights (headed by guarantees that protect religion, speech, press, assembly, petition, association, and academic freedom) all accord with the underlying regard for the dignity and worth of the individual's contribution to and potential for self-governance, as commonly accepted prerequisites for a functioning democracy.

---

6. Erving Goffman, *The Nature of Deference and Demeanor*, 58 Am. Anthropologist 473, 477 (1956).

7. Olmstead v. United States, 277 U.S. 438, 478 (1928) (Brandeis, J., dissenting).

8. *See* Planned Parenthood v. Casey, 505 U.S. 833, 847 (1992).

🏵 Self-Actualization and Renewal

American democracy's highest aspirations, after warding off the dangers of political factions outlined in Madison's Federalist No. 10,[9] is described by American psychologist Abraham Maslow in his research on the hierarchy of human needs.[10] In logical succession, beyond survival needs in the physiological realm (bodily sustenance and security) is the need to belong (acceptance and affiliation), followed by the need for self-esteem (achievement, competency, approval, and recognition). After an individual's needs are met at each of these levels, Maslow's initial conceptualization included only one growth need: self-actualization. Self-actualized people are solution-focused appreciators of life who have a higher regard for matters of personal growth and peak experiences. Greater fulfillment and actualization of an individual's potential often leads to a transcendence of self-interest with ego gratification being replaced by the desire to assist others in the realization of their higher potential. The first presidential act of Barack Obama was a proclamation declaring January 20, 2009 the *National Day of Renewal and Reconciliation.* In part, he affirmed:

> [The] story of America is one of renewal in the face of adversity, reconciliation in a time of discord, and we know that there is a purpose for everything under heaven. On this Inauguration Day, we are reminded that we are heirs to over two centuries of American democracy, and that this legacy is not simply a birthright—it is a glorious burden. Now it falls to us to come together as a people to carry it forward once more.[11]

---

9. James Madison, *Federalist No. 10: The Utility of the Union as a Safeguard against Domestic Faction and Insurrection*, DAILY ADVERTISER, Nov. 22, 1787.

10. *See* ABRAHAM MASLOW, MOTIVATION AND PERSONALITY (1954).

11. http://www.whitehouse.gov/blog/a_national_day_of_renewal_and_reconciliation/.

Moral Philosopher Judith Wagner DeCew persuasively argues that the value of privacy lies in the freedom and independence afforded to the individual.[12] Professor James Q. Whitman concluded that privacy's advocates who justify proposals for regulation in the interests of dignity and personhood invoke nothing more than an intuitive sense of dread that feeds the pervasive human anxiety about the horrors of privacy violation.[13] In reaching this conclusion, Whitman narrowly focuses on the lack of consensus around what is deemed private, describing the debate largely as a matter of contrasting sensibilities between the United States and the European Union. He cites the ancient practice of defecating in the public square (in certain European cities) as a key example of differing notions of privacy.

However, this example fails to incorporate the relationship between privacy and the core values promoted by a free speech and press on both continents. Whitman may be correct in his assessment that most of the free world could care less whether a person uses hemorrhoid cream, or that the person would be mildly horrified to have the information appear in the pages of a book about his life. However, the dignity interest imperiled by such a revelation has little to do with community standards concerning where on the "barometer of embarrassment" this particular piece of information should fall. Rather, the unauthorized exposure and unfettered control over the use of private information arouses deeper concerns about the motive and context under which publication is sought.

These factors may only be adequately addressed by declaring cognizable jurisdiction over the use and dissemination of this and all other information not justifiably in the public interest. Otherwise, we have endorsed (albeit inadvertently) the very violations of

---

12. Judith W. DeCew, *The Priority of Privacy for Medical Information*, 17 Soc. Phil. & Pol. 213–18 (2000).

13. James Q. Whitman, *The Two Western Cultures of Privacy: Dignity Versus Liberty*, 113 Yale L.J. 168, 179 (2004).

fundamental interests in dignity, self-governance, and freedom from coercion in the exercise of civil and political rights upon which this nation declared its independence.

Regulations that remedy undue invasions of privacy provide necessary safeguards relevant to civic responsibilities. The loss of civility is to be expected in a courtroom where an adversarial system is employed to enforce the rule of law, but this has relatively little impact on our understanding of what the U.S. Constitution requires. Justice Breyer reminds us that the Constitution creates a coherent framework for a certain kind of government (i.e., the framework primarily relates to the political order, and may only tangentially relate to the social values Whitman believes to be the driving force behind the relative differences in comparative privacy law).[14] The Articles of the European Declaration of Human Rights are clear on the importance of political rights and their correlation to issues of privacy and dignity, and they offer a consistent approach that is far more respectful of the egalitarian nature of the democratic process.

✍ A Case in Point: Who is Caroline of Monaco?

21st Century Woman
Daughter of the late HSH Prince Ranier III of Monaco
Wife
Mother
Philanthropist

Superficial reviews of Caroline von Hanover's life in relation to others verify these descriptions as significant aspects of it, even as

---

14. *See* STEPHEN BREYER, ACTIVE LIBERTY: INTERPRETING OUR DEMOCRATIC CONSTITUTION (2006).

they fall remarkably short of explaining who she is. Only Caroline knows what best defines her life and contributes to who she is as a person. She is a citizen of Monaco who also has a home in France. The fact that she is a member of a royal family merely demonstrates that we are all born into particular circumstances. Free citizens are guaranteed, as a matter of civil and human rights, the opportunity to place those circumstances into a larger perspective, and to determine how our socioeconomic status will ultimately manifest in our individual lives. A society's constitutional protections for freedom in matters of conscience, association, and privacy are uniquely relevant in examining connections between the sphere of our birth and the journey that defines our personal mission flowing from our respective identities.

✺ Free Development of Personality

As it acknowledges an interest in the free development of personality, the U.S. Supreme Court has recognized constitutional rights to associational freedom in both personal and political contexts. According to DeCew, in relation to that freedom, the fully formed autonomous citizen is guaranteed privacy for purposes of insulation.[15] The need to formulate a coherent identity through autonomous development in moving toward or away from our family, friends, or society is the substance of the respect and esteem we value in self-conscious beings. Scholars examine Abraham Maslow's theory on the hierarchy of needs as being consistent with Jean Piaget's cognitive development theory, but in contrast to Lev Vygotsky's social constructivist approach and Lawrence Kohlberg's planes of moral adequacy.

---

15. *See* Judith W. DeCew, In Pursuit of Privacy: Law, Ethics, and the Rise of Technology (1997).

If we deconstruct popular theories of cognitive, moral, social, and cultural factors to explain human development along life's continuum—especially in search of a constitutional principle that favors the right of the individual consistent with a *well-balanced* society—all theories collide to some extent. Yet they also converge at significant junctures on the path toward self-actualization. The primacy of the individual's occasional need to break free from dysfunctional restraints and to desire equal opportunities to be simply be left alone is where the Constitution, as *the* great social contract, works best. Individuals, as self-conscious beings with legitimate needs for self-respect, sense of independent value or worth, and formation of a coherent identity also require freedom to form or to reject varied and complex relationships with others.[16]

If there is a *story* that ultimately answers the question of who Caroline is, the question is: Why is there debate about its ownership? Whose story is it to tell? No single or combined set of circumstances, attributes, or characteristics should rightfully alter the nature of her constitutional rights as a citizen in a free society. Article 12 of the Universal Declaration of Human Rights confirms her status:

No one shall be subjected to arbitrary interference with his privacy, family, home or correspondence, nor to attacks upon his honor and reputation. Everyone has the right to the protection of the law against such interference or attacks.[17]

The European Court of Human Right's fortification of the link between privacy and reputational interests is far-reaching and beneficial to the great social contract. It strengthens the core of antidefamation law insofar as it acknowledges that an important reason the law protects reputation and privacy surrounding the

---

16. *Id.*

17. Universal Declaration of Human Rights, G.A. Res. 217A, at 71, U.N. GAOR, 3d Sess., 1st plen. mtg., U.N. Doc. A/810 (Dec. 10, 1948).

development of a person's personal and political consciousness is to "safeguard the essential dignity and worth of every human being."[18] Europe's highest court found constitutional validity in societal recognition that private life includes both the individual's physical and psychological integrity. A right to develop relationships with others for emotional fulfillment enhances individual personality as a genuine part of the private domain. The assurance afforded by Article 8 of the Convention is primarily intended to guarantee personal development in relation to others that is free from outside interference.[19] Thus, it offers protection for the zone of interaction with others that, while occurring in a public context, still easily falls within the sphere of "private life."

The fundamental importance of privacy for development of every human being's personality extends beyond nuclear and extended family circles to include communal and social dimensions. Those known to the general public are entitled to as much protection of and respect for their personal choices as we accord the average, unknown individual. The U.S. Supreme Court would better serve our democratic aspirations if it adopted a concept of private life similar to that of the European Union, which formally incorporates certain information and photographic images into protected aspects of personal life. This zone of developmental privacy was designed to secure personhood. Even if it would not rise to high-priority level in war-torn Bosnia, it is positively

---

18. Rosenblatt v. Baer, 383 U.S. 75, 85 (1966) (Stewart, P., concurring).

19. Convention for the Protection of Human Rights and Fundamental Freedoms, Art. 8, 213 U.N.T.S. 221, E.T.S. 5 provides the following:
   1. Everyone has the right to respect for his private and family life, his home and his correspondence.
   2. There shall be no interference by a public authority with the exercise of this right except such as is in accordance with the law and is necessary in a democratic society in the interests of national security, public safety or the economic well-being of the country, for the prevention of disorder or crime, for the protection of health or morals, or for the protection of the rights and freedoms of others.

supported by centuries-old standards of necessity in the formation of republican forms of government and is in accord with evolving standards of decency in modern democratic societies.

⁄⁄. Equal Protection under the Law

There is every reason to expect that Caroline von Hanover will continue to be a subject of enormous media attention even after her death as the German court correctly characterizes her as a "figure of absolute general interest."[20] In short, she is one of those "individuals who, by birth, professional position, or personal achievements are exposed to increased public interest over a long period of time."[21] Colloquially, we would say she is "famous." In the United States, where she is entitled to dual citizenship, she notably possesses fewer basic rights of privacy.

This unhappy development results from the extension of a rule designed to deal with official abuses during the civil rights movement. In the aftermath of the landmark case of *New York Times Co. v. Sullivan*,[22] federal courts began imposing additional burdens upon individuals with von Hannover's status. Under U.S. law, her classification as a public figure would automatically remove the general protections enjoyed by average citizens. The additional steps of proving that the information published about her was false, and that the publisher either knew that it was false or proceeded with reckless disregard as to validity, amount to an effective denial of celebrity privacy in stark violation of the constitutional mandate for equal protection under the law.

---

20. *See* BverfG, Apr. 26, 2001, Order of the 1st Chamber of the First Senate: Photographic Reporting and Protection of Privacy, 1BvR 758/97, The Federal Constitutional Court, http://www.bundesverfassungsgericht.de/en/decisions/rk20010426_1bvr075897en.html.

21. Daniel Kaboth, *Germany: The Publicity of Privacy*, LEGAL WEEK, July 29, 2004.

22. New York Times Co. v. Sullivan, 376 U.S. 254 (1964).

With perhaps deeper respect for the constitutional order, European courts acknowledge that distinctions drawn between figures of contemporary society and those highly visible, politically active, elected, or appointed persons must be clear and obvious. In a State governed by the rule of law, individuals are entitled to precise clarification as to when and where they are in a protected sphere or, on the contrary, in a sphere in which they must expect interference from others, especially the tabloid press. If the development of the personality cannot be properly protected unless the individual has a space in which he or she can relax, meaningful access to that space would not include the additional burden of tolerance for a brood of photographers, cameramen, or other aspects of the industry that sponsors such excesses.

ℳ Individual Autonomy

U.S. history shows the ebb and flow of demands for privacy sparked by reports of abuse by state and local governments. Privacy advocates largely only see the need to carry forth the debate in terms of what is at stake for each new generation in terms of data control. Rarely is privacy characterized as the right of the people as a necessary means to a constitutionally desirable end: production of a self-governing entity capable of providing meaningful consent to those who govern. As an illustration, if the political and ethical discourse on privacy were divorced from the potential effect that any policy would have on abortion rights, we might be further along as a nation.

Nevertheless, when calls for expansion occur at critical historical junctures amid revelations of governmental violations, the judiciary is the first-response team. For example, in 2008 U.S. District Chief Judge Vaughn Walker issued a ruling[23] in a matter where

---

23. *See* Order dated July 2, 2008 in *In re:* Nat. Security Agency Telecomm. Records Litig., U.S. Dist. Ct., N.D. Cal., Case M:06-cv-01791-VRW.

citizens brought suit against the US government for illegal spying. He found that in 1978, Congress had clearly set out the rules for wiretapping inside the United States, and that former President George W. Bush's claims to have inherent authority outside of those rules lacked support under the Constitution. American history confirms the founding political philosophy concerning the need for protection from such claims.

Constitutional principles embodied in the First and Fourth Amendments maintain necessary prohibitions on accessing details about an individual's private life so as to preserve free expression, support autonomy, and encourage self-governance.[24] Thus, although control over an individual's public image is helpful in establishing social relations, it is the coercion of the individual that represents a greater societal harm that threatens to undermine our Constitutional framework. DeCew warns:

> Threats of information leaks, as well as threats of control over our bodies, our activities, and our power to make our own choices, give rise to fears that we are being scrutinized, judged, ridiculed, pressured, coerced or otherwise taken advantage of by others. Protection of privacy enhances and ensures the freedom from such scrutiny, pressure to conform, and exploitation.[25]

Why should the law be concerned about individual autonomy? The simple answer is that it is the basis of our social and political contract. The European Court's validation of interdependency among privacy and reputational interests in constitutional democracies is comprehensive in nature. Protection is required for the development of personal and political identity, the safeguarding of dignity, and the promotion of self-realization that tends to broaden civic engagement. Tristram Engelhardt notes that political

---

24. DeCew, *supra* note 15.

25. *Id.* at 213.

culture is the point of view from which we examine social norms. "The ties of civil friendships" in social democracies demand public consensus regarding the rationale for privacy insofar as a commitment to the unity of a democratic polity first requires recognition of the other as an equal citizen. Consistent with this view, Alan Westin describes privacy under liberal democratic theory as also promoting recognition for the "good life" apart from political participation.

We the People have a continuing obligation to justify the various roles assumed by the State. If the noble and benign advancement of ordered liberty is mandated by constitutional edict, then the formation of laws that ensure public safety and promote the general welfare will result from an authority that is continually and meaningfully granted and exercised through enlightened public participation.

However, Engelhardt wonders whether that overstates the need for recognition of privacy as a matter of human or fundamental rights as compared to mere social value or questions of etiquette.[26] Noting that whenever stakeholders in a controversy do not share the same moral understanding, they nonetheless collaborate to reach consensus based upon mutual authorization, Engelhardt concludes it is "out of this grounding in persons and their residual rights over themselves, that rights to privacy in the sense of rights to be left alone have a cardinal and original standing."[27] As a practical solution to an intractable problem, such patterns are widely observed; however, routinely characterizing privacy as the mere right asserted against the State to be left alone, rather than freedom from every unauthorized gaze and protection from coercion, resembles a plea for civility from non-governmental entities upon which no democratic nation can reliably depend.

---

26. H. Tristram Engelhart, Jr., *Privacy and Limited Democracy: The Moral Centrality of Persons*, 17 Soc. Phil. & Pol. 120–121 (2000).

27. *Id.*

Moreover, the sting of intrusion is noticeably absent with some of today's technologies. A person can be *left alone* in the traditional sense only to later discover that long-range digital audio/visual devices have enabled observation, recording, storage, and transmission of the person's most intimate acts to virtually everyone surfing the World Wide Web. The justification of privacy as a necessary precondition for the development of other rights stemming from a general moral authority that relies upon mutual consent regrettably leads to underestimation of antidemocratic forces.

⑩ Apathy and Diversions Regarding Participatory Democracy

Two corresponding phenomena have developed that dilute a collective commitment to participatory democracy. The first is the decline of protections for whistleblowers, investigative journalists, professionals, and average citizens who question official actions and/or rote explanations of extraordinary events and circumstances. The second is the sheer volume of articles that—in purporting to define what is really at stake when we talk about the loss of privacy—explicitly denigrate the value of individual autonomy and self-determination. Most of the critiques in legal academia focus exclusively upon informational privacy, noting the causes for alarm have escalated in recent years. Most people are appalled at the growing prospect of identity theft and the range of measures we are expected to take to prevent financiers from issuing credit accounts in our names or providing unauthorized access to key confidential financial information, bank accounts, and the like. Medical and other service providers issue periodic warnings that current law mandates our personal data be subject to disclosure in any number of circumstances.

The merging of public and private databases and information sharing among government, marketing, service, and financial institutions has produced a data web containing information that in decades past could only be gleaned from reading a person's diary or accessing confidential personal and financial records. Opportunities to store DNA samples and certain genetic identifiers abound. Nearly everyone is equipped to take a photograph using cell phone technology. It seems all but certain that we will all be photographed given the convergence of photo identification on bank-issued cards, driver's licenses, voter identification cards, cameras in the courtroom, and ongoing surveillance of public and private buildings and interstate highways. All processes leading to application for a professional license require fingerprinting (as do many employers) in addition to background checks. Various forms of electronic surveillance and our increased reliance upon multimedia communication devices make tracking our pathways the rule rather than the exception. Employer monitoring of phones, fax, computer, and Internet use has increased ten-fold during the past 10 years. Legal scholar Julie Cohen notes that the digitized network that has revolutionized the costs and methods of collecting, exchanging, completing, and processing available information in countless databases must be understood in the context of its nature as a catalyst for the erosion of the privacy we have long held dear.[28]

✿ The Cost of Diminished Privacy

As privacy dialogues discount the natural consequences of laws that weaken individual sovereignty with a sharp focus on identity theft, U.S. citizens rank diminishing privacy rights high among their list of concerns. Yet they remain reluctant to demand the kinds of safeguards available in Europe, which protect more than an individual's social security number and extend more fully into the heart of democratic order, taking into account matters of agency and

---

28. Julie E. Cohen, *Privacy, Ideology, and Technology: A Response to Jeffrey Rosen*, 89 GEO. L.J. 2029 (2001).

personhood in relation to citizen participation. Moreover, concerns about identify theft do not address the irony of designating privacy as a top priority in the midst of increased demands to peer into the lives of other people. Chapter Two chronicled trends marking the shift away from traditional psychoanalysis as talk-show therapy ushered in a culture of confession. The public began to discount the value of one-on-one therapy with a trained counselor or the group support of working through 12 clearly defined steps. Instead, they were encouraged to find a television audience and rise above their ordinariness, all the while honing the ability to shock and awe.

Privacy regulations should necessarily exclude circumstances where individuals voluntarily offer information for public consumption. For example, one study of virtual communities found anonymity on the Internet offers some members genuine opportunities to work on their self-identity via the degree of self-expression and social interaction that is mostly available in these groups, and that despite the inherent risks, they consciously, knowingly, and presumably voluntarily choose to bring the "private" into the public realm. Jeffrey Rosen observes:

> Thanks to the Web, private citizens now have the same technological opportunities as celebrities to expose and market themselves to strangers, with similarly unsettling results. Consider the proliferation of blogs, the personal Internet journals that often combine political musings with intimate disclosures about daily life.
>
> There are more than a million and a half of them, according to one of the latest estimates. Some are devoted exclusively to public affairs while others are nothing more than published diaries. (A site called Diarist.net collects more than 10,000 journals from self-styled "online exhibitionists.") Often, these diaries are virtually unreadable examples of self-display, dreary accounts of navel-gazing whose primary function seems to be therapeutic. But they reflect a desire for public attention so

powerful that it erases the boundaries between public and private.[29]

The consequences of living in a tell-all society with its voracious appetite for scandal and gossip are predictable in social and political terms not only for celebrity life, but for the lives of average Americans. Thus, it comes as no surprise that "unauthorized" and mostly defamatory disseminations concerning the private lives of ordinary citizens are also in constant supply.

At this point in time, the American public seems genuinely confused about what is legitimately part of the public domain. In a review of Jeff Rosen's work detailing proposed solutions to the privacy dilemma, scholar Julie Cohen criticizes the notion that sex may be a common denominator in vetting the source of the public's seamless fascination with other people's lives. From the prurient spectator at one end of the spectrum and the Bible-toting enforcer of public morality on the other, there are many reasons for the current social impulse to pry. Cohen sees a far more complex dynamic at work that requires a comprehensive assessment of what motivates those who collect and store information and how they intend to use it.[30]

The problems of unwanted disclosure in the liberal state originated with corporate expectation of entitlement in free market economies. Access to consumer information demanded under the supposed duty to maximize shareholder profit became part of the lexicon of corporate analysts in the language of risks, estimates, and projections. This is precisely where constitutional mandates are most heavily implicated. Individual control over personal information (including religion, choice of intimate partner, political affiliations, financial holdings, and consumer preferences) may be

---

29. Jeffrey Rosen, *Continental Divide*, LEGAL AFF. (Sept./Oct. 2004).

30. *Id.* at 2031. Herein, Cohen looks to the profit motive as the primary indicator of the challenge faced by those seeking to regulate information gathering.

necessary to avoid discrimination, embarrassment, or damage to a person's personal and professional reputation.

✺ Stemming the Tide of Exposure

Unfortunately, measures designed to effectively counter the assault on privacy may be destined for obscurity unless public apathy is tackled. The lack of sweeping proposals suggests there is neither the political will nor public demand. If the historic 2008 presidential election has shown us anything at all, it is that the demand for change must come with an all-hands-on-deck approach from the American people. It took a groundswell of watchdog organizations, an alert core of serious journalists, and five-hour lines at the polls to secure the promise of relief from years of heavy-handed political and economic corruption and public manipulation. With the clearly defined objective of stemming the tide of exposure, the quality of Rosen and Cohen's work suggests they could easily pull together a transition team to craft solutions that would solve 90 percent of the problem.

Yet until now, the clear message to average consumers is that concern for privacy beyond identity theft may not be justified. And if some are convinced—as many on the talk show circuit seem to be—that caring less about their own privacy can bring tangible rewards, then they are far less likely to respect another's choice to set boundaries around their private lives. Thus, getting *any* proposals before Congress (much less effective ones) may not be in our immediate future. Such measures would still have to travel through and survive the scrutiny of the federal courts. In this regard, U.S. citizens are in a diminished posture than the people of the European Union. In the name of freeing the press, federal courts routinely and systematically reduce monetary judgments against culpable media defendants in ways that allow bean counters to assess the likely damage of publishing a particular story based upon the sensitivities of federal judges rather than the rights of the American people.

By giving the media wholesale license to look for and expose celebrity scandals, inconsistency, perversions, and neuroses, media moguls were given free reign to create, perpetuate, and manipulate the public's voyeuristic tendencies. Even those who refuse to buy sleazy tabloid magazines fail to object to their pervasive presence. At the local supermarket, we feel lucky to find even one tabloid- and candy-free checkout line when common sense dictates that in a functioning democracy, it might be the other way around. We are reluctant to question whether sugar addicts and voyeurs should be the ones forced to wait in the longer lines. We witness the media raids on the private lives of individuals, yet we rarely speak out. It is as though we have lost our sense of where to draw the line. Thus, a profiteering press spent more time reporting the nuances of Britney Spear's custody battle and tracking her every move, and less time on the excesses of the mortgage industry, with little or no regard for what those problems might mean to the world economy in the years to follow. Now standing so far removed from its heritage, the press hardly seems to be an "estate" worth preserving.

✺ Constitutive Freedom

The right of the people to choose privacy versus disclosure cannot be wholly characterized as a slippery slope. One person may desire a life of seclusion and her sister a life of publicity, while their brother prefers privacy regarding some issues and publicity as to others. The ability to choose is necessarily embodied within the right of personal liberty. As a species of "constitutive freedom" with intrinsic and instrumental value, these choices may not be arbitrarily denied without damage to democratic institutions.[31] There are overlapping, complex issues related to consent and choice when one

---

31. *See* PREBEN BERTELSEN, FREE WILL, CONSCIOUSNESS AND SELF 114 (2003).

person is a celebrity and the others are not, but that does not—and should not—change the basic landscape.

For example, Cohen argues that marketers who are paid to predict consumer choices are also heavily invested in shaping future preferences and opportunities in ways that a liberal ideology concerning the autonomous individual will not redress.[32] As seen with laws against deceptive advertising, less odious appeals and manipulation of information for emotional effect quickly pick up where actual deception leaves off. An examination of the core of First Amendment protections in general—and freedom of the press in particular—are necessary first steps in the process of examining the implications of privacy regulation in the interests of constitutional democracy. Scholars have likened the protection of corporations as virtual citizens under the Constitution to a speeding train down a steep and winding curve toward the destruction of democratic order. What say ye about using freedom of the press to strip citizens bare in a multibillion dollar industry that was originally established and subsequently protected in order to inform and warn about the dangers of an overreaching government and business alliance?

Such historical and social antecedents to the freedom granted the press only exacerbate the constitutional damage wrought by the current state of decay in many facets of media. It is important to look at the genesis of *infotainment* alongside the rise of sensationalism in general public media beyond the tabloid press for a close examination of its effects on the public at large.

---

32. Cohen, *supra* note 28.

FIVE

The Emergence of Infotainment

Bereavement is stark, gritty, harrowing. It's like a sledgeham-
mer to the gut that leaves you wondering, "Why?" Funerals
should reflect that roller-coaster thrill-ride. In this age of fast
food and hip hop, why are they still about stilted eulogies, and
cheesy floral arrangements. And what about those colonial-
facade funeral homes? Frankly, Scarlett, I don't give a damn
what funerals have been. I care about what funerals can be:
some of us have some serious modern grieving to do here![1]

—Aaron Reuth

It is a joke—we think (?) Comedic entertainment has played a crucial role in the dissemination of ideas and shaping of attitudes in
the political arena. Judicial endorsement of constitutional protections for infotainment began with formal notice that broadcasting
ideas in an entertaining format might be more effective for alerting
an audience to information they consider important or interesting.
The impact has been noteworthy throughout history. The book
Because I Tell a Joke or Two tracks the evolution of comedic influence among British social classes in relation to such variables as
geographic location, sexuality, ethnicity, and age. The work was
intended to show "how comedy has been used to sustain, challenge

---

1. http://www.theonion.com/content/node/48977.

and to change power relationships in society."[2] One result of commercial reliance upon the age, sex, and income-targeted demographic model was the emergence of programming that echoed social discourses among specific groups.[3]

In just three short months during fall 2008, the American public easily absorbed the deluge of banter around the fake credentials of "Joe the Plumber" and vice presidential candidate Sarah Palin's shopping sprees, hunting expeditions, and mothering habits, as well as the groundswell of awards and kudos for the media personalities, entertainment specialists, and comedic journalists who *exposed* them. Obliging aficionados alongside those seeking material facts about the leading contenders for the oval office received the "Royal Treatment."[4]

> The foolishness of the jester, whether in his odd appearance or his levity, implies that he is not passing judgment from on high. . . . Rather than contradicting the king, the jester will agree with a harebrained scheme so wholeheartedly that the suggestion is taken to a logical extreme, highlighting its stupidity. The king can then decide for himself that maybe it wasn't such a good idea after all.[5]

Expansive guarantees for editorial opinion, parody, and satire in Western societies were formulated in a far different political culture. Current levels of public enchantment with the masters of slam and smack is at an all-time high. Rewarding form over substance is the sine qua non of greater media exposure. It was entirely

---

2. STEPHEN WAGG, BECAUSE I TELL A JOKE OR TWO: COMEDY, POLITICS AND SOCIAL DIFFERENCE (1998).

3. *Id.* at 194.

4. *See* BEATRICE K. OTTO, FOOLS ARE EVERYWHERE (2001) (in particular, note Chapter 7, *Stultorum Plena Sunt Omnia, or Fools are Everywhere*).

5. *Id.* at 245–46.

predictable that the blurring of lines between news and entertainment, mainstream and tabloid journalism, and celebrities and political figures would produce a society bedazzled by show business and dizzying celebrity worship.

Recent public opinion polls confirm that interest in the comedic jousting about the qualifications of candidates for high office has surpassed conventional avenues of inquiry, thereby changing the rules of political engagement in ways that might leave some competitors open to unfair attack.[6] Several years running, some of the most powerful news organizations in the United States have honored more comedians for their electoral influence than the journalists covering the White House. Stand-up comics now leverage a degree of power in shaping our collective destiny that is unlike any other time in our history.

The rise of the infotainment culture, like all centrifugal forces, has its genesis in the illusions the media creates around politicians and celebrities. Professor Heather LaMarre and others completed a study in April 2009 titled "The Irony of Satire, Political Ideology and the Motivation to See What You Want to See in *The Colbert Report*." The authors report that conservatives believe Stephen Colbert is himself a conservative who only pretends to be joking. Liberals believe that Colbert uses satire and is not offering serious or heartfelt political statements.[7] The ceaseless posturing of today's media personalities erect mirages around which citizens of the world happily order and reorder their lives.

At a "Stand for Change" rally hosted by American University in Washington, DC, on January 28, 2008, the late Senator Edward M. Kennedy, Representative Patrick Kennedy, and Caroline Kennedy

---

6. Laura Pappano, *Looking for Madam President*, July 25, 2004, http://www.boston.com/news/globe/magazine/articles/2004/07/25/looking_for_madam_president/.

7. Heather LaMarre et al., *The Irony of Satire, Political Ideology and the Motivation to See What You Want to See in* The Colbert Report, 14 INT'L J. PRESS/POLITICS 212–31 (2009).

endorsed Barack Obama for president. In her remarks introducing her uncle, Caroline Kennedy observed:

> Over the years, I've been deeply moved by the people who've told me they wish they could feel inspired and hopeful about America the way people did when my father was president. This longing is even more profound today. Fortunately, there is one candidate who offers that same sense of hope and inspiration and I am proud to endorse Senator Barack Obama for President.[8]

Their endorsements raised the number of comparisons between Obama's imminent victory and the "golden age of Camelot" that marked the pinnacle of America's adoration of their commander in chief.

Public media is charged with the duty to pose legitimate questions surrounding the extent to which serving the public interest and preserving family legacies can peacefully coexist without undermining the normal vetting process. But when Caroline Kennedy became a front-runner for a New York senatorial seat, the speculation merely increased. One writer observed that Kennedy was rumored to be a fiercely committed custodian of her family's legacy. Threats loomed large about a potential end of the Kennedys' legendary devotion to public service in the Senate, given that Ted Kennedy, one of the longest-serving senators in U.S. history, was terminally ill when his niece's candidacy was announced. One writer concluded that with plans to enter the race for New York's vacant Senate seat, Caroline Kennedy would have had little choice but to "hitch her clan's wagon to the hottest political star in decades."[9] He then posed the question of whether Obama's energy

8. Neely Tucker, *Barack Obama, Camelot's New Knight*, WASH. POST, Jan. 29, 2008, C1.

9. Michelle Cottle, *Why Caroline Kennedy Needs Barack Obama: Securing a Future for the Family Brand*, THE NEW REPUBLIC, July 1, 2008.

could sustain the aging Kennedy brand and if the magic of Camelot would rub off on the first world leader of African descent.

✵ "It's the Format, Stupid"

A significant development in public media is the notable decline in the popularity of the traditional press corps and the subsequent rise of programming such as BBC Radio 4's *The Department* (voted UK Radio Station of the Year in 2008) and the political phenomenon driven by the "Colbert Nation" in the United States. The retooling of conventional news programming became swift and certain as parent companies came to grips with shrinking profit margins. The commanding influence of infotainment has been reported in academic journals as well as the popular press. One article noted: "A Sunday edition of the *New York Times* devoted more than two full broadsheet pages to 'The Daily Show', a faux news program that 'has earned a devoted following that regards the broadcast as both the smartest, funniest show on television and a provocative and substantive source of news. [They speak] truth to power in blunt, sometimes profane language, while using satire and playful looniness to ensure that the political analysis is neither solemn nor pretentious.'"[10]

The show is bolstered by a loyal demographic of viewers. Candidates with serious political aspirations are also taking note of *The Daily Show's* spin-off, *The Colbert Report*, which spawned the afore-mentioned Colbert Nation. One study published in the journal of the American Political Science Association concludes that candidates appearing on Comedy Central Network's *Colbert Report* raised 44 percent more money than their opponents within 30 days

---

10. Norman Soloman, *Dubious Praise for "The Daily Show"*, Media Monitors Network, Sept. 12, 2008. *See also* http://usa.mediamonitors.net/content/view/full/54683.

of their appearance.[11] Producers Stewart and Colbert, along with British satirist and *The Daily Show* spoof correspondent Jon Oliver, have proven to be a political force of consequence, far different from the fleeting popularity of standard cable comedic fare. With a list of Emmy nominations and two Peabody Awards for political coverage during the past two presidential cycles, *The Daily Show* producer Jon Stewart also published a best-selling parody of a social studies textbook, *AMERICA: A Citizen's Guide to Democracy Inaction.*[12]

∰ Late Nite's Targets

Today's evening and late night cable television hosts develop 90 percent of their programming around politicians and celebrities. Even when purporting to cover important issues for the general public, they lean toward lurid portrayals, insisting upon a central villain among the cast of characters in unfolding scandals in order to boost ratings. In a statement provided to CNN, the mother of former California congressman Gary Condit confides that when the media spun Chandra Levy's disappearance into a salacious tale after Condit admitted to having an "affair with the 24-year-old intern, he was branded for life with a scarlet letter."[13]

The adversarial-style reporting often ignores psychological research on the social impact of over-the-top sensationalism. International copycat effects of media portrayals of school shootings offer a cogent example. Although there is undoubted benefit to knowing the facts in these cases, extended forays into every detail with lurid speculations in the rush to break the story accomplishes little beyond profiteering. Comedic invitations to enter the public

---

11. James H. Fowler, *The Colbert Bump in Campaign Donations: More Truthful than Truthy*, 41 POL. SCIENCE & POL. 533–39 (2008).

12. JON STEWART, AMERICA: A CITIZEN'S GUIDE TO INACTION (2004).

13. http://www.cnn.com/2009/POLITICS/02/23/gary.condit.now/.

dialogue with coarse, obscene, or racy commentary and innuendo are known to injure rather than enhance public knowledge. This is particularly true when criminal charges are involved. Premature exposure of photographic evidence, relentless tracking of private citizens, unapologetic intrusion upon individual privacy, and crude gossipmongering weakens public understanding while providing few (if any) opportunities for meaningful resolution of complicated issues.

A March 2009 example involves two hip-hop entertainers under the age of 21. The National Training Institutes' National Alliance to End Domestic Abuse hosted a workshop to fill the void. Workshop organizers advertised as follows:

> Using recent events involving criminal charges of domestic violence against Chris Brown for his role in the physical beating of pop star Rihanna, this teleconference will explore the media's coverage of high profile cases involving sexual and domestic violence and its impact on our understanding of crimes against women.[14]

Constant speculation on how the story might impact the respective careers of the two was only the tip of the iceberg. The public endured audience opinion polls and reporters tracking every move of Brown and Rihanna along with discussion of whether they appeared to still be together, what precipitated the incident, who were the top contenders for the "other woman" who allegedly sent Brown a racy text message, and its precise content. The imagery was astounding: footage of the couple earlier that evening, leaked photos and information from the Los Angeles police report, so-called expert testimony about whether Rihanna was an emotional captive and whether she was in touch with members

---

14. http://www.jwi.org/site/c.okLWJ3MPKtH/b.5017177/k.A1E8/Mar_24_2009_ The_Chris_BrownRihanna_Case.htm.

of her family, and the role played by Sean [aka Puff Daddy/P Diddy] Combs, who offered one of his houses to Rihanna and Brown as a safe haven from paparazzi. In contrast, consistent with the Alliance goals, meaningful public dialogue would have addressed "how language used in the public and judicial writing about violence against women can dramatically affect our cultural understanding of the crime, often leading to a misunderstanding of the truth and even a perpetuation of harmful stereotypes and myths about women."[15]

One obvious question, virtually ignored to this very day, is why the case was treated as one of domestic violence to begin with, when the parties were neither married nor living together. Alliance leaders correctly identified the issue of helping "parents and teens understand the magnitude of the problem of teen dating abuse; and how we can use high profile cases as an opportunity to engage in discussions with each other about the true nature of teen dating violence."[16]

🎞 The Actor and His Cause

Widespread interest in the personal choices of the rich and famous is natural, according to one member of the House of Lords, because information about them often serves as a point of crystallization for the general public's adoption or rejection of a lifestyle or point of view by example or counterexample. There is often no greater value to a worthy cause than a well-known celebrity. The opportunity to bring public awareness and action to a pressing social need is present, yet the media often uses the opportunity to relate their public efforts to the actor's personal stories, lived experiences, or deeply held convictions in ways that focus more upon the star than the

---

15. *Id.*

16. *Id.*

cause and therefore never spark important debates throughout all levels of society. For example, actor George Clooney was praised for skipping the Oscar Awards to meet with President Obama to discuss the genocide in Darfur, Sudan.[17] House Speaker Nancy Pelosi met with actor Brad Pitt to discuss the "Make it Right" campaign, launched in 2007, for construction of affordable and environmentally sustainable housing for the low-income residents of New Orleans rendered homeless by Hurricane Katrina.[18] The actors are commended for their efforts in most quarters, but the media simply by-passed a golden opportunity for an openly robust debate on the merits of their cause. In a similar vein, analysis of an actor's active promotion of a worthy cause based upon vicarious experience has been examined from an entirely different perspective. Scholar Patricia William describes surrogate advocacy as part of the larger problem of commodification of equivalencies in the construction of American political discourse. In chapter two of her groundbreaking book, *Alchemy of Race and Rights: A Diary of a Law Professor*, Williams notes that in the United States, wealthy presidential candidates merely purchase the image of true American and routinely deny it to others, as they seek out accomplished speechwriters and acquire them like chattel, placing reality on the auction block by increasing the fungibility of meaning.[19] As a consequence, concepts such as dishonesty and irresponsibility are rendered cliché. Citing the display of movie star Jessica Lange testifying before members of Congress about the condition of farms in the United States because she had *played* a farmer's wife, Williams asked, "What on earth does *testimony* mean in that context?"[20]

---

17. http://www.cbsnews.com/stories/2009/02/24/politics/main4823508.shtml? source=RSSattr=World_4823508.

18. http://www.msnbc.msn.com/id/29535786/.

19. Patricia Williams, Alchemy of Race and Rights: A Diary of A Law Professor (1991).

20. *See* Esther Leslie, Hollywood Flatlands: Animation, Critical Theory, and the Avante-Garde (2002).

Columnist Bob Dart in a piece entitled *Star Power Gives Congress a Thrill* is quite candid about what it means:

> During a rural recession in 1985, the House Agriculture Committee dramatized the plight of farm families at a hearing. But rather than summoning actual suffering farmers, the panel brought in several millionaire actresses who had portrayed farm wives in movies or on TV. Testimony on the problem was provided by [Jessica Lange, Sissy Spacek, and Jane Fonda]. Sally Field couldn't make it, but her statement was read to the committee. . . . The simple reason that stars are called to testify at hearings is that those are the hearings that news crews cover.[21]

✺ Celebrity Commodification: An Invitation or Violation?

In the United States and European Union, the question often arises as to whether celebrities have voluntarily placed themselves in the no holds-barred zone of inquiry whenever they answer personal questions or openly affiliate with a group or cause. Thus, for example, the question of the public's right to hear evidence that the Church of Scientology is a "dangerous cult" depends upon the focus of the article. Buyer beware, undeserved tax-exempt status, criminal tendencies, and need for parental oversight may be plausibly advanced by the general media in the name of guarding the public interest. However, hanging John Travolta and Tom Cruise out to dry because they believe is not a reason that comfortably fits on the list as they have not volunteered to promote a cause in a sequence that parallels Clooney or Pitt. The "badges and incidents" of popularity that move individuals from the ranks of mere citizens to individuals

---

21. Bob Dart, *Star Power Gives Congress a Thrill*, Cox News Service, June 11, 2002. *See also* http://sci.Rutgers.edu/forum/showthread.php?t-11135.

invoking envy, adoration, and curiosity will automatically result in greater pressures on their privacy. However, when the pressure becomes so intense that there is virtually no immunity from defamation and invasion of privacy for celebrity citizens, we are in violation of the social compact.

Quintessentially, as courts refuse to first assess whether public broadcast of private facts involving a celebrity constitutes a matter essential to the public welfare (and then impose liability when it does not), we face a continuing host of problems. Beyond the sensationalism, distortions, and distortions and attenuation of public discourse, it is no secret that inadequate legal remedies and lack of accountability in this realm has led to an exponential rise in the number of social and actual fatalities.

✷ Infotainment's Rising Death Toll

Immediately following the 1997 death of Diana Spencer, Princess of Wales, media critics expressed formidable outrage at the excesses of the tabloid press, targeting paparazzi antics like intercontinental ballistic missiles. However, the critics' failure to grasp the larger significance of Diana's status as a *person of interest* resulted in relative silence throughout the years when the shaping of public opinion and judgments about her morals most affected the quality of her life. Spencer was—and became, in the words of Britain's public media moguls—*The Devil's Own Princess.*

As captioned by London's largest-selling papers, *The Sun* and *The Daily Mirror*, Spencer came under unprecedented attack for taking her sons to see a movie the editors claimed "glamourises the IRA." Her judgment was called into question along with her fitness as a parent and status as a role model. She apologized for causing any distress. Subsequent news reports focused upon the plausibility of her statements concerning her prior knowledge of the movie's content, which was labeled as terrorist propaganda. The favorable coverage emphasized that a series of coincidences resulted in her decision to go, thereby implying that attendance was anything but a considered, justifiable choice by a mother of two young men destined to become part of the next generation of leaders and ambassadors in the free world. Instead, readers were assured that she was not really "paying attention," that "rainy weather" restricted the royals to indoor fun, that they "often visit the cinema," that Brad Pitt and Harrison Ford are among "the boys' favorite actors," and that the time of the show was "convenient for getting them back to school on time."

Is it safe to assume that she would have never been allowed to call a press conference to announce that she considered it for five incredibly long days and ultimately decided that her sons needed to understand how important it is for Europe to find a way of mediating this tension so as to avoid the level of conflict that exists in the Middle East and other parts of the world? Or could she have stated her belief that this particular movie, on this day and time, was the best way to broach a topic that causes so much anxiety in so many quarters?

Critics were equally silent on the matter of publicity surrounding allegations related to the paternity of her youngest son. After one paper led with the story, the others showcased the lead while distancing themselves on the issue of plausibility. *People* magazine posted the following: "*It must be a slow news day. New York Post* columnist Neal Travis has headlined his column with the outlandish supposition that Prince Harry of England, 14, is actually the son of the late Princess Diana and her onetime lover James Hewitt. 'The boy looks awfully like James,' says one observer. 'It's not just the red hair—Diana's family, the Spencers, contains a few redheads . . . But you put a picture of Hewitt next to that of Harry and you'll see what everyone's talking about.' According to the official record, Prince Charles is the father of Harry."[22]

A slow day? These reports were not news. They were designed to entertain in the form of vigilante reporting. We may never know the *truth* the journalist was after, but it would hardly be worth losing

---

22. *Prince Harry: A Love Child?*, PEOPLE, Jan. 18, 1999.

sleep over. The unyielding constitutional support for the role of editorial opinion, invasive speculation, parody, hyperbole, and satire has escaped rigorous legal examination. Some take as an article of faith that this type of expression is completely outside the bounds of regulation. Sweeping aside general industry support for (and universal interest in) fact-based, newsworthy, evenhanded presentations of ideas that might be useful in a general debate, editors of large-scale public media outlets have increasingly crossed a dangerous line between their so-called truth finding and dissent and the promulgation of hatred. Their hubris, naïveté, and presumptuousness exact an increasingly burdensome tax on our collective nerves, regional economies, diplomatic relations, and human lives.

🎞 When Satire Goes Too Far

Five recent satirical expressions merely confused rather than clarified the public's interest in the subject matter at hand. While racial and religious vilification led to increasingly catastrophic results.

New York Post *in Racism Row Over Chimpanzee Cartoon*

At first glance, the main editorial cartoon in today's New York Post seemed like just another lurid reference to the story that the tabloid had been covering with breathless abandon for two days running—the shooting by Connecticut police on Monday of a pet chimpanzee that viciously attacked his owner's friend. [23]

The caption cast the cartoon in a more sinister light. "They'll have to find someone else to write the next stimulus bill," it read, prompting accusations that the Post was peddling a longstanding racist slur by portraying president Barack Obama, who signed the bill into law yesterday, as an ape.[24]

---

23. Oliver Burkeman, *New York Post in Racism Row over Chimpanzee Cartoon*, THE GUARDIAN, Feb. 18, 2009.

24. *Id.*

New Yorker's "Terrorist" Obama Cover Under Fire

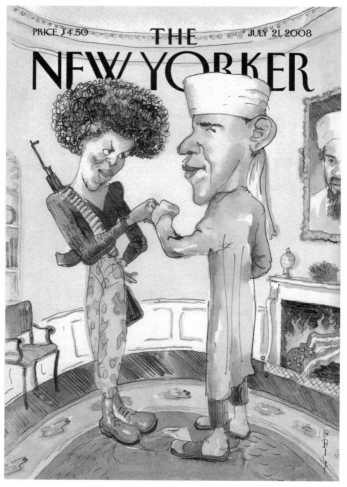

Drawing by Barry Blitt, © *The New Yorker Magazine,*[25]
Conde Nast Publications.

---

25. THE NEW YORKER, Cover, July 21, 2008 "The Politics of Fear" (drawing by Barry
Blitt). http://www.newyorker.com/magazine/toc/2008/07/21/toc_20080714.

[The July 2008 cover was described as depicting the Obamas] as terrorists in the oval office. Obama is in Muslim clothing; Michelle, in an Afro and military garb, has an AK-47 slung over her shoulder. Naturally, the fist bumping is there, along with a portrait of Osama Bin Laden and an American flag roasting in the fireplace.[26]

Candidate for Top Republican Post Gifts "Barack the Magic Negro" CD to His Constituents

Paul Jenkins summarized the important issues: In the aftermath of an electoral landslide where Obama has an approval rating 3 to 4 times that of the extremely unpopular sitting Republican president (G.W. Bush), the last thing the GOP needed to embrace was an act that suggests they have no intention of accepting Obama's presidency.

Like a restricted country club that would rather die than change, the Republican Party is marginalizing itself for the sake of the white men who run it. "Barack The Magic Negro" and Palm Beach aryanists are just the more bizarre manifestations of a party that has wallowed for so long in the privileges of its white male supremacy that it does not even realize that everyone has left the plantation, and they are not coming back.

The core play in the GOP playbook for 44 years has been white supremacy. They don't have a play in their playbook that doesn't start with the exploitation of racial divisions.[27]

Attacks on Obama's support for an economic stimulus plan did not begin or end with a dead chimpanzee. When Charlie Crist, the Republican governor of Florida, endorsed the plan, the

---

26. Paul Lewis, *New Yorker's "Terrorist" Obama Cover under Fire*, THE GUARDIAN, July 14, 2008.

27. Paul Jenkins, *The GOP's White Supremacy*, THE HUFFINGTON POST, Dec. 30, 2008. *See also* http://www.leadershipcultivation.com/2008/12/paul-jenkins-the-gops-white-supremacy.html.

South Florida *Sun Sentinel* published the following cartoon of Crist, which was widely perceived as depicting Crist in blackface. The apartheid-driven Jim Crow era in the United States arising just before the Civil War engulfed a social and political phenomenon prescribed by law and cemented by popular culture. Minstrel character Jim Crow created in the 1830s by Thomas D. Rice was modeled after an elderly crippled Black slave who sang and shuffled. Rice's performance of Jump Jim Crow, a white man in blackface, was widely acclaimed throughout the United States and England. The visibly dark-skinned Crist as depicted in the drawing was explained by the *Sun-Sentinel* editor as a "misinterpretation of Chan's cartoon. The governor's complexion is a play on his tan, and is not meant as a racial slur."[28]

Crist Lapdog Cartoon [29]

28. http://blogs.trb.com/news/opinion/chanlowe/blog/2009/02/charlie_crist_ and_the_stimulus.html.

29. *Id.*

Tensions have always surfaced in democratic nations as governments attempt to deal with symbols associated with their sordid histories of religious and racial persecution. The default approach in the West has been to calculate the likely political consequences of the perception or reality of official endorsement and quickly divert public attention to the next celebrity scandal. Increasingly, that calculation has proven faulty and the official response continues to lag. A significant shift has occurred in terms of public acceptance of the old standby approach of describing isolated incidents, followed by one highly visible gesture as a quick response. This became evident when Fox News cancelled the show of anchor E.D. Hill for coining the phrase "Terrorist Fist Jab" in reference to a ritually affectionate public display (fist bumping) by the Obamas throughout their campaign for the White House.

⁂ The Cartoons that Traveled the Globe

The Face of Mohammed
(Muhammeds ansigt translated)

When a Danish author complained he could find no one to illustrate his book on Mohammed, Danish newspaper editors at *Jyllands-Posten* contacted 40 illustrators asking for depictions of Mohammad. Twelve responded and the drawings were published, reportedly to test whether the threat of Islamic terrorism had limited freedom of expression in Denmark.[30] With full knowledge that in the Islamic faith, it is blasphemous to create images of the Prophet, the editors ostensibly undertook publication to make a point about free speech. Publication led to outrage,

---

30. *See* Paul Belian, *Jihad against Danish Newspaper*, THE BRUSSELS J., Oct. 22, 2005, http://www.brusselsjournal.com/node/382.

causing five thousand protestors in Denmark along with millions worldwide to demand an apology.

In a public statement, the managing editor offered his view of what he undoubtedly viewed as a simple truth:

> We live in a democracy. That's why we can use all the journalistic methods we want to. Satire is accepted in this country, and you can make caricatures.[31]

The Danish Imam replied: "This type of democracy is worthless. . . . Muslims will never accept this kind of humiliation. The article has insulted every Muslim in the world."[32] Indeed it did, because the BBC reports the following timeline of subsequent events:[33]

30 Sept 2005:	Danish newspaper *Jyllands-Posten* published 12 cartoons of the face of Mohammed
10 Jan 2006:	Norwegian Papers: *Magazinet, Aftenposten and Dagbladet* republished the cartoons
31 Jan:	Danish newspaper *Jyllands-Posten* editor Carsten Juste apologises
1 Feb:	French newspaper *France Soir* republished cartoons
	German newspaper *Die Welt* republished the cartoons
	Italian newspaper *La Stampa* republished the cartoons
	Spanish newspaper *El Periodico* republished the cartoons

---

31. Attributed to Editor-in-Chief Carsten Juste.

32. *See* Belian, *supra* note 33.

33. http://news.bbc.co.uk/1/hi/world/south_asia/4715084.stm.

	Dutch newspaper *Volkskrant* republished the cartoons
4–5 Feb:	Attacks on Danish embassies in Damascus and Beirut
6–2 Feb:	Twelve killed in Afghanistan as security forces try to suppress protests
13–15 Feb:	Violent protests break out across Pakistan

However, it was the incident of February 1, 2006, that inflamed the dispute that threatened to destroy Denmark as collusion among editors across Europe led to mass republication of the images. Editors were protesting official demands for a public apology from the managers of *Jyllands-Posten*. Despite public perception about their prolonged silence, a week passed before the Minister of Foreign Affairs Per Stig Møller and Danish Prime Minister Anders Fogh Rasmussen held a press conference to issue a public statement.

As Western commentators churned up the blogspheric pressure, lamenting the hotbed of radical Islamist threat to civilized society, they missed the reaction of third-party observers. European news editors talked about their rights while denying their responsibilities, and in the process provoked all manner of diplomatic and economic sanctions. Syria and Saudi Arabia recalled their ambassadors. Libya closed its embassy in Copenhagen. Iraq sent an envoy. Danish–Swedish dairy giant Arla Foods watched sales plummet in the Middle East. In pure economic terms, between the effects of the sweeping boycott of Danish products and services, disruption to European tourism, and the millions spent to secure Western embassies the impact was significant. If *Jyllands-Posten* wanted to claim a rightful place among members of a Fourth Estate worth protecting, perhaps it could have called for and published the very best caricatures of the idiots responsible for the U.S. subprime mortgage derivative investment packages being sold worldwide.

Sarcasm aside, the bloodshed, deaths, and violent protests were thoroughly covered in the mainstream press—however, the millions who turned out in very loud but nonviolent protests were virtually ignored. It would be easy to conclude the protests were evidence of the growth of Islamic influence in the United States and Europe while overlooking that they were also fueled among large segments by the anger at what the cartoons represent, particularly given the precarious nature of relations between the West and the Muslim world.[34] For example, a Jordanian newspaper published the Danish caricatures to show readers "the extent of the Danish offense."[35]

✹ The Apology that Wasn't

> We express our regrets to the Muslim community and all people who were shocked by the publication[36]

> —*Jyllands-Posten* Editor Carsten Juste

Representatives from the French paper *France Soir* originally said the decision to publish the images was intended to show that "religious dogma" had no place in a secular society. Fewer than 24 hours later, French-Egyptian owner Raymond Lakah fired managing editor Jacques Lefranc "as a powerful sign of respect for the intimate beliefs and convictions of every individual."[37] Dalil Boubakeur, president of the French Council of the Muslim Faith, described republication as an act of "real provocation towards the millions of Muslims living in France." However, editors at Germany's *Die Welt* argued that this exercise of the "right to blaspheme" in the

---

34. http://news.bbc.co.uk/2/hi/europe/7251378.stm.

35. *This is How the Danish Newspaper Portrayed Prophet Muhammad, May God's Blessing and Peace be upon Him*, SHIHAN, Feb. 2, 2006 [The Shihan ran three, one depicting the Prophet wearing a turban shaped like a bomb with a burning fuse.].

36. Charles Bremner, *Press Digs in over Islam Cartoons Fury*, THE TIMES, Feb. 2, 2006.

37. *Id.*

West was justified in the interest of examining whether Islam was capable of coping with satire.

Top Danish officials issued public statements one week after the cartoons exploded across European newsstands. The mixed messages provide useful insight as to what finally brought them to the microphone while the order of sentiments expressed is indicative of their true sentiments.

The remarks of both Prime Minister Anders Fogh Rasmussen and Foreign Affairs Minister Per Stig Møller are reprinted in full below.

Prime Minister Anders Fogh Rasmussen on 7 February 2006

The violent arson attacks on several European embassies demonstrate that this is not a matter between the Muslim world and Denmark alone.

It has been a great comfort to my government and the Danish people to receive widespread international support in this difficult situation. We are working in close cooperation with friends and allies in Europe and the United States as well countries and organizations in the Muslim world.

I am happy to inform you that just a few minutes ago President Bush called me. The President called to express support and solidarity with Denmark in light of the violence against Danish and other diplomatic missions.

We agreed that the way ahead is through dialogue and tolerance, not violence. And we emphasized that freedom of press and respect for all faiths are crucial values.

We share with the Muslim countries a common interest in calming down the situation. We want cooperation, not conflict.

The European Union is now considering ways to re-establish a dialogue with countries in the region building on the long existing friendship between Europe and the Muslim world.

Today I want to appeal and reach out to all people and countries in the Muslim world: Let us work together in the spirit of mutual respect and tolerance. We need to solve this issue through dialogue, not violence.

We are today facing a growing global crisis that has the potential to escalate beyond the control of governments and other authorities. Right now, radicals, extremists and fanatics are adding fuel to the flames in order to push forward their own agenda. For that purpose they are portraying a picture of Denmark and European countries that is not true.

Today the people of Denmark witness with disbelief and sadness the events unfolding in the world. We are watching Danish flags being burned and Danish embassies being attacked. We are seeing ourselves characterized as an intolerant people or as enemies of Islam as a religion.

That picture is false. Extremists and radicals who seek a clash of cultures and religions are spreading it. I would like to emphasize: Denmark and the Danish people are not enemies of Islam or any other religion.

Danes have for generations fought for political liberty, human rights and democracy and for economic freedom, free trade and a free and civilized world. We will continue to do that. It is a part of our history and a fundamental part of our society today.

Denmark is one of the world's most tolerant and open societies.

We believe in freedom of expression.

We believe in freedom of religion and we respect all religions.

We believe in dialogue between cultures.

We oppose violence and hatred.

And we believe in equal rights for everyone irrespective of gender, religious belief, political conviction or ethnic background.

Let me remind you: It was a free and independent newspaper that published the cartoons. Neither the Danish government nor the Danish people can be held responsible for what is published in a free and independent newspaper.

Let me also remind you that the newspaper has already apologized for the offence caused by the cartoons.

I have also made it clear that the Danish government does not have any intention whatsoever to offend Muslims or believers in any other religion. On the contrary, we do respect people's religious beliefs.

I am appalled that we are in a situation where lies and misinformation not only tarnishes the image of Denmark but also spurs violence abroad.

But we are confronted by misinformation passed on by mobile messages and web logs at such high speed that it is picked up and acted upon before we have a chance to correct it.

So for the record let me reiterate: There has been no burning of the Quran in Denmark. If any person attempts to do so the police authorities will react immediately.

These are trying times for the Danish people. On several occasions I have appealed to the Danish people not to be provoked by the events abroad. I have called on all parties to abstain from any statement or action that will create further tension. I am proud to say that all people in Denmark have been acting with calm and dignity using their democratic rights to state their opinion.

I also welcome strongly the moderate statements from many Danish Muslims. They represent the vast majority of Muslims in Denmark, who day by day make an important contribution to the Danish society.

Minister of Foreign Affairs Per Stig Møller on 7 February 2006

Events in the last days have been very serious indeed, and I am saddened to note that the unrest seems to be spreading further east. The Danish government is doing its utmost to minimize the consequences. In doing so, the government counts on the goodwill and good offices of our friends and partners around the world to talk down the tension and animosity.

Today, I am able to tell you that Javier Solana, the EU High Representative, will soon be traveling to the region. I spoke to Javier Solana again this morning. I am sure that his visit will be a positive and important contribution. More than that, it could be the foundation for a more constructive dialogue.

Clearly, Denmark has somehow become a symbol for frustrations that go well beyond the original cause. I want to be very frank and open with you: We in Denmark do not recognize ourselves in the images currently associated with Denmark.

Denmark has always emphasized the need for an international system based on tolerance, justice and the rule of law.

A very powerful example of this is the Road Map for the Middle East Peace Process. We initiated the Road Map in 2002. The goal is—and remains—a Palestinian state living side by side with Israel in peace and security.

Denmark has for many years been the biggest per capita contributor of development aid worldwide. We have for many years given large sums to the Palestinians aimed at improving lives for ordinary Palestinians.

Denmark is also engaged in a wide dialogue with the Arab world. We want to improve our understanding of the history, culture and religion of our Mediterranean neighbors.

The core values of our society are reflected in this effort: Denmark only supports initiatives that the Arab people are themselves supporting. In short: We do not want to impose ourselves!

I expect Muslims and their leaders around the world to look beyond the big news headlines and the inflammatory rhetoric.

I am all the more sad to see that misinformation continues to set the agenda in parts of the world. It is frustrating to have to repeat what should be adamantly clear to everybody: the Danish government respects Islam as one the world's major religions.

And once again I have to restate and re-emphasize that the Koran has not been burned in Denmark. Such a repulsive act would be strongly condemned by the government. It is simply illegal and perpetrators would be punished. Governments should act decisively to help us counter false rumors. And they should definitely not be spreading them themselves.

Much is at stake right now. We all have a responsibility to avoid that the situation escalates. Dialogue based on mutual respect is the only way forward—it really is that simple.

✵ Who Are You Going to Believe? Me or Your Lying Eyes?

Back in September 2005, various chairs of Muslim councils predicted and warned officials that the cartoons would be deeply offensive, but rather than opening up for immediate debate the question of whether the so-called right to give offense is consistent with claims of egalitarian democracy, the mainstream press continued the assault. The day after the apology, when the large group of papers republished the cartoons, the BBC produced the following chart entitled "Art and Blasphemy Charges."[38] The contents readily suggest that the case has already been made for just how unreasonable these people are:

1989: Iranian spiritual leader Ayatollah Khomeini calls on Muslims to kill British author Salman Rushdie for alleged blasphemy in his book *The Satanic Verses*

2002: Nigerian journalist Isioma Daniel's article about [the] Prophet and Miss World contestants sparks deadly riots

2004: Dutch film maker Theo van Gogh killed after release of his documentary about violence against Muslim women

2005: London's Tate Britain museum cancels plans to display sculpture by John Latham for fear of offending Muslims after July bombings

---

38. http://news.bbc.co.uk/2/hi/europe/4670370.stm.

Shortly after the mass republication in early February 2006, an interviewer asked *Jyllands-Posten* culture editor Flemming Rose if in retrospect he would still have commissioned and published the cartoons. Rose replied that posing such a hypothetical was:

> [L]ike asking a rape victim if she regrets wearing a short skirt at a discotheque Friday night. In that sense, in our culture, if you're wearing a short skirt, that does not necessarily mean you invite everybody to have sex with you. As is the case with these cartoons, if you make a cartoon, make fun of religion, make fun of religious figures, that does not imply that you humiliate or denigrate or marginalize a religion.[39]

None of the coverage of these remarks focused on the two most salient factors: (1) that not one objective observer believed the images published were simply poking fun at religion or religious figures, and most importantly, (2) that every editor who went on record following publication admitted they published the cartoons with the intent to offend and to blaspheme, as well as to show Muslims (perhaps better than they could tell them) what is "means" to live in a democracy. The British Parliament debated the controversy and confirmed its support of Denmark. Moreover, none of the Western officials indicated there was any need to reconsider exactly what they meant as they claimed broad support for freedom of speech.

All this occurred while historian David Irving is locked up in Austria for denying the Holocaust. Many would rightfully argue that given Austrian history, the law on Holocaust denial as applied both there and in Germany makes perfect sense because of the nations' special responsibilities.[40] But how special are they? Do we not all

---

39. *Danish Editor Behind Prophet Drawings Says He'd Publish Iran's Holocaust Cartoons*, Associated Press, Feb. 9, 2006.

40. *See* http://news.bbc.co.uk/2/hi/middle_east/4740020.stm, wherein Paul Reynolds addresses the spread of protests against the cartoons of Muhammad as another manifestation of globalization.

bear similar responsibilities for redressing injustices around the world? Holocausts, genocides, and demonizations of another's god or goddess are surely matters of the highest public concern.

🕮 Examining the Value of Satire

Questions are long overdue regarding the value of satire as a tool of mainstream media for sparking debate about matters of public concern. Critics believe many of these cartoon-caricatures are deployed like mini-time bombs with an overall effect that offers more division and distraction than insight into fundamental issues at crucial points and times.

Representatives from *Reporters Without Borders* reported that the reaction in the Arab world "betrays a lack of understanding" of press freedom as "an essential accomplishment of democracy."[41] Borders notwithstanding, the actions of the press may have sparked additional outbreaks of violence. The legendary wrong turn may well have been the hubris of the European press corps to assume that it was their place to defend the limits of freedom and challenge dissent in any manner they chose. The bomb throwers were a very small subsegment of the entire outraged world. Why in the name of freedom would editors choose to focus on them, to extend the microphone to the voices of violence, to frame the majority of public debate around criminal acts, and to use them as an excuse (yet again) to ignore everyone else while openly disparaging an entire group of believers?

The old mechanisms of credentialing and labeling are wearing thin. Mainstream media outlets warn the public away from the environmentalists, the socialists, the radicals and Islamic terrorists

---

41. http://news.bbc.co.uk/2/hi/europe/4670370.stm.

by labeling them crazy without meaningful debates of the issues. The unequal distribution of power that allowed a handful of major corporations to gain control of most of the public media while ignoring the public interest will not and cannot last.

Provocative speech is recklessly deployed then defended as the only guarantor of freedom from orthodoxy. In a March 2008 interview with *Jyllands-Posten* culture editor Flemming Rose, he explained:

> I don't think that you should offend people just for the sake of offending them or make a provocation just for the sake of making a provocation. But I think we'll have to be very clear that in a democratic society, you do have many rights—the right to vote, the right to free movement, the right to assembly, freedom of religion, free speech etc. . . . But the only right you do not have is the right not to be offended.[42]

The notion that the "right to give offense" is necessary to preserve speech rights has itself become the very orthodoxy our right to free speech is supposed to check. Luckily, because this so-called right is responsible for so much wanton destruction of communities, it is now coming under closer scrutiny. The European Court of Human Rights noted in *Murphy v. Ireland* that greater latitude is "generally available when regulating expression in relation to matters liable to offend intimate personal convictions within the sphere of morals or, especially religion."[43] If freedom means anything at all, it must embrace those of us who reject the unsubstantiated view that unbridled liberty in the realm of speech and press is the most crucial factor in building and sustaining an egalitarian society.

---

42. Editor behind Cartoon Controversy Discusses Islam, Free Speech, http://www.rferl.org/content/article/1079705.html.

43. Murphy v Ireland (2004) 38 EHRR 13 (para. 67).

SIX

Public Figures or Public Property

Public men, are, as it were, public property, and discussion cannot be denied and the right, as well as the duty, of criticism must not be stifled.[1]

—Beauharnais v. Illinois

First it was the public square, and later the public forum: open spaces such as parks, sidewalks, streets, libraries, and other accessible publicly owned properties where management and control reposes with government officials for the common good.[2] The public square was not quite the free-for-all release or exercise of the "right to offend," but more traditionally seen as "congregations of civic minded, politically structured subjects intent on resolving differences by reasoned, democratic means."[3] As the public media began to mediate this process, the tendency to appropriate wider experiences for conversion into human interest stories also tended to individualize social problems and promote a fondness for ignoring systemic and structural problems while looking upon

---

1. Beuharnais v. Illinois, 343 U.S. 250 (1952).

2. Jamin B. Raskin & Clark L. LeBlanc, *Disfavored Speech about Favored Rights:* Hill v. Colorado, *the Vanishing Public Forum and the Need for an Objective Speech Discrimination Test*, 51 AM. U.L. REV. 179, 180–81 (2001).

3. Review of MARY ESTE, THE AESTHETICS AND POLITICS OF THE CROWD IN AMERICAN LITERATURE, 2 http://muse.jhu.edu/journals/modern_fiction_studies/v052/52.1tandt.pdf.

startling events as isolated incidents.[4] The national preoccupation with presenting stories without their lessons not only fails to deliver with respect to the goals of democratic processes, but introduces confusion about what is rightfully considered part of the public sphere.

If public men and women are public property, this certainly calls for more serious consideration of how a person becomes a public figure. One example (presented fully below) was the patently narrow media focus on Caroline Kennedy's family history while ignoring her political and philosophical views as a candidate for the United States Senate. The republic's requirement that its citizenry be willing, able, and ready to hold its elected officials accountable can be quickly compromised when a candidate can achieve office through public canonization or lose it because of public demonization rather than electoral due process. That celebrities and public figure have to endure excessive amounts of personal scrutiny is evidence of the extent to which the lives of public figures have been unfairly converted to public property.

From a constitutional perspective, the currency and relevance of the "public's right to know" is the weak link in the analytical chain. It is inextricably bound to notions of government accountability, transparency, and the regulatory apparatus found in sunshine laws. Public rights as they pertain to government records and processes are designed to enable journalists, historians, consumer advocates, and watchdog groups to monitor official conduct. However, in logical sequence the plaintiffs featured throughout this book question how the "public's right know" serves as sufficient justification for displaying an individual's life in unscripted segments of video clips offered up for commentary by a round table of professional comedians.

---

4. BENNETT & ENTMAN, MEDIATED POLITICS, COMMUNICATION IN THE FUTURE OF DEMOCRACY 68–69 (2001).

⅏ Extension and Amplification of the Publisher Malice Standard

Public Officials

New York Times Co. v. Sullivan established a publisher malice standard that certainly has an intuitive ring. Limiting the extent to which government officials can obtain damages for slightly erroneous reports critical of their administration and performance of official functions seems both necessary and proper. Preventing local jurors from bankrupting national newspapers in retaliation for their coverage of the extreme violence attending Southern resistance to the Civil Rights Movement under the guise of defamation law provides free speech with the essential breathing space deemed vital and consistent with long-standing democratic traditions. Defamation presents a relatively easy case in this context, while invasions of privacy present more temporal and weighty concerns.

For example, the value of medical privacy has long been a staple in the pantheon of American values. Yet this was hardly apparent when debate surrounding the public's knowledge of former Vice President Dick Cheney's history of chronic heart disease received less media coverage than former New York Mayor Rudolph Giuliani's prostate cancer. Where no clear partisan jockeying is at play, relevant questions of physical and mental health in assessing political fitness are rarely broached. Are these matters of public concern or private medical conditions?

Britain's publicly supported television stations are under a mandate to avoid tabloid-style journalism, and its private, for-profit television news station "is under a closely monitored and regulated obligation to provide large amounts of high quality news and public affairs."[5] Thus in the United Kingdom, even where the private lives of public officials intersect with their public duties, relevant details

---

5. *Id.* at 392.

surrounding their infraction (absent excess voyeurism) are the only elements deemed crucial for the public at large—and only to the extent they bear upon responsibility for the management of public resources.

Agents of federal, state, and municipal governments in the United States are closely scrutinized in relation to matters that impact their fitness for office. The scandal involving the former Democratic governor from New York, Eliot Spitzer, provides a relevant example. Spitzer was forced to resign from office in May 2008 after rumors surfaced that he would soon be indicted for patronizing a high-paid call girl. Three local news editors called for his resignation while top officials in the New York Republican Party threatened impeachment proceedings if he failed to resign within 48 hours.[6] The *New York Times* reported that Spitzer's "signature issue was pursuing Wall Street misdeeds, and as attorney general [he] prosecuted at least two prostitution rings [while heading] the state's organized crime task force."[7] In 2004, "Spitzer spoke with revulsion and anger after announcing the arrest of 16 people for operating a high-end prostitution ring" in the state.[8] A mere four years later, he appeared to have softened his stance and the press had a field day.

Judges occupy a special position in society because as with politicians, they are expected to uphold the public trust, enforce the rules, and extend equal protection to all citizens. Nevertheless, the private choices and decision-making processes of U.S. judges are rarely ever subject to intense public scrutiny. Even when their actions substantially relate to performance of their official duties, criticism of justices on high courts generate more debates about

---

6. Dean Bartlett, *FAQ: The Spitzer Affair*, THE WEEKLY STANDARD, Mar. 11, 2008. *See also* http://www.npr.org/templates/story/story.php?storyId=88094617.

7. Danny Hakim & William K. Rashbaum, *Spitzer is Linked to Prostitution Ring*, N.Y. TIMES, Mar. 10, 2008.

8. *Id.*

the propriety of criticizing judges and threats to judicial independence than demonstrations of loyalty to the principle governing enforcement of the rule of law. For example, an Oklahoma judge was convicted for using an electronic masturbatory device under his robe while presiding over two murder and one civil trials.[9] The issue clearly relates to fitness for office because we would like to think our judges are actually listening to the evidence and testimony before they decide cases. Thus, media coverage of the issue of fitness is more important than salacious details. The case rightfully garnered only a few days of press coverage, and thankfully failed to produce any groundbreaking TV specials on the "world's most perverted judges." Ultimately, judicial mis-conduct deserves far more attention than it currently receives.

ABC News reported on January 23, 2006, that when John Roberts was sworn in by the president of the United States as the 17th chief justice, every member of the U.S. Supreme Court was present except for Antonin Scalia.[10] Scalia was on a tennis court at the Ritz-Carlton Hotel in Bachelor Gulch, Colorado, attending an all-expense paid trip sponsored by the archconservative legal lobby known as the Federalist Society.[11] Scalia is rumored to have snubbed the new chief justice because he was passed over for the position. He did not call in sick that day; he merely offered that he was "out of town with a commitment that [he] could not break."[12]

For well over 20 years, researchers have documented the conflicts of interest stemming from federal judges accepting expensive vacations at some of the world's top resorts for seminars purporting to "educate" them, which are sponsored by interest groups that represent parties before the courts. They have affected entire

---

9. *Judge Suspected of Masturbating in Court*, REUTERS, June 24, 2004.

10. http://sweetness-light.com/archive/why-did-abcs-nightline-lie-about-scalia.

11. *Id.*

12. *Id.*

substantive areas of judicial decision making.[13] Numerous studies already detail the serious conflicts of interest and perceptions of impropriety that arise when judges go on these private trips.[14] Members of Congress have spoken out against these trips and introduced legislation to ban them altogether. Ethics experts, judges, public interest groups, and more than 30 editorial boards have strongly criticized these programs without there being significant media interest or public debate concerning these conflicts. From a political standpoint, these dynamics create multilayered effects that, in relation to celebrities in particular, promote the public's naive acceptance of media power to victimize some people (mainly celebrities) as long as they leave other, though far more relevant targets alone.

Candidates for Public Office

Shortly after the U.S. Supreme Court introduced the *New York Times* "actual malice" standard, which makes it nearly impossible for elected or appointed officials to recover on claims of defamation, the test was extended to candidates for public office. Legally designated candidates for public office in the District of Columbia are those who announce an intention to run for public office, possess the qualifications for the office under the applicable law, are placed on official ballots or entered into the nomination process, and have publicly committed to seeking election after making a substantial showing of a bona fide candidacy.[15] These include a hefty degree of involvement in activities commonly associated with political

---

13. Doug Kendall, *NOTHING FOR FREE: How Private Judicial Seminars Are Undermining Environmental Protections and Breaking the Public's Trust*, Community Rights Council, July 2000.

14. *Id.*

15. 47 USC § 151.

campaigns, including speeches, distribution of literature, press releases, selection of campaign committees, and setting up of headquarters.

Once a person qualifies as a candidate, public scrutiny begins. Criminal convictions, background, credit checks, and voting records have long been part of the national dialogue pertaining to suitability for high office. (Candidates for office in South Carolina were also subject to mandatory drug testing, although soon after the South Carolina Supreme Court declared the law unconstitutional.)

It may be that few people understand the injuries sustained at the intersection of defamation and invasion of privacy as well as the women in the news during the 2008 presidential election cycle. Conservative vice presidential candidate Sarah Palin once declared:

> It's a sad state of affairs in the world of the media today, mainstream media especially, if they're going to rely on anonymous bloggers for their hard news information; very scary. Reporters, especially, not taking one extra step to get to the facts and report the facts, but instead continuing to spread things that are not true. Is it political? Is it sexism? What is it that drives someone to believe [and] perpetuate the worst?[16]

No legitimate researcher has found an overall heavy-tilting partisan bias in favor of conservative or liberal media. Nor is it certain that socioeconomic class privilege was an important distinguishing characteristic in the national media's treatment of Palin in comparison to Caroline Kennedy-Schlossberg, a fixture among New York's liberal sociopolitical elite. Both women took a pounding from the talking heads opposing their political parties. Abusive and condescending diatribes about these women from several quarters

---

16. Howard Kurtz, *Online, Sarah Palin Has Unkind Words for the Press*, WASH. POST, Jan. 9, 2009.

underscore the gendered-skewed nature of the national dialogue. In short, neither candidate received objective treatment from most quarters. Studies about the wide-ranging effects of gender-bias have yet to make their way into the national conversation about fairness and equality. Ultimately, American voters rejected Palin on the merits; Kennedy withdrew from consideration.

Candidates vying for the seat of former New York Senator (now Secretary of State) Hillary Clinton were given a 28-page questionnaire pertaining to personal finances, associations, and general conduct. Caroline Kennedy, a well-known privacy advocate who has always guarded her own, was thought to have withdrawn from consideration after learning that her responses might become public under New York's freedom of information laws. A useful starting point in the analysis of Kennedy's reticence as a candidate for New York's top job are well summarized in a January 2009 feature in *New York* magazine. The source of her obvious dilemma was described as:

> [K]ennedy's lifelong avoidance of anything resembling a personal question—and [belief]] that politics is about issues. She had never come to terms with the fact that the reason she was in line for the job was that she was, well, a Kennedy, and that people loved Kennedys, what they ate, where they lived, what they felt about their triumphs and tragedies. Whereas she'd based her entire life on witholding such information. . . . This is New York, and they're gonna come after her. It's not just going to be about abortion and Indian Point [leaky nuclear] power plant. It's gonna be all the things that nobody has dared to ask her. . . .[17]

She was never able to integrate her dominant instinct for privacy with her newfound willingness to live in public. There is no

---

17. Chris Smith, *The Zany Adventures of (Senator) Caroline Kennedy*, N.Y. MAG., Jan. 24, 2009.

more personal issue than trying to transform yourself into a new person.[18]

Intrusions upon familial privacy and defamatory publications affect candidates for public office in much the same way as ordinary citizens for all of the same reasons. To classify the intentional spewing of misleading statements during a highly charged public vetting process as a "legitimate and necessary" price to pay for those who wish to manage the public largess ignores the central issue: how can we introduce meaningful consequences for the purposeful injection of patently false and demeaning statements into the stream of public discourse?

Even more agonizing is the likelihood the American public may actually care more about what Kennedy wears and eats and how she endured her brother John F. Kennedy Jr's premature death than if and how she would use the resources of a U.S. senator to deal with a nuclear hazard that endangers significant portions of the northeast region of the country. If this view is confirmed, it would represent a stinging indictment of contemporary civic republicanism from both a classical liberal and a pragmatic consequentialist perspective.

General Purpose Public Figures

The publisher malice standard was later extended to include public figures. Surprisingly, it was a case involving the late televangelist Jerry Falwell against *Hustler* magazine for an ad parody that defamed his relationship with his deceased mother that best demonstrates the effects of this extension.[19] The U.S. Supreme Court noted that the case was one of first impression insofar as it dealt with a state's

---

18. *Id.*

19. Hustler Mag., Inc. v. Falwell, 485 U.S. 46 (1988).

authority to provide a remedy for the tort of intentional infliction of emotional distress resulting from publication of a parody considered grossly repugnant in the eyes of most.

In rejecting Falwell's tort claim, the Court declared that robust political debate was bound to produce speech critical of those who are "intimately involved in the resolution of important public questions or, by reason of their fame, shape events in areas of concern to society at large.[20] Such criticism has been deemed a prerogative of American citizenship."[21] The Court went on to concede that inevitably, this criticism would not always be reasoned or moderate, as public figures as well as public officials will be subject to "vehement, caustic, and sometimes unpleasantly sharp attacks."[22]

The reasoning is sound, but the Court's expansion of the malice standard to this tort exacerbated the emerging doctrinal weaknesses. Demanding proof of malicious intent (defined as publication of false statements of fact with prior knowledge of falsity or reckless disregard in light of suspicion as to its veracity) before allowing public figures to recover damages for dignitary harms that relate to their private life has yet to be adequately explained or sufficiently applied in U.S. courts.

Limited Purpose Public Figures

Notwithstanding these deficiencies, in addition to elected and appointed officials, candidates for office, and general public figures, the malice standard was later extended to *limited purpose* and *involuntary* public figures. In 1980, Candy Lightner's 13-year-old

---

20. *Id.* at 51, citing Assoc. Press v. Walker, *decided with* Curtis Publ'g Co. v. Butts, 388 U.S. 130, 164 (1967).

21. *Id.*, citing Justice Frankfurter in Baumgartner v. United States, 322 U.S. 665, 673–74 (1944).

22. New York Times Co. v. Sullivan, 376 U.S. 254, 270 (1964).

daughter Cari was killed by a drunken hit-and-run driver as she walked down a suburban street in California. Candy then founded Mothers Against Drunk Drivers to raise public awareness of the serious nature of driving while intoxicated and to promote tougher legislative penalties.[23] As a national spokeswoman, her privacy protection is limited under U.S. law. Any legal challenge to published errors pertaining to her drinking habits, whether she has ever been found driving while under the influence, or any misinformation related to her choice to lobby for the American Beverage Institute (a trade group of restaurant and hotel executives responsible for distribution of large quantities of liquor each year) would be subject to the actual malice standard.

The problem in this case is that although information concerning her lobbying efforts is clearly part of the public domain, how might a court approach the need to weigh the effects to her reputational interests and to her cause if it failed to punish false reports about a DUI or similar charge? The "more speech" paradigm—the assumption that as a public figure on the issue of drunk driving she will automatically be given many more opportunities to effectively refute such allegations—fails to comport with modern reality.

Private Citizens Involved in Matters of Public Concern

The constitutional lines have been blurred even further. Private citizens who are involved deliberately or by fiat in the loosely defined category of "matters of public concern" are also forced to endure added trauma. In 1955, *Life* magazine published a story about a stage play based on real-life escaped convicts who held a

---

23. Stephen L. Isaacs & Steven A. Schroeder, *Quiet Victories: What We Can Learn from Success Stories in Health*, 13 THE RESPONSIVE CMTY. 60, 95 (2003).

family hostage.[24] The inaccuracies and embellishment that further supported the plaintiff family's claims for privacy invasion were dismissed by the U.S. Supreme Court insofar as the family could not prove actual malice. As involuntary public figures they could neither successfully recover for libel nor intentional infliction of emotional distress.

Similarly, former U.S. Marine Oliver Sipple reached out to help a passerby when a shot was fired at former U.S. President Gerald Ford in 1975. Sipple's heroism was reported in the news alongside details about his homosexuality. In Sipple's suit against the *San Francisco Chronicle*, the court declared that Sipple had become a public figure, and thus questions about his "character" were deemed newsworthy.[25] Yet *newsworthy* as a legal concept remains vague. Indeed, this final all-absorbing extension of the malice standard captures the ubiquity of category of "citizens involved in matters of public concern." It casts a net so wide that virtually everyone is now required to prove malice before recovering for either defamation or public disclosure of private facts.

Consider these February 2009 national headlines: "The pilot who guided a crippled US Airways jetliner safely into the Hudson River—saving all 155 people aboard—became an instant hero Thursday, with accolades from the mayor and governor and a fan club online."[26] Chesley B. Sullenberger III, affectionately known as "Sully," was the pilot of Flight 1549. In less than 24 hours, he endured two of the most traumatic back-to-back experiences of his life. First, he performed a "crash-landing on water, called 'ditching.' [A] largely

---

24. *True Crime Inspires Tense Play: The Ordeal of a Family Trapped by Convicts Gives Broadway a New Thriller*, "*The Desperate Hours*", LIFE, Feb. 1955; *see also* Time, Inc. v. Hill, 385 U.S. 374 (1967).

25. Sipple v. Chronicle Pub. Co., 154 Cal.App.3d 1040 (1984); *see also* Daniel J. Solove, *The Virtues of Knowing Less: Justifying Privacy Protections against Disclosure*, 53 DUKE L.J. 967 (2003).

26. Amy Westfeldt, *Hudson River Hero is Ex-Air Force Fighter Pilot*, Associated Press, Jan. 16, 2009.

untested tactic that is considered one of the most difficult and dangerous things a pilot can do."[27] His courageous feat caused the second experience: a public media foray into the details of his entire personal and professional life in the midst of a full-scale investigation of both Sully and his crew by the National Transportation Safety Board.[28]

𝍦 Public Figures Profiled

General purpose public figures are presumed to possess significant power and influence. They thrust themselves to the forefront of public controversies with the intent of exerting their influence during resolution of key public questions. Public debate of their activities and positions on matters involving the economy, environment, and similar domains are fair game because they actively seek to influence public debate. As political figures they are similar to, actively connected with, and willingly used by appointed and elected politicians in nearly all instances.

Joe the Plumber and the Art of Political Mirage

Samuel Wurzelbacher became a national figure after he was referred to as "Joe the Plumber "21 times during a 2008 presidential debate and declared the winner of the debate by Republican candidate John McCain. Wurzelbacher burst onto the national stage as the new "icon of the authentic working-class voter"[29] because in a

---

27. Debbi Baker, *US Airways Pilot a Mix of Modesty and Professionalism, Says Coronado Friend*, Union-Trib., Jan. 16, 2009.

28. *Id.*

29. Carla Maranucci, *Story of Joe the Plumber Springs Many Leaks*, S.F. Chron., Oct. 17, 2008.

reportedly unscripted moment, he confronted Obama about his tax plan, declaring that Obama's raising of taxes on those earning more than $250,000 per year would thwart Wurzelbacher's efforts because he was "getting ready to buy a company that makes $250,000 to $280,000 a year."[30] The registered Republican then joined the bus tour of the McCain campaign.

Afterwards, his every movement including past voting record, circumstances of his divorce, the birth of his son, his military record, and "all things personal" became media fodder. A few problems emerged: his name was not Joe, he was not a licensed plumber, and his earning capability did not even approach $250,000 a year. After the AP, bloggers, investigators, librarians, and the *Chronicle* turned up court documents and birth records, they reported that he owes the state of Ohio about $1,200 in personal income taxes, another $1,200 to St. Charles Mercy Hospital, and that there is an "active lien on his residential property."

His former residency in the home states of both McCain and Palin and admission that he was hoping to catch Obama off guard underscores that old and newly created pubic figures are staples in the political chicanery that has permeated U.S. politics since the birth of the nation. Its proliferation can be directly traced to the frenzied style of "breaking news" coverage CNN started 28 years ago as the first 24-hour cable program. The news-for-profit formats heralded a precipitous decline in journalistic standards.

The beyond-saturation phenomena has left one segment of the nation vulnerable and suspicious, with rising levels of cynicism and voter apathy, fearful of the great political hoax, while the other segment remains all too eager to judge and cast a vote according to whims dictated by the mass media. Helping the public to decide whether *Joe* is who he claims to be and the veracity of his message concerning the tax hike were matters of legitimate public interest. But when Wurzelbacher learned the media was interviewing all of

---

30. http://www.nytimes.com/2008/10/17/us/politics/17joe.html.

his neighbors and former associates in several states, digging up old photographs and inquiring into the character of his 13-year-old son, and as YouTube parodies littered the Internet and the door-stepping continued unabated, he remarked that he might be in over his head.

In March 2009, Wurzelbacher filed a lawsuit against the director of the Ohio Department of Job and Family Services and her two assistants.[31] He is suing for privacy violations that include the gathering and dissemination of personal information in a records search that allegedly caused him emotional distress, humiliation, and embarrassment.[32] Wurzelbacher may be able to sustain a cause of action against an agency director caught digging up his personal information for the press. But if he prevails, the victory would most likely be related to agency policy and a forced settlement while ignoring the publishers, who in all probability are at least equally culpable.

Similarly, merely erroneous statements in publications critical of governmental administration are an inevitable part of news reporting. When observed, journalistic standards require reporters to follow proper protocol in obtaining and reporting the news that keep imprecision at a tolerable level. Even politicians and public figures with official duties in European countries have been successful in pushing for more precise classifications as to which topics constitute matters of public interest and those that primarily relate to their personal lives.

For example, years ago unauthorized recordings surfaced of telephone conversations between England's Prince Charles who is considered a public figure with official duties, and his fiancée at the time, Lady Diana Spencer. Publishers sought to have these

31. Read more: http://www.nydailynews.com/news/us_world/2009/03/05/2009-03-05_samuel_joe_the_plumber_wurzelbacher_sues.html#ixzz0G4WtP3 uy&B.

32. *Id.*

conversations classified as a matter of public concern because they contained a blunt assessment of the head of Australia's government. A German court held that the conversations were private and procured illegally through an unauthorized wiretap, and thus were not subject to publication on both grounds.[33] European journalists often envy the one-sided interpretation of the right to free expression in the United States because it allows the tabloid media-machine to publish with impunity under the guise of public interest.

✳ Classification of Celebrity Citizens

At the nucleus of all the constitutional transitions and fog surrounding justifications for a lower standard of protection is the wholesale classification of all celebrities as general purpose public figures without a legitimate basis. Although the courts have customarily recognized the public's interest in learning as much as possible about the views of candidates for public office, they have historically been more protective of the average citizen. Those who are well-known have had to endure pressures upon their privacy and the misreporting of significant facts in the rush and excitement that surrounds pop icons. Yet the road leading from an occasional error linked to a trio of errant photographers, to a stampeding paparazzo camped outside every possible venue, to supply imagery for the stories appearing in today's tabloids, has been a treacherous one indeed. Unfortunately, the legitimate reporting of the details related to a public incident involving a celebrity as a journalistic means for arousing public interest and action regarding a social problem morphed into the present tendency toward the general reclassification of celebrity morals and lifestyles as a *matter of public concern.*

Disparate treatment from this misguided transformation has introduced a chaotic level of reasoning in lower courts and represents a near-wholesale commoditization of another's life. Instead of an

---

33. http://www.time.com/time/magazine/article/0,9171,953753,00.html.

objective presentation of factual data beneficial to the general welfare, the American public is bombarded with diatribes laced with misinformation and innuendo. The deluge of value-centric, ideologically driven commentary that is overly critical and mocking in tone but without obvious connections to the duties of elected or appointed officials attenuates the quality of public discourse.

As guardians of individual rights, courts are obligated to ask whether widespread dissemination of information concerning an individual's private life is justified as a matter essential to the public welfare. If so, then its serious nature and severity require some measure of objectivity, respect, and consideration of the long-term consequences of the release of inaccurate information or factual information in a false light. Merely publicizing information about Tiger Woods's infidelity with intent to ridicule and disparage him demonstrates how current media trends are inextricably linked to the social pathologies produced in argumentative, judgmental, and voyeuristic cultures.

Among the several factors that should naturally fall outside of constitutional consideration in defining the realm of celebrity privacy include estimation of the numbers of "ordinary citizens" who may be influenced by celebrity choices, and the motives of publishers who lack direct consent to publish private facts. In the case of *Campbell v. MGN Ltd.*,[34] several members of Britain's House of Lords erroneously equated celebrity status to that of a role model. This development calls into question the entire doctrinal basis for stripping the so-called involuntary public figures of their protected status through no purposeful acts of their own. Locking all celebrities into the public figure category and taking away their constitutionally mandated protection is part of the legal fiction that obfuscates deeper questions of social and moral responsibility. The justification is nebulous at best, if for no other reason than it contravenes the very equal protection standards for which this

---

34. Campbell v. MGN Ltd. [2004] UKHL 22.

country is now famous. A quick overview of what celebrities endure, starting with the stalking of the paparazzi, begs the question of whether the current tabloid feeding frenzy has been justified on the theory that they are public figures, or in practice because we have secretly determined that they are essentially public property.

Public property is managed by the government for the use and enjoyment of the public. In general, we think of parks, playgrounds, libraries, colleges, universities, and high schools as traditional venues for public fora. Recent presidential elections in the United States have featured structured debates and less-formal town hall meetings in many of these locations. Similarly, environmentalists exert considerable influence when they lobby Congress to maintain recreational opportunities on public lands. Wilderness areas and our national forests are mostly preserved for human recreation and as a national wildlife refuge. Thus, public property is preserved for public use and pleasure. But have we reached the constitutional moment when celebrities and their families are required to make themselves, their life stories, and their daily decision-making available for similar use?

There was a period when child stars and the children of stars were given a reprieve from the hunt. Alas, a new era is dawning where the boundaries protecting children have nearly disappeared. Actress Julia Roberts has requested that U.S. lawmakers ban paparazzi from taking photos of children to dissuade the practice of critiquing and comparing famous offspring in the tabloid press. The former rule dictating a hands-off approach (although the media would pounce as soon as their targets turned 18) has been replaced with a new formula for mix and malign. For example, Kathie Lee Gifford sued the *National Examiner*, naming her 10-year old son as plaintiff, after the paper ran the headline: "Kathie Lee Wrecking Cody's Life! Pushy Mom's Creating a Monster."[35]

---

35. *Gifford Settles with* National Examiner *over Story on Son: Tab Accused TV Personality of Turning Boy into Brat*, EDMONTON J., Apr. 4, 2002, at C3.

✐ Public Access to Private Information

The very question of how to celebrate the addition of a new family member has become part of the so-called "baby wars." The UK's *Independent* was quick to report that when "Angelina Jolie finally emerged from the hospital in Nice yesterday, following the birth of twins Vivienne Marcheline and Knox Leon last week, the waiting paparazzi were none the richer for it."[36] Why? Because first photos were promised to a U.S. magazine for £6 million. The story concludes that Jolie and Pitt were right to donate the money to charity to avoid the major PR faux pas of many new celebrity parents who appear "grasping by pocketing a fat fee, or annoying an eager public by refusing to let the world see the much-hyped infant for months."[37]

Now celebrities are continuously measured and compared to those among them who live to show, tell, and reveal all, but this was not always the case. For those who may have been unaware of just how quickly and permanently things have changed, consider how juxtaposing our concept of public figures in the United States with our treatment of and the rules regarding access to public property provides a superior means for evaluating this issue. One blatant example involves actor Tom Cruise and the fallout over the choice he and his fiancée made to shield their newborn daughter from the public eye.

✐ Where is Suri Cruise?

Weeks before her arrival, Andrew Morton, the top creator of unauthorized celebrity "tell-all" books, alleged that some members of

---

36. Rachel Shields, *Angelina Makes Good PR Move by Dodging Paparazzi*, THE INDEPENDENT, July 20, 2008.

37. *Id.*

Scientology believed that Cruise's fiancée had been impregnated with frozen sperm from the founder of Scientology L. Ron Hubbard. Morton declared: "In her more reflective moments, Katie might have felt as if she were in the middle of a real-life version of the horror movie 'Rosemary's Baby,' in which an unsuspecting young woman is impregnated with the devil's child."[38] Morton's scathing "pre-birth announcement" was a portent of the bloggerspheric rant that would inevitably follow. The rumor mill churned out speculation that the newborn was deformed, that she did not actually exist, that the pregnancy was a hoax, and that the infant was only being concealed in an effort to generate a bidding war for the first photos. Introduced by a comparison to another famous newborn, one blogger wrote:

> Staring at the People magazine cover of Angelina, Brad and baby Shiloh—the one that set Time Warner Inc. back 4 million big ones—I was inspired to ponder just what exactly happened to all of those pictures (you know, the ones that don't exist) of Tom Cruise's and Kate Holmes' female offspring Suri. She was born on April 17. For those of you keeping score, that was precisely 56 days and nights ago. I believe that's around 18,749 months in Scientology years. Translated, this kid ain't g'tting' any younger— and yet there is no visual public record of her existence. This is not to infer that there is no Suri Cruise and that she was simply manufactured as a marketing tool to boost the promo for "Mission Impossible III." But you know, hey, National Enquiring minds want to know: where is this kid? Trapped in some L. Ron Hubbard parallel universe? I think the Cruise–Holmes duo owe it to their fans to sell some cheesy shots of their infant to the highest bidder and then use the cash to help line the coffers of Tom's favorite church.

---

38. *See* Mike Baron, *Katie Holmes, Tom Cruise Baby Suri Not His? Likened to Anti-Christ*, THE POST CHRON., Jan. 7, 2008.

When celebrity friends shared that they had not yet been invited to visit the newborn, a few were permitted to visit and publicly reported her magnificence. However, soon after media pundits began referring to the "purported birth of one Suri Cruise."[39] When no photographs appeared after four months, the media hounded the couple round-the-clock as if they were international fugitives holding up in a cave in Colorado. The discovery of Saddam Hussein in an eight-foot bunker on a farm near Tikrit generated less media attention.[40] One commentator seemed relieved to place the photos in proper context: "*So This Is What We've Waited 4 1/2 Months To See:* Yes, Suri looks like a baby, a pretty cute one, even. Now . . . can we move on to securing the homeland and finding that cure for cancer?"[41]

Cruise was eventually nixed by Paramount Studios, whose executives may have also insisted that the couple display the baby out of fear the media flack might negatively impact the release of his hit film, *Mission Impossible III.* As compared to the money spent to produce and promote the film, it was not the box office sensation Paramount hoped it would be. Within the overall context of Paramount's announcement that Cruise's contract would be terminated, a curious subtext emerged related to the prior executive decision about backing Mel Gibson in the wake of his public meltdown. One commentator observed that it is Richmond's Rules of Transgression:[42] Hollywood will forgive anything except being unsuccessful, and America will forgive anything except being unrepentant.

---

39. *Id.*

40. Susan Sachs & Kirk Semple, *Ex-Leader, Found Hiding in Hole, is Detained Without a Fight*, N.Y. TIMES, Dec. 14, 2003.

41. www.pastdeadline.com/2006/04/katie_holmes_gi.html,   http://www.pastdeadline.com/tom_cruise/.

42. *Id.*

Celebrity entitlement to a private life was a nonissue before the cultural transitions preceding our conversion into a tell-all society. However, homogeneity of social thought and the pervasiveness of privacy intrusions has leveled the mere mention of celebrity privacy invasion by way of a defensive refrain that it is the price of being rich and famous.

With advancing technologies, it has increasingly become the price a person pays for any public attention, wanted or unwanted. A stark recent example unfolded as one woman consented to TV interviews, accepted government funds for her disabled children, and exercised her constitutional rights to procreate. When Nadya Suleman asked for donations to help with the rearing of her 14 children after giving birth to the first set of octuplets in U.S. history with a meaningful chance of survival, a feeding frenzy began that shows the breadth and depth of our collective overreaction to risk.[43] It also demonstrates a lack of doctrinal cohesion in circumstances involving targeted vilification and harassment of private citizens supposedly involved in matters of public concern.

✳ Nadya Suleman's Story in Context

When a native California woman gave birth to octuplets on Janurary 26, 2009, the facts surrounding her life came fast and furiously. Her name is Nadya Suleman, she is 33, single, celibate, has six children at home ages two through seven, unemployed, used invitro fertilization, claims to have used the same sperm donor for all 14 of her children, has a monthly income of roughly $3,000 (nearly $500 per month in food stamps and $2500 in disability payments from three of her children), has hired a publicist, will likely generate a medical

---

43. http://www.dailymail.co.uk/news/worldnews/article-1142566/The-mother-baby-bumps-Octuplets-mum-bares-ENORMOUS-stomach-just-days-giving-birth.html.

bill for taxpayers in the amount of $1.3 million to cover the birth and pre-release infant care, and requires another $1.3—$2.7 million to raise them.

Suleman's mother granted a media interview indicating that she was less than happy about the new additions to the family, calling the pregnancy unconscionable and stating her daughter was not equipped to handle 14 kids. After trailing her about town on a single day, one tabloid reported that the new mother got a manicure and purchased videogames. We learned that she has numerous unpaid parking tickets and has had to seek a gag order to prevent her mother from speaking about her any further. The veracity of every public statement made by Suleman was opened for review. Her viewpoints and explanations were greeted with suspicion, and there was a groundswell of speculation about her psychological stability. Journalists probed whether she received assistance from a Protestant congregation, whether her doctor is under review for medical ethics violations, whether she has had plastic surgery, and whether she believes she is a "twin soul" of Angelina Jolie.

The Los Angeles police were called in when Suleman's publicist quit after receiving more than 55,000 emails, stacks of snail mail, and numerous death threats. Messages from all over the states included threats to rip out Suleman's uterus, expressed hopes that her publicist would die, and suggested that Suleman be anesthetized and put down like a dog. Los Angeles police likened the furor to that expressed during the trial of O.J. Simpson.[44] Both publicist and client had to move to an undisclosed location, and the dogs owned by the publicists had to be placed in a kennel for their protection. When interviewed, Suleman's publicist acknowledged that the only thing that kept her from jumping out of a window was the fact that they also heard from so many people offering support,

---

44. Molly Hennessy-Fiske, *Publicists for Octuplets' Mother Quit over Death Threats*, L.A. TIMES, Feb. 15, 2009.

including a family with a farm in the Midwest who offered a permanent home to Suleman and her children.[45]

As Suleman's story unfolded, a question arose: how did we get from the miracle of life to death threats faster than the speed of sound? Koreans observe Samch'il-Il, the 21st day of a new baby's birth. Relatives and family members get together, celebrating the baby and praising the mother's labor.[46] The Western Australian capital of Perth is famous for its naming ceremonies. "In many cultures, a child is not recognized until it is named. Different names have different meanings and it is thought that a name can imbue an individual with some of the characteristics associated with the meaning of the name."[47] In the United States, we have baby showers, christening ceremonies, and charity for those blessed by the miracle of multiple births. Not more than a dozen years before Suleman's case, the birth of septuplets in Iowa garnered these headlines and story, "Septuplets Sleep Quietly as a Parade of Gifts Rolls In":[48]

Slumbering peacefully in seven incubators, the McCaughey septuplets passed their first day outside the womb Thursday in surprisingly good health, unaware as a nation showered their suburban Des Moines family with money, flowers, quilts and a monster van big enough to ferry a Scout troop. While doctors and nurses at Blank Children's Hospital monitored the infants around the clock, keeping tabs on their weakened breathing functions on a day considered the most critical to their survival, companies and donors rushed forward to provide Bobbi and Kenny McCaughey with a staggering array of amenities to help them care for their brood. Kenny McCaughey, 27, a Chevrolet

45. http://news.yahoo.com/s/ap/20090212/ap_on_re_us/octuplets_4.

46. http://www.lifeinkorea.com/culture/ricecake/RiceCake.cfm?Subject=rituals.

47. http://www.aspirecelebrancy.com.au/ceremonies.php.

48. Stephen Braun, *Septuplets Sleep Quietly as a Parade of Gifts Rolls In*, L.A. TIMES, Nov. 21, 1997, A26.

billing clerk who was at his 29-year-old wife's side during her caesarean section on Wednesday, seemed pleasantly stunned when he emerged from the Des Moines hospital to accept some of the donations. "Wow!" the father said as corporate officials paraded before him with offers of the van, bank donations and a year's supply of groceries. "This is one of the most blessed events I've ever encountered."

In similar news: "Identical Quads Born to Canadian Couple, in US": "A Canadian woman delivered four identical daughters in a Montana hospital. . . . The newborns were able to breathe on their own and are now doing fine. The odds of giving birth to naturally conceived identical quadruplets is one in 13 million."[49] On May 8, 1997, Jacqueline Thompson and her husband Linden were the first African-American couple to give birth to sextuplets, all of whom survived. Theirs was the first natural and longest sextuplet pregnancy in the United States. Yet the Thompson children drew far less attention than the Iowa couple identified above. Even though the Iowa couple used invitro fertilization, the outpouring of company endorsements and donations to help pay the cost of raising seven children was unprecedented. Gifts for the Thompson children came only after they were featured on *The Oprah Winfrey Show*.

Fertility experts have raised a fair number of medical and ethical concerns.[50] Assisted fertility is ultimately about the quality of normal births—it is not a numbers game. As a matter of public interest, survival rates, medical costs (who is picking up the tab), and quality of life all factor into the equation.

One Internet discussion of the moral issues involved from a Christian point of view deemed the McCaughey septuplets "Gifts of

---

49. http://www.newser.com/story/5985/identical-quads-born-to-canadian-couple-in-us.html.

50. Shari Roan, *Multiple Births, Multiple Risks*, L.A. TIMES, June 25, 2007, F1. *See also* http://archives.cnn.com/2001/US/07/14/septuplets.mother/index.html.

God after All." Why? The list of answers read more like justification: (1) there is no moral consensus around overpopulation, or serious proposals to limit American families to a set number of children; (2) fertility drugs are a standard treatment for infertile women; (3) selective abortion is not an option for everyone; (4) the couple's insurance paid their medical bills, and (5) the mother underwent tubal ligation following the delivery of the last child. In short, the couple fulfilled "the ordinary requirements of responsible parenthood."[51]An updated report seems to concur.[52] According to the septuplet's Sunday school teacher, all the McCaughey kids are outgoing and sociable. They no longer need the crowd of volunteers that fed, burped, changed their diapers round-the-clock, and accompanied the family every time they left the house. By the time the children were age nine, their parents were even able to get a babysitter while they went out for dinner to celebrate their 13th anniversary.[53]

Public dialogue about Suleman indicates that her case is best analyzed through a historic socio-reproductive lens. Media pundits, as the self-ordained framers of public debate, emerged front and center. Fox News personality Bill O'Reilly has called on the state of California to remove all 14 of Suleman's children, suggesting that something about her circumstances renders her an obviously unfit mother. Kathryn Joyce's February 2009 article "Eight Is Not Enough? The Big Families We Love to Hate"[54] provides unique insight: "vocal commentators across the ideological spectrum" condemn Suleman, despite fascination with The Learning Channel's reality show featuring the 18-child Duggar family. "The Duggars are grounded in and motivated by the pro-patriarchy Quiverfull Movement (where

---

51. http://www.parkridgecenter.org/Page136.html.

52. *A Septuplet Celebration: The Septuplets at 9*, LADIES HOME J., Dec. 2006.

53. *Id.*

54. Kathryn Joyce, *Eight is Not Enough? The Big Families We Love to Hate*, REPRODUCTIVE HEALTH, Feb. 5, 2009.

children are deemed to be blessings from God, while rejecting the use of any form of birth control including natural family planning and sterilization), with its emphasis on female submission and male headship." *Jon and Kate Plus Eight*, "another reality TV show about a large family . . . also presents a traditional picture of large family life, with married heterosexual parents and a stay-at-home mother."

Though it's now impossible to separate the public reaction to Suleman's delivery from the swirl of facts and speculation about her motivations and mental health, it seems clear enough that much of the ire directed at her is due to her unorthodox family situation and her singleness most of all. While many observers are concerned with her apparent inability to support such a large family, the fact that she is unmarried has alone been cause enough for others to declare her family a situation of de facto child abuse.

After what Joyce refers to as a "brief moment of "miracle news," highly moralistic overtones included "discussing whether or not Suleman's pregnancy should have been 'allowed' to take place" or if she should have been forced to abort some of the embryos." "Right-wing California shock jock Bill Handel declared the births 'freakish,' and announced that people were 'ready to boycott any corporations that help the octuplets or their mother.' There were no corporate endorsements. One blog, speculating about Suleman's ethnicity, brought issues of race and class to the forefront. Conservative blogger Phyllis Chesler first referenced Osama bin Laden's large family before speculating about the influence of Suleman's Palestinian lineage on her procreative choices by stating: "Once this gets out—will she become a poster child/mother for . . . free baby formula and diapers? Or for Jihad?"

Regrettably, the constant attacks reduced public notice of the phenomena that promotes celebration of very large families produced by Christian religious conviction and "extreme tradition-alism in marriage roles that holds women's prolific fertility up not as one option to choose but as the *only righteous path* for true believers." Quiverfull is celebrated while Suleman is condemned. One woman became the poster child for parental abuse and neglect while movements go undebated that insist on "large and labor-intensive broods of children" for all women and raises daughters to see this as the only blueprint for their lives.[55]

An entry in one blog sums it up perfectly: Nadya Suleman is easily the most vilified mother in recent history when public media has "stopped at nothing to portray her as an irresponsible nitwit too crazy to know what is in her own best interests."[56] Simultaneously, spending tax dollars for her children was portrayed as anathema "when they would be so much better spent on fat pensions for bureaucrats who don't serve the public need, foreign wars of aggression that have left untold numbers dead and damaged, and bailing out companies like AIG who are once again begging (private jet anyone?). . . ."[57]

> Nadya is in deep financial trouble, the home that she lives in is about to be foreclosed on and the hospital has threatened to refuse to release her children to her. The website that she created to give people the opportunity to help her struggling family has been ridiculed and all avenues of support have been radically slammed in her face.[58]

Disagreement about the legal and cultural norms that transformed Nadya Suleman into public enemy number one while subjecting her every thought and action (past, present, and future) from any and every possible source of information and speculation contributes very little to the privacy debate. However, upon returning

---

55. *Id.*

56. http://menstrualpoetry.com/porn-industry-ready-exploit-nadaya-suleman.

57. *Id.*

58. http://www.womanist-musings.com/2009/02/now-porn-comes-calling-for-nadaya.html.

to the question of human dignity, the early and disparaging dehumanization of calling her "Octomom," the dominance of pseudopsychologists and outraged doctors, along with numerous death threats and calls to boycott anyone sympathetic to her children, all need further study and public exploration by responsible researchers.

As this spectacle unfolded during the spring 2009 semester, the overwhelming student response to the question of what Suleman did to warrant such abuse came from one of the most vocal and thoughtless students: "she receives public welfare, and should have to pay for her choices, we cannot afford to do a single thing that would encourage other women to follow in her footsteps." None of the science about the so-called range of choices, probability of copycats, facts about the nature and sources of her income, or the diametrically opposed public reactions to these children in comparison to other multiple births seemed to soften the most hardened believers. For those of us saddened by the current state of public discourse, but equally hopeful for the future of Noah, Maliyah, Isaiah, Nariyah, Jonah, Jeremiah, Makai, Josiah, and their six siblings (Elijah, Joshua, Jacob, Aidan, Caleb, Amerah and Calyssa)—who are *not* the "Octo-spawn" but just children, there is money to be donated, books to write, and laws and culture to redirect.

✷ Venom and Hyperbole Around Tiger Woods

Recent articles about Pro golf legend Tiger Woods roundly offer the most venomous commentary featuring endless hyperbole. Misappropriation of his likeness and images of his family members in pursuit of financial gain appear to be the editorial marching orders of the day. Character assassination is plentiful, as writers describe his "diabolical cunning", the terminal velocity of his fall from grace, and his inability to accept himself as a lesser being.[59]

---

59. James Moore, *To an Athlete Screwing Up Young,* 12 Dec 2009, *available at* http://
www.huffingtonpost.com/jim-moore/to-an-athlete-screwing-up_b_ 389908.html.

There are rumors of widespread respect for his talent for the game coupled with disdain for his arrogance.[60] Lies, half-truths, and innuendo are flying about like projectiles from an air ball machine. In barely six weeks time, Woods's brand has supposedly nose-dived from the "cleanest, safest athlete in the world" to that of world-class whore who "slept with every cocktail waitress with collagen lips from Las Vegas to Dubai."[61] One writer remarked, "It feels like the OJ thing" except blacks won't defend him. In short, there will be no chorus of support "standing firmly and loudly behind" the Cablinasian because he "rejected his black heritage on Oprah in 1997," now "people see him for what he really is, a fraud."[62]

After spending an entire career exploring the value of free speech and individual rights in a democracy, and observing the pervasive effects of stereotyping, it seems all but certain that Tiger's infidelity and lack of black support are the least of his problems.

The main problem is that an unrelenting press core has invaded Woods's privacy. At the intersection of the privacy invasion, defamation of his character and widespread assault on his familial dignity is a stinging indictment of the constitutional reach of the public figure doctrine. Rumors about deal making for an expose of nude photos prompted application for an injunction against publication, which was granted by UK's High Court Justice David Eady.[63]

A flock of women in five years, including one ex and two porn starlets could not possibly be worth the non-stop coverage that it has garnered. Over-the-top characterizations and speculation

---

60. *Id.*

61. James Bernard, *Ad rant: Tiger Woods Fell Victim to His Branding,* 15, Dec, 2009, *available at* http://www.walletpop.com/blog/2009/12/15/ad-rant-tiger-woods-fell-victim-to-his-own-branding/.

62. Terence Moore, *Where are Tigers Cablinasian Backers*, 08 Dec 2009, *available at* http://golf.fanhouse.com/2009/12/08/where-are-tigers-cabalasian-backers/.

63. Jason, Lewis, *Tiger Woods's Lawyers Act Over Nude Pictures That Don't Exist*, MAIL ONLINE, December 13, 2009, *available at* http://www.dailymail.co.uk/news/article-1235251/Tiger-Woods-lawyers-act-nude-pictures-dont-exist.html.

about whether he pursued the supposed sins of his loins with the tacit consent of a woman with whom he shares a home, along with their two children, is NOT at this moment, and may never become, a matter of public concern.

The tabloid machinery churns out celebrity narratives with questionable photos while deliberately overshadowing interest in their talent.[64] One writer notes that Brad Pitt and Angelina Jolie are "far better known for their life together" than any of their performances on film and stage. Public media outlets spend a hefty amount of their resources seizing upon the fruit of the kind of paparazzi stalking and harassment that literally drove Britney Spears over the edge. An injunction was also issued in the UK preventing the British Press from publishing details concerning Spear's treatment in a rehab center.[65] Just one year ago, tabloid producers seized upon the death of John Travolta and Kelly Preston's son Jett to pry into their lives, marriage and religious beliefs, with little regard for their loss.

There is an urgency surrounding the need to address the harmful and mercenary exploitation of today's so-called public figures. Limiting the harm of the global tabloid market requires greater consistency in legal doctrine in the Western world. Thus, it will most likely begin with a critical examination of why the U.S. Supreme Court has thrown every artist and athlete into the public figure category. Only one writer acknowledged that Woods is not "a politician, priest or morals crusader."[66] She then posed the question of how he or anyone else might expect to maintain privacy while playing footsy with tell-all exhibitionists. Enjoining "photographic evidence" is an appropriate place to begin. Playmates aside, defense

---

64. Neal Gabler, *The Greatest Show on Earth, In defense of our Brangelina-loving, Jon and Kate-hating, Tiger-taunting, tawdry tabloid culture*, NEWSWEEK, Dec 12, 2009, *available at* http://www.newsweek.com/id/226457.

65. *Id.*

66. Julia Baird, *Privacy a Forgotten Virtue, Tiger is an athlete, not a politician*, NEWSWEEK, Dec 14, 2009, *available at* http://www.newsweek.com/id/225792.

of the press for raising awareness of the so-called spoiled athlete's syndrome, where accountability lags for inappropriate behavior, is an equally weak justification for trampling upon Woods's familial dignity. It is not within the media's jurisdiction to hold Woods "accountable for his actions." The legitimate focus of the press, under long-standing constitutional edicts, are public officials in the discharge of their public duties. The UK is favored with a justice system where this is properly understood and enforced.

𝄞 European Respect for Private Life

In Europe, the balancing of every person's right to privacy with free expression (as part of the fundamental commitment to fostering democratic society) is guaranteed in the Convention on Human Rights. These rights require neither absolute deference nor hierarchical ordering as they are of equal value. Thus, the right to privacy afforded by Article 8 of the European Convention on Human Rights not only protects an individual against interference by government authorities, but against interference by private persons or institutions, including agents of mass media.

Under European law, individuals who are classified as public figures in the United States are described as figures of contemporary society. Removing the label *public* is vital because we are examining protections for people rather than regulating use of common space. European citizens are afforded respect for their private lives inside and outside of their homes.

Signaling an important shift in privacy enforcement, European courts banned the publication of photos taken outside the home when it was objectively clear the subject was seeking privacy. The ECtHR in *Case of Von Hannover* reasoned that when an individual feels confident and secure in a semi-sheltered environment, the natural tendency is to relax and behave "as we all do, depending on the situation most assuredly in a manner in which they/we would not behave in a public place." Thus, publishing secret photos or those taken by catching the subject unaware amounts to an unlawful interference. Moreover, European laws restricting privacy invasions are generally applied without resort to extensive analysis of whether the target understood herself to be in a "public place" and does not foreclose protection to persons "of contemporary history." Otherwise, anyone could be photographed anywhere in public and exploited by the press, which itself is a growing problem in the United States.

One judge stated that the public's lawful interest in celebrities may extend to information about their public behavior in general. The question presented is when the public is deemed to have a legitimate interest in judging whether the personal behavior of a celebrity "convincingly tallies" with the person's public image.[67] Given that the law must draw a viable line, it appears to do so for those who are charged with felony crimes or with the notion of outrageous behavior, which is usually covered somewhere in misdemeanor criminal statutes (i.e., public drunkenness, public nudity, indecent exposure, dangerous jaywalking, public disturbances, and so forth). Public behavior is not always intended to be publicized, but is mostly an issue of spatial awareness, communal standards, and propriety. However, the nature of lawful public interest beyond items similar to those noted above is not clear.

In June 2007, the German Federal Court of Justice held in favor of the girlfriend of singer and songwriter Herbert Groenemeyer in ruling that publishing photographs of the couple during their holidays in Rome violated their privacy rights under the Convention. Without a connection to a contemporary event or voluntary involvement in a discussion of general interest, such publications are unacceptable. Although some lyrics of Herbert Groenemeyer's songs allude to private events, his girlfriend was not deemed to have waived her privacy rights.[68] In *Case of Von Hannover*, the ECtHR

---

67. *Id.*

68. http://www.bundesgerichtshof.de/.

declined to rule that all actions and photographs taken outside the home of a figure of contemporary society could be widely publicized without the person's consent. Had it done so, people would have been afforded very limited protection of their private lives or the right to control the use of their own images.

Constitutional recognition of privacy, autonomy, and freedom of choice in intimate associations protects the individual from unreasonable intrusion in secluded space, misappropriation of an individual's name or likeness, extensive publicity of elements of a person's private life, and publicity presenting the subject in a false light. These protections extend to all citizens. Legally mandated zones of privacy include boundaries for the safety of persons, their property, and their personal and familial dignity. Therefore, although public figures have increasingly become the target of media gamesmanship in the United States, European courts have taken judicial notice that although valuable for everyone, these guarantees may be even more essential for figures of contemporary society.

SEVEN

U.S. Courts' Normative View of Media Invasion

UNLIKE THE EUROPEAN UNION, there are no high court (i.e., U.S. Supreme Court) rulings featuring celebrity plaintiffs in cases involving defamation or invasion of privacy. It is nearly impossible to track the evolution of a suit launched by a high-profile celebrity through a lower court (where we would expect to find the legal reasoning and justification for the verdict) to the ultimate imposition of a final judgment supported by an opinion issued from a U.S. Circuit Court of Appeal. Most celebrity cases settle out of court with swift dispatch. One exception was the $1.6 million judgment obtained by actress–comedian Carol Burnett in 1981 against the *National Enquirer* for falsely reporting that Burnett was falling-down drunk at a prestigious award dinner that was later reduced to $800,000 on appeal.[1]

In their respective jurisdictions, the U.S. Circuit Courts of Appeal are the courts of last resort, before appeal to the U.S. Supreme Court. By and large, the paucity of guiding doctrine can be attributed to denial of petition for a writ of certiorari by the Supreme Court.[2]

---

1. Robert Lindsey, *Carol Burnett Given $1.6 Million in Suit against* National Enquirer, N.Y. TIMES, Mar. 27, 1981, A1; *see also* Alex Beam, *Tabloid Law*, THE ATLANTIC, Aug. 1999.

2. Less than five (5%) of petitions for writ of certiorari are granted by the U.S. Supreme Court, a number that is even more drastically reduced when the Court analyzes *in pauperis* petitions. *See* Saul Brenner, *Strategies in Certiorari Voting on the United States Supreme Court*, 51 J. POL. 828–840 (1989).

Chapter Six detailed the peculiarities surrounding classification of every artist, athlete, actor and musician as all-purpose public figures. Akin to elected and appointed public officials and candidates for office, all celebrities must establish that published falsehoods were motivated by actual malice under the heightened standard of clear and convincing evidence.

Along this evolutionary path, public interest in the free flow of legitimate information appeared to mandate such a standard. To require proof of a publisher's knowledge of falsity or reckless disregard (including downright avoidance) of the truth about official conduct is consistent with the goals of democracy. Evidence of reasonable investigation and reliance upon reputable sources when undertaken in good faith appropriately shields the press from undeserved liability. The dilemma in the United States has arisen in those instances where publishers lie outright and admit to fabrication of not just one, but a series of articles, presumably for pecuniary gain. As the courts began to shift emphasis away from the rights of the individual toward unfettered publication, the real winners became the shareholders of corporate media empires. Legal remedies began to resemble qualified immunity from the type of legal damages that would and should have a true deterrent effect. The late Justice Byron White concurring in *Rosenbloom v. Metromedia*, predicted this constitutional trajectory:

[The ruling in] *New York Times Co. v. Sullivan* was the wiser course, but I am unaware that state libel laws with respect to private citizens have proved a hazard to the existence or operations of the communications industry in this country. Some members of the Court seem haunted by fears of self-censorship by the press and of damage judgments that will threaten its financial health. But technology has immeasurably increased the power of the press to do both good and evil. Vast communication combines have been built into profitable ventures. My interest is not in protecting the treasuries of communicators, but in implementing the First Amendment by insuring that effective communication which is essential to the continued functioning of our free society. I am not aware that self-censorship has caused the press to tread too gingerly in reporting "news" concerning private citizens and private affairs, or that the reputation of private citizens has received inordinate protection from falsehood. I am not convinced that we must fashion a constitutional rule protecting a whole range of damaging falsehoods, and so shift the burden from those who publish to those who are injured. . . . [T]oday's experiment rests almost entirely on theoretical grounds, and represents a purely intellectual derivation from what are thought to be important principles of tort law as viewed in the light of the primacy of the written and spoken word.

% Dignitary Protections under U.S. Law

The origins of the right to privacy as covered in Chapter Four relate to its primacy in a representative democracy. Tort law has been the traditional vehicle for redressing injury, and its dignitary protections cover zones of freedom from observation, intrusion, or attention, which have instrumental and functional value in safeguarding reputation, earning capacity, and meaningful opportunities for self-governance. The rights of autonomy indispensable to freedom of personal and political choice embody protection from coercive interference from government officials as well as from individuals acting alone or in concert with others. The Constitution as a matter of civil and political rights demands that we give account of our behavior and take reasonable precautions to avoid harmful and reckless trampling upon another's rights and interests. This is the underlying rationale for modulating publisher liability commensurate with the degree of fault involved.

Defamation consists of broadcasting an intentionally false communication, including single statements of fact or opinions laced with facts, about individuals that injures their standing in the community, with the typical communicative effect of exposing them to public condemnation, shame, ridicule, humiliation, or contempt. Whether dispensed in the form of libel (written communication) or slander (oral communication), the injury to personal and professional reputation is associated with the communication's widespread dissemination. The malevolent character of certain statements rise to such a contemptible level of offense that damage to the subject's reputation is presumed. False allegations relating to taboo sexual exploits, involvement in criminal activity, or affliction with a loathsome disease are regarded as defamatory per se. For example, actor Josh Hartnett sued the British tabloid *Daily Mirror* in September 2008 for falsely reporting that a Soho London hotel's closed circuit television cameras captured him having sex with a mystery lady in its public library. By December 2008, the publisher was required to pay a libel judgment and issue a public apology.[3]

Unlawful intrusion into the personal life of another occurs through disruption of other people's solitude or trespass upon exclusive space for purposes of exposing them to unwarranted publicity. For example, former presidential candidate John Edwards became a primary target in the *National Enquirer's* tabloid makeover. Assuming the mantle of investigative reporting, headlining one "world exclusive" after another as political bombshells, it claimed to be the first to uncover Edward's cheating on a cancerstricken wife. The paper announced the birth of his "love child," who unnamed sources believe he fathered even though another man stepped forward to claim paternity. It also advertised "never before seen spy photos" of Edwards at The Beverly Hilton while visiting the child at 2 a.m. along with reports of the commotion that erupted as photographers who allegedly caught him sneaking out through the hotel basement, chased him into a bathroom where he waited until hotel security was able to escort him out. The story of course, was rounded off nicely by a criminal complaint filed against

---

3. Roger Pearson, *Josh Hartnett Wins Libel Payout for* Daily Mirror *Sex Slur*, PRESS GAZETTE, Dec. 11, 2008.

hotel guards for unlawful detention of the photographers, the first birthday coverage of the tot, and an exclusive interview with the "mistress."[4]

Interference with the right to seclusion in the celebrity context is often accomplished through constructive invasions of privacy. Legislation known as the New York and California paparazzi statutes penalize the combining of physical dexterity (such as scaling a 17-foot wall) with use of enhanced auditory, visual, or electronic devices to peer into another's private space.[5] European celebrities enjoy similar protections; for example, actor Sienna Miller sued the UK's *News International* in July 2007 for invasion of privacy after it published nude photographs of Miller and actor Balthazar Getty on a yacht in Italy.[6] British tabloids *News of the World* and the *Sun* had made a habit of intruding upon Miller's privacy by publishing stories about her love life and sneaking onto movie sets to take shots of her when she was filming nude scenes for the movie *Hippie Hippie Shake* and semi-nude ones for the movie *Factory Girl*. London'sHigh Court held the magazine liable for invasion of privacy, ordered deletion of the photos from its archives, and enjoined republication.[7]

Gaining access to a home, garage, office, car, storage unit, locker, or other restricted space by fraud or misrepresentation, or abuse of a limited-purpose valid authorization with the intent to acquire private information or images is actionable, regardless of whether any material obtained was later broadcast or actually induced disparaging or hostile feelings against the subject. A typical example of this was featured in the December 2008 lawsuit instituted by Madonna against a leading British tabloid[8] when the *Mail* published

4. *Spy Photos Love Child*, NAT. ENQUIRER, Aug. 6, 2008.

5. Cal. Civ. Code §1708–1728.

6. Oliver Luft, *Sienna Miller in Tabloid Privacy Complaint over Holiday Pics*, THE GUARDIAN, July 23, 2008.

7. *Id.*

8. Robert Verkaik, *Madonna Sues over Wedding Pictures*, THE INDEPENDENT, Dec. 9, 2008.

private photographs of her 2002 wedding in Scotland to Guy Ritchie. According to her attorney, "pictures of the 'wholly private' event, held in the lavish setting of Skibo Castle in the Highlands, were copied 'surreptitiously' by an interior designer." Designer Robert Joseph Wilber copied the photographs while doing work at her Beverly Hills home and sold them to the publisher for $7,500.

Privacy rights also extend to public disclosure of facts that are likely to cause humiliation. It certainly became a matter of public interest that police questioned former Congressman Gary Condit over the 2001 disappearance of a 24-year-old Bureau of Prisons intern with whom he had been having an affair. Condit's 79-year-old mother acknowledged that "it has been hell at times."[9] Although he was never named as a suspect, "he was branded for life with a scarlet letter." His brother agreed that "unrelenting media scrutiny of the case painted his brother in an irreversibly damning light" that their mother believes has tainted the whole family.[10]

Public disclosure of private facts involves dissemination of information that is not incorporated in any public record or court proceeding, that lacks any direct impact upon the public welfare, and that under general community standards would prove embarrassing to the average person. Breach of confidence is similar to public disclosure except that it provides a claim for circulation of information shared under a reciprocal expectation or unilateral obligation of confidentiality that is later revealed in circumstances proving detrimental to the subject. Dr. Gary Mulhauser, managing editor of a counseling resources Web site, described an alarming discovery in his article "A Fundamental Violation of Trust":

In March 2005, I stumbled upon incontrovertible evidence that a group of six self-styled online therapy "experts" had unwittingly

---

9. http://www.cnn.com/2009/POLITICS/02/23/gary.condit.now/

10. *Id.*

published personal details about their clients on an electronic discussion group hosted on a major web portal. In one instance, the discussion group archive apparently exposed a client's full name, occupation, work and educational history. In another instance, it revealed first name, occupation, work and educational history, medical history, and city of residence of a man openly discussing practices which were punishable by law in his country. And in a third, the therapists' discussions exposed family details and other information about a child and about ongoing legal proceedings concerning allegations of child abuse, including the name of a local child protection agency involved in the case.[11]

Mulhauser later reported that his original article was revised and reposted after he received a request from the British Association for Counseling and Psychotherapy to remove the names of the parties involved in the breach of confidence.

Protections are similarly available from the effects of publicity generated with malicious intent to create a false and misleading impression of another individual. This occurs when valid information or images are presented in a "false light." For example, three escaped convicts held several members of the Hill family hostage in 1952. The family was detained in their Pennsylvania home for 19 hours, after which all members were released without harm. Publicity efforts undertaken in furtherance of production and sale of commercialized accounts of their ordeal caused extensive involuntary notoriety. First there was a novel in which the story line was embellished to include a great deal of violence, then the novel became a play. *Life* magazine wrote a story about the play referencing the Hills that it described as a reenactment, while including

---

11. Greg Mulhauser, *BACP Asks that Names Be Removed from Published Account of Confidentiality Violation by Online Therapists*, Oct. 19, 2006; *see also* http://counsellingresource.com/features/2006/10/19/bacp-ruling/.

photographs that illustrated scenes staged in the home formerly owned by the Hills where their hostage ordeal took place. The victims brought suit against the magazine upon establishing that it knowingly orchestrated the false impression that the play depicted their experience.[12]

The hostage incident was certainly a matter of public concern. At issue in the case was the applicability of a New York law that provided a cause of action to a person whose name or picture is used by another without consent for purposes of trade or advertising.[13] The trial court instructed the jury that liability under the statute depended upon a finding that the *Life* article was published not to disseminate news, but rather as a fictionalized version of the Hill incident for the purpose of advertising the play or increasing the magazine's circulation. Punitive damages were justified if the publisher knew the association to be false or failed to conduct a reasonable investigation in reckless or wanton disregard of family's rights.

The jury awarded compensatory and punitive damages. Though liability was sustained on appeal, the Appellate Division ordered a new trial as to damages at which only compensatory damages were awarded. That decision was affirmed by the U.S. Court of Appeals for the First Circuit. However, the U.S. Supreme Court reversed and remanded, holding that the Hills were required under law to prove actual malice.[14]

Appropriation of an individual's name, image, or likeness for purposes of misrepresenting the person's character, personal history, activities, or beliefs produces tangible reputational harm for which relief is routinely granted. In November 2005, actor Kate Hudson sued the *National Enquirer* after the tabloid published

---

12. Time, Inc. v. Hill, 385 U.S. 374 (1967).

13. New York Civil Rights Law §§ 50–51, governing the *rights of privacy and* actions *for injunction and for damages.*

14. *Time*, 385 U. S. at 387.

photos of her under the headline "Goldie Tells Kate: Eat Something! And She Listens!"[15] Thus, actor Goldie Hawn and her daughter were implicated in a report that Hudson had an "eating disorder that was so grave and serious that she was wasting away, to the extreme concern of her mother and family."[16] Hudson's attorney named two London tabloids, *Heat Magazine* and *Daily Mail*, for reporting that she was dangerously thin and battling anorexia.[17] In July 2006, publisher American Media Inc. "apologised for the deep distress and acute embarrassment caused by the allegations, which it now acknowledges were false."[18]

Laws based upon misappropriation of an individual's right of publicity have both dignitary and proprietary elements. Monetary loss caused by appropriation of personal likeness for commercial exploitation violates the individual's exclusive rights to control of image and operates as do statutes designed to prevent trademark infringement for companies and corporations. Actor Reese Witherspoon sued *Star* magazine in June 2006 after the publisher reported that a "baby bump," "empire-waist dresses," and "baggy clothing" indicated that she was hiding a pregnancy from the producers of an upcoming movie in order to play a certain role.[19] She alleged that the aspersions cast upon her ability to perform her duties on set interfered with working relations. The suit was settled in fall 2006.

Laws prohibiting alienation of affection enables one marital partner to sue a third party whose pernicious interference in an otherwise loving relationship results in the plaintiff's spouse

15. *Kate Hudson Goes to Court over Photos*, Associated Press, Nov. 8, 2005.

16. *Id.*

17. Ciar Byrne, *Actress Hudson Wins Libel Case over being "Dangerously" Thin*, THE INDEPENDENT, July 21, 2006.

18. *Id.*

19. http://www.foxnews.com/story/0,2933,200642,00.html?sPage=fnc/ entertainment/celebfamilies.

leaving the marriage to be with another.[20] When the Missouri Supreme Court abolished the tort, it acknowledged that its original purposes (to ensure purity of bloodlines and discourage adultery, at a time when wives were deemed valuable servants) are no longer relevant in post-modern life.[21] Liability for alienation as a means of preserving a marriage or family has long outlived its usefulness. No-fault divorce and laws governing equitable distribution of marital assets have replaced the primitive concept that husbands and wives have a proprietary interest in the person and services of the other. Arguments for retaining the tort are specious at best as alienation suits are ordinarily commenced after dissolution or separation. Reaction to failure or sense of betrayal that accompanies the realization that a marriage is irretrievably broken indicates that revenge, rather than reconciliation, is often the principal motivation. Affidavits divulging embarrassing details of an illicit affair are unlikely to restore the degree of trust necessary to salvage a union.

In an adventurous moment, an Illinois man named Arthur Friedman reportedly told his wife of 10 years that they needed to spice up their boring sex life, so they began having sex with other couples.[22] She fell in love with one of the men, leading both couples to divorce court. Friedman sued the interloper, Blinov German, in one of a handful of states that still recognize the tort and recovered $4,802.87. However, one lawyer summed it up as follows. "German was not a pirate of her affections . . . her affections were already adrift."[23]

Alienation suits are an interesting breed that have not lost all currency in the American legal system. For example, a Canadian

---

20. Only a handful of states still have "alienation of affection" laws.

21. Helsel v. Noellsch, 107 S W 3d 231 (Mo. 2003).

22. Steve Patterson, *Guy Wants Wife to be Swinger, She Ends Up Cheating, He Sues*, SUN TIMES, July 1, 2007.

23. http://www.infidel-club.com/news.php?item.34.2.

man alleged that his former wife relocated to New Jersey, changed her phone number, blocked e-mails, and cut all of his contact with their two children ages 13 and 9.[24] After locating them through a private detective, the father sued for visitation and to enjoin the mother from further attempts to change the children's last names. Because he no longer had the relationship with his children that he once had, he sought to sue for alienation of his children's affection and for infliction of emotional distress.

Liability for intentional infliction of emotional distress provides damages for injuries arising from calculated or reckless, extreme, and outrageous conduct that causes severe anguish. Plaintiffs carry the burden of demonstrating intentionality, as well as whether the defendant knew or should have known that the particular acts would rise to that level of torment. The character of the conduct, when judged egregious and insufferable under widely approved codes of decency, is the cornerstone of successful lawsuits. Causal connections between the defendant's conduct and the victim's emotional distress must be obvious and direct. However, the U.S. Supreme Court has ruled that public figures must prove actual malice before recovering on claims of intentional infliction of emotional distress, since it is a malice-based claim, the redundancy as a constitutional precept is even more perplexing.

✌ Publisher Immunity Run Amok

What differentiates U.S. law from European law is that although free speech and freedom of the press serve a vital role in insuring liberty of consciousness, the U.S. Supreme Court has yet to enforce as a matter of constitutional right all of the necessary prerequisites to the proper exercise of those freedoms. The Ninth Circuit Court of

---

24. Maria Vogel-Short, *Millionaire Pursues New Marital Tort: Alienation of Children's Affection*, N.J.L.J. (2006).

Appeals issued a ruling in the aftermath of *Sullivan* that mandated due regard for the fact that the First Amendment has never been "construed to accord newsmen immunity from torts or crimes committed during the course of newsgathering. In short, no constitutional provision provides a license to trespass, to steal, or to intrude by electronic means into the precincts of another's home or office."[25]

Common defenses to defamation (advanced largely by media defendants) include assertions that the statements made are true or substantially true. Demonstrably false statements published in certain contexts are nonetheless privileged for reporting purposes. The classic example involves allegations found in court filings during divorce and child custody proceedings. Reporting scurrilous accusations might exact the proverbial pound of flesh from its victim, but news outlets merely quoting an affidavit are neither under any obligation to investigate accuracy nor subject to increased exposure of liability for any damaging effects.

Opinion also enjoys a broad range of constitutional protection depending upon the context in which it is delivered. Brooklyn Law School Professor Gary Minda sued Times Publishing Co. for defamation after obtaining custody of his daughter in family court.[26] (Donna Marie Kostreva was named as a codefendant for e-mailing the column to over one hundred of Minda's associates).[27] The *St. Petersburg Times* had published a story on August 15, 2001 that Minda alleged "in tone and content, falsely suggested that [he] used his alleged legal connections and financial means to overpower and intimidate [the mother]."[28] Under the headline "The Deck Was Stacked Against Unwed Mexican Mother in Custody Battle," the

---

25. David H. Holtzman, Privacy Lost: How Technology is Endangering Your Privacy 102 (2006). *See also* Dietemann v. Time Inc., 284 F. Supp. 925 (9th Cir. 1971).

26. Leanora Minai, *Law Professor Sues Times Publishing, Columnist*, St. Petersburg Times, July 16, 2002.

27. *Id.*

28. *Id.*

story detailed the fight for custody between Minda and 33-year-old Theresa Noelle Ponce.[29] Ponce became pregnant soon after they met and gave birth to a baby girl, which DNA tests confirmed was fathered by Minda. Contrary to its customary practices, the county's circuit judge awarded physical custody to the father and allowed the mother only scheduled visitation. The paper claimed, "Ponce was up against an attorney and law professor who knew how to work the system."[30] *Times* attorney George Radhert stated that the article was largely an expression of opinion.

Depending upon the information, sources, and witnesses, the crucial question in this case is whether the story can be objectively viewed as containing false statements of fact. When the individual making the statement is in a position to know, then its factual validity is more easily imputed. Some jurisdictions weigh the extent to which a derogatory statement advanced as an opinion during trial was nonetheless offered with an implied basis of factual support during its actual dissemination.

✎ Fair Use in the Realm of Public Debate

Publishers and writers often use photographic images without first obtaining permission to republish from the owner of copyrighted material under fair use laws designed to facilitate commentary on matters of public concern. In an interesting twist on these issues, the case of *Hustler v. Falwell* involved a vulgar parody that also displayed an actual photograph rather than caricature of its subject, the late Reverend Jerry Falwell.[31] Two separate editions of *Hustler Magazine* (in November 1983 and March 1984) featured the cameo

---

29. Bill Maxwell, *The Deck Was Stacked Against UnWed Mexican Mother in Custody Battle*, St. Petersburg Times, Aug. 15, 2001.

30. *Id.*

31. Hustler Magazine, Inc. v. Falwell, 485 U.S. 46 (1988).

photo and liquor ad parody with the latter publication being a direct response to Falwell's lawsuit.

As founder of the religious and political coalition known as the Moral Majority, and during his weekly television broadcast *Old Time Gospel Hour*, Falwell spoke out against the magazine and invited others to protest. In the course of his campaign to solicit money and outrage, Falwell staffers mailed three quarters of a million copies of the ad to known supporters. *Hustler* publisher Larry Flynt then sued Falwell for copyright infringement.[32] Upon motion for summary judgment, the court noted that Flynt had made a prima facie showing of infringement but upheld Falwell's distribution as fair use.[33] However, one dissenting judge contended that because Falwell went well beyond "criticizing and commenting on the ad parody and actively sought to exploit the emotional impact of the work in order to raise money," his use was commercial and therefore weighed against a finding of fair use. [34]

The fair use doctrine confers a privilege to use another's copyrighted material in a reasonable manner without their consent. The court described the doctrine as a means of balancing the need to provide individuals with sufficient incentives to create public works with the public's interest in the dissemination of information.[35] Accordingly, the district court dismissed Falwell's action, finding that Flynt's original use of an actual cameo photograph did not amount to misappropriation of Falwell's name and likeness "for purposes of trade" within the meaning of the Virginia statute, which the Fourth Circuit Court affirmed on appeal.[36]

---

32. Hustler Magazine, Inc. v. Moral Majority, Inc., 796 F.2d 1148 (9th Cir. 1986).

33. *Id.*

34. Justice Poole's dissenting opinion noted, "Falwell went beyond simply criticizing and commenting on the ad parody and actively sought to exploit the emotional impact of the work to raise money. This commercial use of the copyrighted work is a separate factor that weighs against a finding of fair use." *Id.*

35. *Hustler v. Moral Majority.*

36. http://www.opengovva.org/content/view/744/5/.

In February 2009, a lively row ensued over what the *New York Times* characterized as a preemptive strike: "Street artist Shepard Fairey filed a lawsuit on Monday against the Associated Press, asking a federal judge to declare that he is protected from copyright infringement claims in his use of a news photograph as the basis for a now ubiquitous campaign poster image of President Obama."[37] Court filings claim that AP officials contacted Fairey with a notice of copyright infringement, demanding payment for his use as well as a percentage of any profits.

✄ Constructive Invitation to Intrude and Frivolous Suits

According to Professor Nat Stern, the torts of defamation and false light invasion of privacy have been rightfully criticized as confusing in theory and arbitrary in result.[38] The case of *Fielder v. Greater Media, Inc.* is a prime example.[39] Here the Michigan Court of Appeals affirmed dismissal of a suit alleging libel and false light invasion when the *Detroit News* reported that baseball player Cecil Fielder's gambling and investment decisions destroyed his fortune and his marriage. As it took some of its information from official records, the defendant publisher argued (and the court agreed) that the paper's factual statements fell under constitutionally protected opinion.

Stern argues that a viable middle ground is warranted in those cases where false light and defamation injuries are substantially the same, and where elements of contributory negligence might exist.

---

37. Randy Kennedy, *Artist Sues the A.P. Over Obama Image*, N.Y. TIMES, Feb. 9, 2009.

38. Nat Stern, *Creating a New Tort for Wrongful Misrepresentation of Character*, FSU College of Law, Public Law Research Paper No. 107, Mar. 2004.

39. Fielder v. Greater Media, Inc., No. 267495 (Mich. App. 2006) (unpublished).

Stern proposes that a new legal claim for *wrongful misrepresenta-tion of character* may clear the path for those seeking to resolve claims where compelling arguments exist on both sides of the case. This would provide a workable alternative for the state supreme courts that do not recognize the false light invasion theory because of its similarity to defamation.[40]

The scholarly debate over imposition of damages has emerged in a robust fashion and mainly focused upon whether private citizens should only be required to prove publisher negligence, and if the communication is sufficiently outrageous, whether a private claimant should be eligible for punitive damage awards. However, scholars have been relatively quiet about the form of appellate review that has developed since the actual malice standard was first deployed to deter what we all know to be the natural threat that defamation suits pose to a free press.

A 2003 story "Libel Suit By Well-Known Children's Recording Artists Dismissed" provides a paradigmatic example.[41] Sisters Chad and Terri Sigafus sued the *St. Louis Post-Dispatch* for information released in the paper's expose about the growth of right-wing hate groups in their community. The article stated that the Christian Identity Movement has spawned some of the most violent domestic terrorists in America, including bombers, arsonists, and murderers.

The self-proclaimed "nationally known recording artists" were deemed public figures because of their 15 albums distributed nationwide, solo musical performances, tours with other artists, authorship of children's books, video performances, and frequent interviews for print and radio media. They were also deemed limited purpose public figures in the context of the news article in question. The court ruled that the teens had injected themselves

---

40. *See, e.g., Denver Publ'g Co. v. Bueno*, 54 P. 3d 893 (Colo. 2002). *See also* BRUCE W. STANFORD, LIBEL AND PRIVACY 572 (Supp. 2d ed. 2004).

41. Barbara Wartelle Wall, *Libel Suit by Well-Known Children's Recording Artists Dismissed*, Gannet, May 2003; *see also* http://www.gannett.com/go/newswatch/2003/may/nw0502-3.htm.

into the controversy surrounding the Christian Identity Movement by performing at numerous public events featuring Movement speakers, and helping to produce a videotape espousing the Movement's views. Concluding that there was no evidence that the articles were published with actual malice, the court held that the teens' performance at a "Gospel Gathering" sponsored by Christian Identity leaders (composed of militant white supremacists and anti-Semites) did not amount to falsely affiliating them with the Movement. Accordingly, the suit was dismissed.

Frivolous libel suits are routinely dismissed. Suits filed by celebrities for what amounts to little more than stinging criticism of personal choices fall into this category under rules establishing protection for opinion. Beyond simple disagreement the privacy violations and defamatory publications featured throughout this book require meaningful redress. Even in those rare instances when a public figure clears the hurdle of demonstrating that a publisher had prior knowledge that information published was false (or in most instances, contrived at the editor's desk), the ultimate penalties amount to little more than a slap on the hand. As a result of automatic appellate review, trial verdicts favoring celebrities for many violations often cost the publisher a fraction of the profit gleaned from its sales figures. If left unchecked, this kind of redress observed in the United States can amount to little more than a wink and a nod in the direction of upholding constitutional protection for dignity and reputation.

🏵 Rationale for De Novo Review

In *Bose Corporation v. Consumers Union of United States, Inc.*,[42] the U.S. Supreme Court reaffirmed de novo review of libel cases. Differing standards among state courts in recognizing traditional

---

42. Bose Corp. v. Consumers Union of United States, Inc., 466 U.S. 485 (1984).

tort claims coupled with insufficient agreement around proper classification of individuals defamed by the press have reverberated throughout this body of case law without due regard for the motive and incentives surrounding grossly defamatory communications. Successful cases have been subject to automatic review by the U.S. Circuit Court of Appeals since 1969.

The Supreme Court announced in *New York Times v. Sullivan* that to ensure adequate enforcement of the actual malice standard:

> Judges—particularly Members of this Court—must exercise [appellate] review in order to preserve the precious liberties established and ordained by the Constitution. The question whether the evidence in the record in a defamation case is of the convincing clarity required to strip the utterance of First Amendment protection is not merely a question for the trier of fact. Judges, as expositors of the Constitution, must independently decide whether the evidence in the record is sufficient to cross the constitutional threshold that bars the entry of any judgment that is not supported by clear and convincing proof of "actual malice."[43]

Thus, successful plaintiffs at the trial level find that upon de novo review, their damage awards against publisher defendants are habitually lowered to a mere fraction of the initial recovery. Scrutiny of the overall impact of de novo review and the impact of those reductions upon the practices of the publishing industry is minimal at best. Scholarly appeals to the Supreme Court to review the process of review are rare. Critiques of the way U.S. law governing the public figure classification evolved in relation to celebrity plaintiffs are few and far between. Prominent scholars of constitutional law have subordinated dialogue around the efficacy and fairness of the

---

43. *Id.* at 510–11.

current system in favor of review of proposals to untangle the web of conflicts imbedded in statutory and common law understanding. Consistent with the preferences of successful media lawyers, we hear far more in academic circles about the importance of a free press and the ignorance of jurors than we learn about proportionate means for protecting citizens from illicit invasion.

⚝ Opinion, Public Records, and Rights of the Accused and Suspected

All criminal trials pose interesting and significant questions of public interest. As envisaged by the statesmen who drafted the Constitution, protections insisted upon and embodied throughout (and epigrammatically upon) the Bill of Rights are heavily weighted on the side of the accused. However, prosecutors acting on behalf of the State are unremittingly vulnerable to the sway of ambition and pressures of political factions. According to Rabbi Wine, beyond political ambition, unfounded zeal, corruption, and longing for star-chamber-style justice have their roots in the harshness of our puritan past, where patriotism is equated with allegiance to God, and where coercion and conformity flourished.[44] Thus, regrettably abuse of prosecutorial discretion is a significant issue in the United States.

However, the rights of the accused, while decreasingly relevant in criminal law enforcement, are nonexistent in the realm of public media. The dangerous intersection for U.S. citizens in the court of public opinion occurs when the victim becomes suspect or there is ambiguity in the relationship between the two classifications. The following cases illustrate key differences on this issue between the United States and European Union.

---

44. Patricia Bonomi, *Under the Cope off Heaven: Religion, Society, and Politics in Colonial America* (1988).

London

The parents of missing toddler Madeleine McCann received a $1.1 million judgment, given to the Find Madeleine Campaign, along with an apology after suing publishers of the *Daily Express* and *Daily Star* newspapers in London. The papers' stories alleged that Kate and Gerry McCann were involved in the disappearance or death of their three-year-old daughter whom police believe was abducted during a family vacation at the Praia da Luz resort in southern Portugal.[45] A spokesman for the McCanns outside the High Court in London stated: "[We] are pleased that the papers have today admitted the utter falsity of the numerous grotesque and grossly defamatory allegations that their titles published . . . We feel it entirely appropriate that the search for Madeleine will now benefit directly out of the wrongs committed against us as her parents."[46]

The front pages of both papers featured an apology for suggesting the couple was responsible for the death of their daughter. Editors admitted there was no evidence to back up a series of articles they had printed alleging the parents had a role in their daughter's disappearance or death: "Kate and Gerry are completely innocent of any involvement in their daughter's disappearance," and adding "we are truly sorry to have added to your distress" and "we assure you that we hope Madeleine will one day be found alive and well and will be restored to her loving family."[47]

Los Angeles

Ongoing legal analysis of celebrity arrests and detentions has become a standard feature since Greta Van Sustern became a nightly television fixture during the "trial of the century,"

---

45. http://www.cnn.com/2008/WORLD/europe/03/19/mccann.newspapers/index.html.

46. http://news.bbc.co.uk/1/hi/uk/7304556.stm.

47. *Id.*

People v. Simpson. CNN markets former prosecutor "Nancy Grace" as television's:

> only justice themed/interview/debate show, designed for those interested in the breaking crime news of the day. Grace challenges guests on the most high-profile legal issues of the day by drawing on her unique perspective as a former violent crimes prosecutor and as a crime victim herself. Nancy Grace provides viewers with a clear understanding of not only the top crime stories, but also the cases often overlooked.[48]

The defendants (and occasionally the victims) featured on Grace's program are invariably tried and convicted during her nightly diatribe.

In March 2009, nationally televised reports of pop singer Chris Brown's court appearance on charges of domestic violence provide a ready example. There were missed opportunities resulting from public media's refusal to provide comprehensive coverage of issues related to violence against women. Cable news networks' ongoing hyper-analysis of high-profile arrests and detentions are sensationalized in ways that enable routine violations of the constitutional rights of the accused to all but escape public notice.

Coverage of Brown's court appearance included the usual array of descriptive excess. Even more surprising is that video footage that included both private and privileged conversations held in the courtroom, replayed on national television without the usual voice-over. In a shocking display of hubris, moments into the broadcast the audience heard audio of a private conversation among Brown, his lawyer, and the victim's lawyer that took place just minutes before his hearing began. In order to disclaim liability, the conversation is alleged to have been "caught" by a microphone. Thus, video clips of Brown and his attorney were played with audio from this conversation and closed caption transcription at the

48. http://www.cnn.com/CNN/Programs/nancy.grace/.

bottom of the screen to provide clarity for the viewing audience. According to the American Bar Association, "protection of communications, as embodied in the attorney–client privilege, has been a bedrock principle of our justice system for hundreds of years. The full and frank exchange of information is necessary to ensure effective legal representation and protection of civil liberties."[49] In Brown's case, the violation of legal protections that privilege communications between lawyers and their clients was greeted with virtual silence. Public media issued no calls for investigation into the type of microphone, owner, or manager of the recording device that casually "caught" the conversation.[50]

Throughout the general reporting of this story, the public was treated to every conceivable theory about the couple's relationship, Brown's prospects for escaping prison and retaining his fan base, whether they would stay together, and whether Rhianna would jeopardize her status as a role model by standing by him. Audience polling and commentary about these questions continued apace without a single call for investigation into the various privacy violations or public interest in understanding how to detect and prevent violence against teen girls.[51] This incident demonstrates just how egregious these violations have become.

✄ Attorney-Client or Reporter Privilege and Post-Mortem Waivers

Public understanding of the role of privilege is less developed and coherent now that questions of privacy, newsworthiness, and public concern have collided on national airwaves filled mostly with radio

---

49. http://www.abanet.org/buslaw/attorneyclient/

50. http://abcnews.go.com/Entertainment/WinterConcert/story?id=7021131&page=1.

51. *Id.*

shock jocks. These soldiers of culture war fortune pull down multi-million contracts to do little more than divide and misinform the public, while National Public Radio's mission to educate and explain falls prey to politicians' threats to decrease public funding. Confusion related to defining matters of public interest and the rationale for certain boundaries is most evident regarding the question of when we choose to recognize post-mortem rights in relation to privacy and defamation.

For example, under Florida law the relatives of a deceased may not pursue a claim for privacy or defamation on behalf of the decedent. Derivative false light claims are only recognized if the statements are exceptionally egregious[52] because public interest in protecting the memory of deceased individuals is not formally recognized. Ironically, it can serve as a basis for a court's refusal to override claims of privilege for certain communications, even when it would undoubtedly serve the public interest.

An interesting case arose in the late 1980s that illustrates key aspects of this quagmire. The investigation by a grand jury into the shooting death of Carol DiMaiti Stuart on October 23, 1989, provides a concrete multidimensional view of the public interest question. Stuart was pregnant at the time of the shooting, and her son Christopher died several days later following delivery by emergency caesarean section. Her husband Charles sustained a gunshot wound but survived.

The case overtook the national spotlight in the news media after various official and civic leaders mounted the soapbox decrying the murders following Charles Stuart's reports that the perpetrator was black. National civil rights organizations called for federal intervention based upon the chaos that gripped the city. Following a federal investigation, police were found to have violated the civil and human rights of scores of Black Americans by tearing through Boston's poor black neighborhoods demanding leads in the case.

---

52. *See, e.g., Tyne v. Time Warner Ent. Co.*, 336 F 3d 1286 (11th Cir. 2003).

Charles went on to identify one black man as the assailant in a police lineup.[53]

Fewer than three months later, the grand jury heard testimony that it was Charles Stuart who had shot his wife with his brother Matthew Stuart participated by concealing certain evidence on the night of the shooting as part of an insurance fraud. Matthew reportedly drove to a prearranged spot in the Mission Hill section of Boston, drove up beside Charles's car, and took a bag from Charles containing Carol's purse, engagement ring, and a gun. On January 3, 1990, Matthew reportedly told the police that Charles shot Carol. Charles committed suicide the next day. The investigation into the shooting death of Carol Stuart then turned toward the conduct of Matthew Stuart and his friend John McMahon on the night of the shooting. More than 80 witnesses had already appeared before the grand jury. The police and assistant district attorneys had interviewed every member of the Stuart family and spoken with "virtually every person that had any connection to Charles, Matthew and John", including family, "friends, girlfriends, employers, and fellow employees."

However, although they were all interviewed, not everyone testified before the grand jury. A summons was issued for David Ropeik, a television reporter for Boston's WCVB. The purpose was to have Ropeik identify the "source close to the Stuart family" quoted in his October 16th broadcast. Ropeik reported that the source told him that Charles Stuart had confessed to murdering Carol, and that his brother Matthew brought the gun to Mission Hill on the night of the murder. The jury watched a videotape of the news report. *Boston Herald* reporter Patricia Mangan was also subpoenaed for the name of source who told her that John McMahon was with Matthew when Charles tossed the bag into the car.

---

53. *See, e.g.*, Sherri Sharma, *Beyond "Driving While Black" and "Flying While Brown": Using Intersectionality to Uncover the Gendered Aspects of Racial Profiling,* 12 COLUM. J. GENDER & L. 275, 291 (2003).

The trial court supposedly weighed the public's interest in obtaining all available evidence in this case against a countervailing interest in the free flow of information. In doing so, the judge failed to discuss the salient facts that catapulted this case to an entirely different level. Beyond issues pertaining to the way police acquire evidence and the role of the press in promoting dialogue, the Stuart case was about a great public hoax. The shocking facts sent waves of reverberation across the nation, with grave consequences to the Boston community and imposition of even greater hardship on black men. Thus, the need to correctly identify what appeared to be multiple conspirators and perpetrators in a heinous crime required a special balancing of interests.

The trial court's mundane explanation identified the first inquiry as "whether the reporters had made 'some showing that the asserted damage to the free flow of information is more than speculative or theoretical.'"[54] A second guiding principle was that police may not rely upon others to do their job and they had already interviewed everyone known to be involved. The over 80 witnesses called before the grand jury were asked under oath about these specific news reports, and no one admitted having knowledge of the underlying facts. The judge therefore concluded that the information sought from Ropeik and Mangan was otherwise available and issued a ruling that protected the reporter's privilege.

The Massachusetts court failed to acknowledge that the truth was a significant competing interest. Virtually ignored was the great benefit to the cause of justice that stems from a law enforcement machinery as vigilant in the search for truth as it is in tearing the city apart and creating widespread racial tensions and discord. Police misconduct in the case presented a crucial matter of public concern relating to issues of accountability. The only competing interest would have been the rights of the accused, which took on

---

54. Mark S. Brodin & Paul J Liacos, Handbook of Massachusetts Evidence (8th ed. 2006).

less importance because he was already dead. And if the reporters had no legitimate source to protect, the public was entitled to know.

Similar issues around privileged communication arose in this case concerning a two-hour meeting that Charles Stuart had with his lawyer shortly before committing suicide. The prosecutors sought a waiver of the privilege to question the attorney. Also at issue was whether Charles Stuart's mother, as executor of his estate, had the power to waive the privilege. Ultimately the court issued a blanket protection. Waiving attorney-client privilege post-mortem to solve this crime and prevent insurance fraud would have been justified since the weight of the public interest favored disclosure over invocation of any of these privileges. If the vital role of the press as "watchdog" entails reporting facts capable of contributing to debates related to government agents in the exercise of their official functions. In the Stuart case, it included police, prosecutorial and judicial conduct.

Safeguarding protections that allow the media to fulfill its essential role is entirely consistent with both curbing publisher transgressions and establishing boundaries that separate matters of public concern from the private and reputational rights of the living. Despite evidence of an overwhelming public need for truth, this case illustrated just how easy it has become for a judge to stifle access to crucial information, presumably to protect the rights of a deceased suspect in the murders of Carol and Christopher Stuart— and in effect the living co-conspirators who worked to obstruct the investigation. Our justice system appears to be in crisis when the courts brook no interference when the press corps seeks constitutional cover for its motivations and methods in "breaking the news." Like the parallel universes of science fiction, murders go unsolved and cities are torn asunder while the unbounded search for truth exposes the "real" conspiracies and cover ups: John Edwards has a love child, and Naomi Campbell's recreational drug use is likely on the decline.

EIGHT

European Courts' Comprehensive Approach to Media Invasion

SEVERAL DISTINCTIONS EMERGE when comparing laws operating in the United States with those in the European Union. In relation to rules that govern stalking, defamation, and invasions of privacy carried out by paparazzi on behalf of public media outlets, the most striking difference is evident in the European Union's concerted efforts to "get it right."

There is no denying that Member States have had a great deal of incentive to do that very thing. Several jarring incidents have produced the requisite motivation. In 2004, widespread protests followed French President Nicolas Sarkozy's endorsement of tax breaks for the wealthy as oil giants prepared to lay off workers "while simultaneously announcing record profits."[1] However, this paled in comparison to the horror following the attacks on the London Underground in 2005.[2] The period 1997–2007 was also the decade of accountability for tabloids and other segments of the press.

It began with public outrage over the sudden death of the former Princess of Wales when paparazzi gave chase as she and her partner left a Paris hotel.[3] The swirl of rumors surrounding the

---

1. http://www.thisislondon.co.uk/standard/article-23664707-details/Police%20 arrest%20300%20in%20Paris%20riots%20over%20economic%20crisis/ article.do.

2. http://news.bbc.co.uk/1/hi/in_depth/uk/2005/london_explosions/default. stm.

3. http://www.cnn.com/WORLD/9708/31/diana.links/index.html.

circumstances of that car crash fed into mounting despair regarding the prolonged silence from Buckingham Palace.[4] The entire crisis led to the production and distribution of the movie *The Queen* in the fall of 2006. Throughout 2007, actor *Helen Mirren* won international acclaim for her performance as head of the British Empire, including the highly coveted Best Actress for a Performance in a Leading Role at the February 25, 2007 Academy Awards.[5] A spokesperson from Buckingham Palace indicated that Queen Elizabeth II might be pleased for Mirren.[6] Ten weeks later, Her Majesty visited the United States for the first time since 1991.[7] According to the ever-popular American movie critic Roger Ebert, *The Queen* "told in quiet scenes of proper behavior and guarded speech, is a spellbinding story of opposed passions—of Elizabeth's icy resolve to keep the royal family separate and aloof from the death of the divorced Diana, who was legally no longer a royal, and of Blair's correct reading of the public mood, which demanded some sort of public expression of sympathy from the crown for "The People's Princess."[8]

Nearing the end of the decade that marked that fateful crash in Paris, members of the European Press again dominated international headlines for an entirely different, though perhaps not unrelated reason. Professor Ulf Hedetoft's 2006 article in *Open Democracy* titled "Denmark's Cartoon Blowback" describes it best:

> The distance from domestic provocation to global outrage is short, as Denmark has found to its surprise and regret in the course of a few short weeks. What the daily newspaper

4. http://www.dailymail.co.uk/news/article-421446/Diana-death-driver-entirely-blame-fatal-crash.html.

5. http://www.cnn.com/SPECIALS/2007/academy.awards/.

6. http://www.telegraph.co.uk/news/uknews/1543864/Queen-pleased-by-Mirrens-Oscar-triumph.html.

7. http://abcnews.go.com/US/popup?id=3135234

8. http://rogerebert.suntimes.com/apps/pbcs.dll/article?AID=/20061012/REVIEWS/61012001/1023.

Jyllands-Posten intended as a public demonstration of Danish democracy and the right to free speech—an exemplary case presented to the Muslim minority in Denmark—was suddenly transformed into a major political, diplomatic, and even economic quandary. The cartoon scandal has come home to roost, proving to doubters . . . that globalisation is a reality in today's world and comprises more than economic adaptation to changing external conditions. Danes have been forced to realise—among other sobering lessons—that the immigrant "little brother" on the inside apparently has powerful kith-and-kin on the outside.[9]

The enormous social and economic consequences attendant to what some might generously describe as momentary lapses in judgment as one newspaper after another, in one country after another, republished the caricatures are unlikely to be repeated any time soon. However, regardless of whether those actions could be accurately described as accidental, inadvertent, or unintentional, the grievous events of that decade originating in France, Britain, and Denmark echoed in reverberations that placed all of Europe in the global spotlight. Unsurprisingly, the tone and tenor of EU debates about the need to "get it right" among its public leaders have been restorative and illuminating. As a result, human dignity, liberty of conscience, free expression, respect for private life, and personal data now are regularly protected by law in ways that are appropriately balanced with societal interests in a broad dissemination of ideas and continual search for truth.

⅏ Human Dignity

During the winter of 2009, a group of U.S. law students were polled about their experiences and participation in public or private

---

9. http://www.opendemocracy.net/faith-europe_islam/blowback_3315.jsp.

discussions related to dignity. Roughly 70 percent had never participated in such a dialogue. Deliberation by those remaining had, without exception, been sparked by debates about an individual's "right to die."

Our discussion moved toward determining if this was a natural right, and, if so, how we might harmonize a natural right to die with the laws governing risk and liability for wrongful death applicable to skydivers and race car drivers, as well as prohibitions on suicide. We then turned toward defining suicide. Who among the famous and infamous would we pronounce dead via suicide: Socrates? Jesus? The 20-year-old about to enlist in the U.S. Marine Corps? Iraqi bombers? Issues of intent, causation, probabilities, and free will were considered without once discussing the *dignity* of these individuals. Thus, the right to die, as such, was quickly shown to be a misnomer unsupported by current legal thinking.

Death with Dignity, on the other hand, is a growing movement in the United States following the success of campaigns for laws permitting physician-assisted suicide in Washington and Oregon. According to the Death with Dignity national Web site:

> The greatest human freedom is to live, and die, according to one's own desires and beliefs. The most common desire among those with a terminal illness is to die with some measure of dignity. From advance directives to physician-assisted dying, death with dignity is a movement to provide options for the dying to control their own end-of-life care.[10]

The unanswered question surrounds the extent to which the American failure to respond to issues related to the dignity of terminally ill patients and their families might correlate with our rarely considering matters of dignity for the living.

---

10. http://www.deathwithdignity.org/.

𝕸 European Charter of Fundamental Rights

The preamble to the European Charter of Fundamental Rights proposed to bring Member States closer in peaceful respect for their spiritual heritage and universal values: on behalf of dignity, freedom, equality, solidarity, democracy, and the rule of law. Preservation and development of those values required measures to strengthen the protection of fundamental rights in light of changes in society, progressive understanding, and the latest scientific and technological developments. While affirming due regard for the powers and tasks of the community and the Union, the Charter decrees that all rights developed over time throughout the interlocking web of Members' courts, treaties, charters, and international obligations would henceforth entail significant responsibilities and duties to others for the sake of humanity and future generations.[11]

The Charter's 54 articles identify fundamental and inviolable rights of the individual to life; dignity; physical and mental integrity; liberty; security; private and family life; marriage and family; liberty of conscience; religious expression; assembly; petition; equality (including gender equality), nondiscrimination; diversity; protections for children and the elderly; integration for persons with disabilities; artistic, scientific, and academic freedom; education; occupational choice; entrepreneurship; voting; property; seeking of asylum, protection against extradition, torture, and slavery; protection of personal data; collective bargaining; worker rights; healthcare; environmental and consumer protection; to hold public office; freedom of movement; diplomatic protection; presumption of innocence; proportionality in criminal offenses and penalties; and protection from abuse.

European laws protect development of personality, respect for private life, and privacy of youth in ways that allow the freest

---

11. http://eur-lex.europa.eu/LexUriServ/LexUriServ.do?uri=OJ:C:2004:310:0041:0
054:EN:PDF.

possible dissemination of ideas and opinions on matters of public interest. Since the passage of both the Human Rights and Data Protection Acts of 1998, there have been more concerted efforts to deal with media intrusion in its two principal forms. The first involves unethical methods for obtaining information through the use of telephoto lens or concealed camera and parabolic microphones to peer into private domains and/or interception of phone, fax, e-mail, and text messages or searching through private spaces; the other involves persistent camping out at the entrances and exits of media targets (known as door-stepping). Lord Wakeham described it as "media scrum" where incessant "gathering at the scent of a story" represents "a form of collective harassment."[12]

ℋ Redress for Media Intrusions and Unlawful Conspiracies

Efforts to eradicate privacy invasions in the United Kingdom include bans on the use of information obtained through illegal payments to the police, private detectives, and other public and private sources. Public awareness about the illegality of these practices is a natural deterrent. A private detective pleaded guilty to 12 offences under the Data Protection Act for compiling phone numbers and bills for editors at *News of the World, People, The Sunday Express*, and *The Mail on Sunday.* A solicitor's employee was nearly jailed for stealing documents relating to a murder case to sell to *The Sun*, the *Daily Mirror*, and *The Express*. A black market for data was created by an agency called "Southern Investigations" as a broker for information from police sources to *News of the World, Daily Mirror*, and the *Sunday Mirror.* Private detectives routinely tapped

---

12. *Conclusions and Recommendations*, Select Committee on Culture, Media and Sport, Fifth Report, (House of Commons, May 21, 2003), ¶¶ 4–7; *see also* http://www.publications.parliament.uk/pa/cm200203/cmselect/cmcumeds/458/45804.htm.

private telephone calls for the tabloid press. The Human Resources directorate at the Inland Revenue admitted that employees sold confidential information from tax returns to outside agencies. The Police Complaints Authority also reported ongoing complaints alleging disclosure of information from its national computer.[13]

The safeguarding of personal information in the hands of current and former employees, is an age-old dilemma for the rich and famous. After 13 years of service, Jane Williams, former assistant to Lady Archer (wife of Conservative Party vice chair Lord Jeffrey Archer) approached publicity agent Max Clifford about selling her stories to the press. During the court hearing, Lady Archer disclosed that Williams had received psychiatric counseling and denied there is any legitimate dispute over the ownership of several diaries and computer files located on the desktop computer used by Williams. Archer asserted they "were not only paid for by me, they were about me, they contained confidential information about me as well as a list of my full-time appointments."[14]

In a similar case, pending the outcome of the trial, Abbie Gibson, former nanny of Victoria and David Beckham, retained the £125,000 she was paid by the *News of the World* for information she provided about the famous pair. According to the lawyer for the Beckhams: "It is uniquely hurtful and distressing to have the person who until the end of March this year was sitting around the breakfast table with them and their children, discussing their daily lives, repeat that information."[15]

Celebrity clients have bombarded British public relations advisers and lawyers with calls after David and Victoria Beckham said they would sue their former nanny for breaking a confidentiality

---

13. *Id.* at ¶ 93 (i–vi).

14. http://www.dailymail.co.uk/news/article-136717/Archers-jailing-brought-great-change-wife.html.

15. http://news.bbc.co.uk/2/hi/uk_news/4496301.stm.

agreement. The celebrities are concerned that tabloid newspapers will be deluged with staff's revelations about their private lives, too. Despite failing to win an injunction to stop the publication of a seven-page expose in Sunday's News of the World, the Beckhams said they planned to sue Abbie Gibson for breach of confidentiality. She claimed to have witnessed a string of rows between the pair.[16]

Former nannies and personal assistants are the primary source of celebrity disparagement. The tales surrounding celebrities involved in legal tussles with these categories of employees are legendary in measure; the more famous cases have involved Madonna, Oprah, Britney Spears, Angelina Jolie, Naomi Campbell, Nicole Kidman, Demi Moore, Rob Lowe, Robert DeNiro, Cameron Diaz, and Jude Law. Despite thorough and artfully crafted confidentiality agreements, all of these celebrities have found themselves ensconced in litigation with former employees who once held respected positions of trust and confidence in their lives.

The Breach of Confidence is more serious because publication or broadcast of intensely personal information into the public domain feeds regional, national, and even international consumption that "can reappear in other stories, however tangentially related, almost indefinitely."[17] Such stories are sure to be repeated and marketed to sell unauthorized biographies. To alleviate some of the burden, the Committee on Culture, Media and Sport recommended the automatic annotation of archives "in all serious cases."[18] After an adverse ruling, publishers would then be responsible for the removal of the offending articles from all publicly available databases. The Committee noted "in one case described to us the

---

16. http://www.theage.com.au/news/World/Celebrities-worried-as-Beckham-nanny-tells/2005/04/27/1114462097728.html.

17. *Conclusions and Recommendations*, ¶ 17.

18. *Id.* at ¶ 82.

offending article was indeed not available on the press database provided through the House of Commons Library. However, the particular inaccuracy had been repeated in an article in the same newspaper on the following day and that reference was returned by a search on the general topic."[19]

⁂ Determining What the Public Has a Right to Know

The landmark cases *Case of Von Hanover* (in the European Court of Human Rights) and *Campbell v. Daily Mirror* (in the House of Lords) are prime examples of the way the courts balance those interests. They represent significant and welcomed developments in European law. As summarized by Lord Justice Sedley in *Douglas v. Hello! Ltd* in 2001, we can recognize the high importance of a free press and the steady flow of information without building a fortress around the press.

> The European Court of Human Rights has always recognised the high importance of a free press of communication in a democracy, but its jurisprudence does not—and could not consistently with the Convention itself—give article 10 the presumptive priority which is given, for example, to the First Amendment in the jurisprudence of the United States' courts. Everything will ultimately depend on the proper balance between privacy and publicity in the situation facing the court.[20]

In similar discussions, Italian Green Party Deputy Mauro Paissan notes that the public "right to know, freedom of expression, [and] transparency are all basic features of a democratic society; however,

---

19. *Id.*

20. Douglas v Hello! Ltd. [2001] 1 QB 967, 1004, para. 135[2].

they may not override the demand for privacy, the right to freely develop one's own personality, to build one's private sphere—to get respect for one's dignity. It is often the case that very private features of a person's life do not add anything at all to the appreciation of a piece of information—indeed, they are only food for voyeurs."[21] The code of ethics adopted in 1993 by the National Federation of the Italian Press and the National Council of the Order of Journalists consistent with the Italian *Garante* identifies "materiality of the information" as a fundamental precept.[22]

The *Garante* is Italy's 2004 data protection code, which brings together all previous laws governing data protection since 1996. Section two outlines its primary purpose: simplification, harmonization, and effectiveness.[23] Disclosure of a name, picture, or purely personal detail must relate to the public interest or remain unpublished. In the United Kingdom, Lord Justice Hoffman declared that even the clear public interest readily established in relation to use of political power is subject to reasonable limits as to the extent of disclosure. A sexual liaison between a politician and someone he has appointed to public office is a significant matter of public concern, but "the addition of salacious details or intimate photographs is disproportionate and unacceptable. The latter, even if accompanying a legitimate disclosure of the relationship, would be too intrusive and demeaning."[24]

Deputy Paissan's article concludes with the two basic premises upon which enforcement of the Italian provisions are based:

---

21. Mauro Paissan, *Privacy Protection and Right to Know. Striking a Difficult Balance*, Spring Conference of European Data Protection Commissioners, May 10, 2007; *see also* http://www.garanteprivacy.it/garante/doc.jsp?ID= 1408388.

22. Charter of Duties of Journalists, National Federation of the Italian Press and the National Council of the Order of Journalists, July 8, 1993; *see also* http://www.media-accountability.org/library/ITALY.doc.

23. http://www.garanteprivacy.it/garante/doc.jsp?ID=1030925.

24. Campbell v. MGN Ltd. [2005] UKHL 61; *see also* http://www.publications.parliament.uk/pa/ld200304/ldjudgmt/jd040506/campbe-2.htm.

(1) Privacy may not be relied upon to hinder the necessary transparency of power; and (2) Journalists are required to make use of their freedom in a manner commensurate with their duty to protect the dignity of individuals. In England, efforts to enforce these provisions included recommendations for a revision of its code of journalistic conduct that would enable solitary journalists to have the backing of the Press Complaints Commission in refusing an assignment on the grounds that it breaches their Code.[25]

ℳ The Public's Interest

Restricting publication of information consistent with the public interest requires some dileneation of those matters that genuinely impact public life:

information necessary or helpful to participating in the democratic process, information about crimes and misdemeanours. [26]

information necessary to prevent the public from being misled by some statement or action of an individual or organisation.[27]

information important to the ability of society and individuals to safeguard health, wealth and safety and generally to the effort of navigating through the complexities of modern life.[28]

This list, from the conclusion and recommendations of the Committee on Culture, Media and Sports specifically excludes

---

25. http://www.garanteprivacy.it/garante/doc.jsp?ID=1408388.

26. *Conclusions and Recommendations*, ¶ 13.

27. *Id.*

28. *Id.*

private material, finding "the lack of knowledge of which could have little significant impact on anyone else's life."[29]

There is an ongoing need to redefine the areas of highest priority in the public's interest. Serious breaches of conduct of officials in the discharge of their duties are the highest priority, but examples abound in each of the categories identified above. We would be hard pressed to argue that the public does not have a legitimate interest in watching video footage of a gang of police officers beating a suspect to death as police are charged with the duty of upholding the public trust in matters of general safety and public order. Despite abhorrence of the use of subterfuge to gain information, a court upheld its use by one Sunday paper to obtain photographs of a Nazi shrine in the home of a member of the British National Party who was married to policewoman with specific responsibilities for the investigation of racially motivated crimes.[30] Exposés of major corporations routinely dumping highly toxic waste into the Danube that leak into municipal water supplies would constitute information that citizens of several European nations would have the right to know. Likewise if the London Bombings Relief Charitable Fund was shown to be inexplicably slow in dispersing the 12 million pounds donated to families affected by 7/7, but quick to give raises and promotions to its CEOs, it would constitute an important matter relative to a general debate about public accountability.

ℳ Role of the Press Complaints Commission

The balance of competing interests in view of a full range of potential solutions requires a determination of where to draw the line

---

29. *Id.*

30. Patrick Barrett, *Policewoman's Complaint against* Sunday Telegraph *Rejected*, THE GUARDIAN, Mar. 25, 2004; *see also* http://www.pcc.org.uk/news/index. html?article=MjEyMg.

between supporting the role of a free press and setting appropriate boundaries for the protection of human rights. Public education campaigns that raise awareness of what the right to privacy entails are important to the extent that ignorance rather than willfulness is partly responsible for some injuries. Facilitating access to the courts through simplified legal procedures related to press offenses is key to ensuring that victims' rights are better protected.

Mindful of the role of lay enforcement, the House of Commons, Culture and Media Committee sought stronger assurances from the incoming chairman of the Press Complaints Commission that its selection process for lay commissioners would be "proper, open and transparent."[31] An audit of the current imbalance and constitution of press commission members indicates that their first order of business might be to ascertain who among them "were there to represent the interests of their trade associations; and how many saw themselves as independent figures in a quasi-judicial capacity."[32] According to the Committee, the Commission "would command more confidence in the independence of its membership if it adopted the following proposals, outlined in paragraph 67 of its Report."

i. Lay members should be sought and appointed for fixed terms under open procedures including advertisement and competition.

ii. Press members should be appointed for fixed terms from across the industry. There should be an explicit presumption that they are not there to represent the interests of their associations but to offer the benefits of their particular experience whilst acting independently as members of a quasi-judicial body.

---

31. *Conclusions and Recommendations*, ¶ 65.

32. *Id.* at ¶ 66.

iii. Press members (and here we include members of the Code Committee) who preside over persistently offending publications should be required to stand down and should be ineligible for reappointment for a period—perhaps the length of a term of office. Persistence could be defined as "three strikes and you're out".

iv. The lay majority should be increased by at least one; as provided for in the PCC's Articles and accepted by Sir Christopher Meyer, the new PCC Chairman.

v. The Appointments Commission should appoint an independent figure, also under the new procedures, to implement the procedural appeals process to which Sir Christopher has referred. To this responsibility we would add the task of commissioning a regular external audit of the PCC's processes and practices—a version of accreditation. While the "standard" would probably be unique to the PCC, the methodology has been pretty well-established throughout the corporate world.

vi. The Code Committee, which at the moment is composed entirely of editors, should be reestablished with a significant minority of lay members.[33]

✻ A Profile of Publisher Redress

Requiring a "profile of redress" commensurate with the prominence of the offending story is perhaps an equitable and effective way to deter future invasions; "a hideous transgression on the front page,"

---

33. *Id.* at ¶ 67.

should be addressed with news of the adverse adjudication on the front page as a means of increasing public confidence in the Commission's work. Annual tables showing how often various publishers and entities have transgressed was also recommended as a positive step toward clarifying the scope of such intrusions. Inclusion of the data on how the Commission categorizes complaints and determines which are pending, resolved, or "not pursued" helps to reveal crucial factors in the process. The most valuable annual reports would be user-friendly and designed in the interest of full disclosure. The Press Complaints Commission, armed with the capability, capacity, and political capital to flex its muscles, is charged with searching out every means for securing a resolution between parties to a complaint.[34] Thus, the relative scope and nature of formal complaints of paparazzi and publisher intrusion are viewed by the public as a significant matter of concern that is not easily swept under the carpet and avoids the specter of *Mirror* editors milking a story round Naomi Campbell's recreational drug use to increase its profit while claiming to be a defender of a free press.

ℳ Unified Approach

Europe's unified approach paved the way for comprehensive solutions. The House of Commons Commission on Culture, Media and Sport "firmly recommend" that the government "bring forward legislative proposals to clarify the protection that individuals can expect from unwarranted intrusion by anyone—not the press alone—into their private lives."[35] This was deemed vital for

---

34. http://www.publications.parliament.uk/pa/cm200203/cmselect/cmcumeds/ 458/45802.htm at 33. *Id.* at ¶ 61.

35. *Conclusions and Recommendations*; *see also* http://www.publications. parliament.uk/pa/cm200203/cmselect/cmcumeds/458/45804.htm.

satisfaction of its obligations under the European Convention of Human Rights. European laws specifically acknowledge that the press is not exempt from relevant privacy provisions, even as the sections on interpretation and enforcement caution courts of justice on avoiding unduly broad interpretations and application of these provisions to journalists acting in good faith. European High Courts have emphasized the requirement that actions involving private information brought upon the claim of breach of confidence give effect to both Article 8 (privacy) and Article 10 (free speech).

Judicial recognition of the interaction between distinct kinds of intrusions upon privacy is illuminating because of the care taken to define specifically what constitutes a matter of public interest while taking due notice of those who court publicity with respect to certain aspects of their lives while retaining privacy in others. In relation to celebrities, these decisions seek to distinguish the interest in preventing disclosure of personal or embarrassing facts from the interest in managing public image and controlling access to and release of photographs for (among other things) pecuniary gain. Photographs are more than a means for conveying factual information because they often capture details of emotion, demeanor, mood, and disposition. Unauthorized displays almost always raise issues of proportionality even as they place into the public domain a permanent record that is difficult to recall in our technologically advanced world. Thus, without compromising the relativism and relevance of truth seeking, fair comment, and various kinds of privilege related to information obtained by or useful to the press and public, lawmakers introduced a consistent set of rules to bar unnecessary disclosures. The cause of action for breach of confidence depends on the nature of the information and not upon whether it is true or false.[36]

Measures proposed in the Assembly that called upon the governments of the Member States to deal with journalists have opened

---

36. Cream Holdings v. Banerjee, [2005] EWHC 372 (QB).

up a broad and useful discussion about the nature of democracy. In the United Kingdom, those charged with studying effective resolutions agree the "key to this system must be that it commands the full commitment of the industry itself as well as the confidence of Government, Parliament and, crucially, the public."[37]

The primary goals were to enhance the independence of the Press Complaints Commission with regards to its procedures, practices, and transparency. One example relates to developing a consistent approach to "foreseeable events that herald intense media activity around people in grief and shock; and for acting as soon as possible after unexpected disasters have occurred."[38] Questions regarding the efficacy of the government's insistence upon the establishment of meaningful criteria for entry into the journalism profession; self-regulation; codes of journalistic conduct; and law courses that highlight the importance of legal rules, the right to privacy, human rights, and journalistic responsibilities have been given thorough and respectful attention in many quarters. However, issues concerning a target's objection that arises in advance of a publication have typically invited a rash of warnings about "prior restraint" or "press censorship."

The Culture, Media and Sport Committee of the House of Commons recommended establishment of a dedicated prepublication team to handle inquiries presented with the relevant editor on matters raised prior to publication. In relation to quelling media harassment, the transmission of "desist messages" from those who do not want to talk to the media are often timely and useful during the prepublication phase.[39] These measures are designed to address many areas where the journalistic Code of Practice falls short, such as publications involved in "serious cases of inaccuracy" or libel, persistent door-stepping, interception of telephone calls, removal

---

37. *Conclusions and Recommendations.*

38. *Id.* at ¶ 20.

39. *Id.* at ¶¶ 20, 62.

of documents and photographs without consent, and identification of victims of sexual assault.[40]

✄ Europe's Collective Commitment

The European experience demonstrates how the will to redress the stalking of not only celebrities but also private citizens involved in matters of public concern lends itself toward greater collective understanding and a commitment to respectful norms. After careful study, the report to the House of Commons stated:

> We were not at all convinced that door-stepping, by a film crew, of people who have refused, sometimes in writing, to be interviewed is really done to give the subjects of a programme a final opportunity to put their side of the story. The motivation is surely less judicial and more about entertaining footage. Such intrusion, and broadcasting the result, should only be undertaken in important cases of significant public interest.[41]

The European Union promotes due regard for another's boundaries, personally identifiable information, and mutual obligations to respect another's honor by rightly classifying each of these as a necessary and constitutive element of the comprehensive plan for bringing public bodies and laws of Member States into compliance with the mandates of the Convention:

> The dignity of human beings is inviolable. All public authorities have a duty to respect and protect it.[42]

---

40. *Id.* at ¶ 90.

41. *Id.* at ¶ 92.

42. European Union, *Charter of Fundamental Rights of the European Union*, Art. 1, Human Dignity, Official Journal of the European Communities, 18 Dec. 2000 (2000/C 364/01); *see also* GERMAN CONST. Art. 1.

Everyone shall have the right to the free development of their personality provided that they do not interfere with the rights of others or violate the constitutional order or moral law.[43]

Everyone has the right to respect for his private and family life, his home and his correspondence. There shall be no interference by a public authority with the exercise of this right except such as is in accordance with the law and is necessary in a democratic society in the interests of national security, public safety or the economic well-being of the country, for the prevention of disorder or crime, for the protection of health or morals, or for the protection of the rights and freedoms of others.[44]

Marriage and family enjoy the special protection of the State. The care and upbringing of children is the natural right of parents and a duty primarily incumbent on them.[45]

Everyone shall have the right freely to express and disseminate his or her opinions in speech, writing and pictures and freely to obtain information from generally accessible sources. Freedom of the press and freedom of reporting on the radio and in films shall be guaranteed. There shall be no censorship. These rights shall be subject to the limitations laid down by the provisions of the general laws and by statutory provisions aimed at protecting young people, and to the obligation to respect personal honour.[46]

The Copyright Act provides that images can only be disseminated with the express approval of the person concerned. Except for images that portray an aspect of contemporary society, on

---

43. GERMAN CONST. Art. 2.

44. European Union, *Charter of Fundamental Rights of the European Union*, Art. 8, Right to Respect for Private and Family Life.

45. GERMAN CONST. Art. 6.

46. *Id.* Art. 5.

condition that publication does not interfere with a legitimate interest of the person concerned.[47]

The collective commitment between European legislative and executive organs of governances guarantees respect for private and family life, home, health, and correspondence, and extends these protections to artists, musicians, sports figures, and others well-known to the public. These judicially constructed classes of persons are able to recover damages when publishers defame them and report details related to their private lives without their consent.

These issues are examined in a comprehensive fashion by opinions explaining the House of Lord's ruling in favor of International Fashion Model Naomi Campbell, against the *Daily Mirror*. The case is a paradigmatic example of the nuances that influence judicial opinions in celebrity privacy cases.

In 2004, The House of Lords handed down its judgment in *Campbell v. MGN Limited*. The opening opinion describes the plaintiff follows:

"Naomi Campbell is a celebrated fashion model. Hers is a household name, nationally and internationally. Her face is instantly recognisable. Whatever she does and wherever she goes is news."

The facts are undisputed. On 1 February 2001 the *Mirror* newspaper carried the following headline on its front page: *Naomi: I am a drug addict*. The article was supported on one side by a picture of Miss Campbell as a glamorous model, and another described as slightly indistinct where she was dressed in baseball cap and jeans, over the caption "Therapy: Naomi outside meeting." The article disclosed that she had been attending Narcotics Anonymous meetings for three months to beat her addiction to drink and drugs.

---

47. Von Hannover v. Germany, 2004-III Eur. Ct. H.R. 284.

She was pictured entering what the paper described as a women-only gathering of recovered addicts: "With a net worth of £14million she is treated as just another addict." Citing a close source as stating that: "She wants to clean up her life for good," the publisher offered youth and naïveté as the culprit, blinding her to the danger of alcohol and drugs; both known to be widely available in the fashion world. Her spokeswoman at Elite Models declined to comment. Inside the paper, spread across two pages, the writer continued with praise for efforts to reform her "wild lifestyle." Describing a previous incident where she was rushed to hospital to have her stomach pumped. The writer claimed that Campbell claimed to have had an allergic reaction to antibiotics and that she never had a drug problem: but "those closest to her knew the truth."

Several pictures showed her on the doorstep of a building embraced by two people whose faces had been pixelated. Standing on the pavement was a board advertising a named café. The article did not name the venue of the meeting, but anyone who knew the district well would be able to identify the place shown in the photograph. Lord Nicholls described the general tone of the article as sympathetic and supportive with, perhaps, the barest undertone of smugness that Miss Campbell had been caught out by the *Mirror*. The story contained several inaccuracies.

Campbell sued the publisher of the *Mirror*. The newspaper then retaliated with additional stories using the same photos, but with very different headlines. On 5 February 2001, in large letters, '*Pathetic*', above a photograph of Campbell over the caption *Help: Naomi leaves Narcotics Anonymous meeting last week after receiving therapy in her battle against illegal drugs*. The text of the article was headed: *After years of self-publicity and illegal drug abuse, Naomi Campbell whinges about privacy*. An editorial in the same edition with the heading *No hiding Naomi*, concluded with the words: "If Naomi Campbell wants to live like a nun, let her join a nunnery. If she wants the excitement of a show business life, she must accept what comes with it." Two days later, on 7 February, the *Mirror* returned to the attack with an offensive and disparaging article. Under the heading *Fame on you, Ms Campbell*, an article referred to her plans "to launch a campaign for better rights for celebrities or artists' as she calls them." The article included the sentence: "As a campaigner, Naomi's about as effective as a chocolate soldier." Thus, her choice to exercise her free speech rights was ridiculed by the editors with racial metaphors.

Campbell's lawsuit sought damages for breach of confidence and compensation under the Data Protection Act 1998. The article of 7 February formed the main basis of a claim for aggravated damages. When her claim was upheld, the newspaper appealed her small award of £3,500. That award was later discharged by an appellate panel. Campbell then appealed to the House of Lords, pursuing the claim for breach of confidence, and misuse of private information. In the realm of celebrity privacy, *Case of Von Hanover* is the first of several important European victories. When the House of Lords ruled in Campbell's favor against a London tabloid, it firmly established a significant trend of welcomed developments in European law.

The full story of tabloid media invasion is beautifully illustrated in the series of back-to-back articles that the *Mirror* published about Campbell. She prevailed, according to court's majority, because all citizens deserve privacy with respect to their medical condition. The Lords noted that the *Mirror* editors chose to include a lengthy discussion of the impact of Campbell's prior statements denying drug use and her status as an international fashion model to justify their decision to ignore her rights of citizenship. The purpose of the publications was apparent. An editor at a conference table with a bulging file effectively dredged up all of the information from previous publications and feigned empathy for her plight, before quickly revealing a vindictive and predatory nature at the first sign of her objection to the violation of her rights as an individual. The purported "need to set the record straight" snowballed into multiple opportunities to exact revenge for having to defend the law suit. Mockery, promises to continue the barrage, and a racially derogatory assault was the papers response to her effort to heighten awareness of the habitual intrusion upon the privacy of the rich and famous. Subsequent stories represented a vicious attack upon her dignity. The high-court found that rather than reporting straight facts, the articles included "a good deal more about men with whom she had been associated and other past incidents, taken no doubt from a bulging cuttings file."

It is a general principal that information about whether a person is receiving medical or similar treatment for addiction, and in particular details relating to such treatment or the person's reaction to it, is considered confidential. "Public disclosure disrupts treatment and/or its benefits for the media target and other people who may retreat from treatment out of fear of exposure." The guiding principle is straight forward, reasonable and uncontroversial in scope and application.

The London paper advanced a peculiar justification, which some judges found compelling. According to one member of the Court:

> The facts are unusual because the plaintiff is a public figure who had made very public false statements about a matter in respect of which even a public figure would ordinarily be entitled to privacy, namely her use of drugs. It was these falsehoods which, as was conceded, made it justifiable for a newspaper to report the fact that she was addicted.

It's difficult to tell from the record how the question of drug use first surfaced in Campbell's interviews with the media. Evidence of an interview where she denied using drugs coupled with rumors that her trip to the hospital might have been drug related, do not rise to the level of "Falsehood" to which the public interest entitles the press to "put the record straight." Unless Campbell had spearheaded a "Just Say No" campaign, and became politically active in raising money and awareness on the dangers of drug abuse and held public forums declaring that she has been able to resist temptation and never used drugs a day in her life, the validity of the public's interest in knowing whether she lied about her use of drugs is far from certain. Absent information related to abuse coupled with trafficking in illegal substances, there is no viable connection to matters of public concern and Campbell's medical condition. The conclusion that Campbell's drug use would have been deemed private matter if she were an ordinary citizen, or public official in the absence of a contrary denial makes perfect sense. The notion that she forfeited her right to privacy because she stated that her hospitalization was unrelated to drug use at a time when it may or may not have been true, and in the absence of a charge of criminal fraud or perjury, borders upon the absurd. Surely rights against self-incrimination in the court of public opinion fall within the realm of privacy rights and reputational interests that promote human dignity, and which courts have a duty to respect.

European judges are undoubtedly grappling with what we all understand to be a distillation of complex issues, but at least the judgements are consistent with their Convention. Consider the multiple characterizations of the salient issue in the Campbell case, although evidence of publisher malice was clear and direct.

Lord A:

> The case is about a public figure who has sought publicity about various aspects of her private life, including her use of drugs, in respect of which she has made a false claim.

Lord B:

> A public figure chose to present a false image and make untrue pronouncements about her life. This model went out of her way to say that, unlike many fashion models, she did not take drugs. By repeatedly making these assertions in public she could no longer have a reasonable expectation that this aspect of her life should be private. Public disclosure (contrary to her assertions) that she took drugs and had a serious drug problem for which she was being treated was not disclosure of private information.

Lord C:

> The business of fashion modeling is highly competitive and con-
> ducted under the constant gaze of the media. Public reputation
> as a forceful and colourful personality adds value to physical
> appearance. Much good can come of this, if the process is care-
> fully and correctly handled. But aspects of her exploitation of her
> status as a celebrity has attracted criticism. She has been manip-
> ulative and selective in what she has revealed about herself. She
> has engaged in a deliberately false presentation of herself as
> someone who, in contrast to many models, has managed to keep
> clear of illegal drugs. The true position, it is now agreed, is that
> she has made a practice of abusing drugs. This has caused her
> medical problems, and it has affected her behaviour to such an
> extent that she has required and has received therapy for her
> addiction.

Any one of these characterizations could be true, and they could
all be false, but in any event they hardly warrant constitutional
notice. To conclude that Campbell sought publicity about her drug
use, went out of her way to deny that she took drugs, exploited her
status, has been manipulative and selective in what she revealed, or
deliberately and falsely presenting herself, sounds like the high
drama of justification. As I examined the record, the only factual
description of her actions was that "she publicly denied any involvement with illegal drugs, in a television interview after an admission
to a clinic in America in 1997."

Thus, the proper question before the Court was twofold:

1. Should the fact that she previously denied drug use be enough
   to catapult her into another category of citizens for whom
   general privacy rights no longer apply?

The answer may be yes for highly visible, politically active,
elected or appointed persons. But not for those who by accident of
birth or through personal achievements are exposed to increased

public interest over a long period of time, the assault on individual autonomy, dignity and self-esteem is obvious.

2. If one is unsure as to whether the public had a legitimate interest in knowing, should the paper have confined itself to the bare proven facts: she lied, or was it was entitled to reveal full-blown details with photographs of Campbell and others leaving and entering treatment?

According to one judge, the division of opinion was over whether the newspaper went too far in publishing associated facts about her private life: if the fact that she lied justified exposing that she had been involved with drugs and was seeking treatment, then "it was not necessary for those purposes to publish any further information, especially if this might jeopardise the continued success of that treatment."

The House of Lords was unanimous as to the means for striking a balance between the right to privacy and the right to freedom of expression. The Court determined that there was "an unlawful invasion of privacy in publishing:

1. The fact that she was attending meetings at NA
2. Details of attendance and what happened during the meetings
3. Photographs taken in the street without her knowledge/consent.

One Lord asked if the civil and political values which underlie press freedom make it necessary to deny citizens the right to protect their personal information? He notes that "while there is no contrary public interest recognised and protected by the law, the press is free to publish anything it likes, subject to the laws of defamation."

But when press freedom comes into conflict with another interest protected by the law, the question is whether there is a sufficient public interest in that particular publication to justify curtailment of the conflicting rights. Free speech weighs little in the balance against the privacy of personal information.

There is no public interest in publishing to the world the fact that a citizen has a drug dependency. Major headlines with photos that reveal the location of the meetings, "add to the potential harm, by making her think that she was being followed or betrayed, and deterring her [and possibly others] from going back to the same place again."

One Lord conceded that celebrities pay a special price in this regard:

Paradoxically, for [celebrities], there are few areas of the life of an individual that are more in need of protection on the grounds of privacy than the combating of addiction to drugs or to alcohol. It is hard to break the habit which has led to the addiction. It is all too easy to give up the struggle if efforts to do so are exposed to public scrutiny. The struggle, after all, is an intensely personal one. It involves a high degree of commitment and of self-criticism. The sense of shame that comes with it is one of the most powerful of all the tools that are used to break the habit. But shame increases the individual's vulnerability as the barriers that the habit has engendered are broken down. The smallest hint that the process is being watched by the public may be enough to persuade the individual to delay or curtail the treatment. At the least it is likely to cause distress, even to those who in other circumstances like to court publicity and regard publicity as a benefit.

The weight to be attached to these various considerations is a matter of fact and degree. Not every statement about a person's health will carry the badge of confidentiality or risk doing harm to that person's physical or moral integrity. The risk of harm is what matters at this stage, rather than the proof that actual harm has occurred. People trying to recover from drug addiction need considerable dedication and commitment, along with constant reinforcement from those around them. That is why organisations like Narcotics Anonymous were set up and why they can do so much good. Blundering in when matters are acknowledged to be at a 'fragile' stage may do great harm. Publication of the details of the appellant's course of treatment at NA and of the photographs taken surreptitiously in the street of her emerging from a meeting went significantly beyond the publication of the fact that she was receiving therapy or that she was engaged in a course of therapy with NA. It revealed where her treatment was taking place and the text went into the frequency of her treatment. In this way it intruded into what had some of the characteristics of medical treatment and it tended to deter her from continuing the treatment which was in her interest and also to inhibit other persons attending the course from staying with it, when they might be concerned that their participation might become public knowledge.

Everyone is entitled to respect for his or her private and family life, home, health and correspondence. A publisher will be held liable for intrusions into an individual's private life without consent. Members of the press persistently claim that celebrities, as role models, ought to be held to different standards. If we believe that to be true then we must seriously address the irrational state of media law that has placed the fox in charge of the hen house. For it is the law which automatically places celebrities in the category of "public figures" coupled with a media machine that converts them into "role models" against their manifest intentions. Therefore, we have a mass media industry that molds public opinion and appetites, while claiming that the public has the *right to know* about the role models that it has created, as it continues to feed and capitalize on artificially stimulated voyeuristic tendencies. The House of Lords concluded that guarantees of freedom for the press and coverage of matters of serious public concern, carry express "duties and responsibilities" which assume even more significance when there is question of attacking the reputation of private individuals and infringing the "rights of others."

⁂ Rejection of U.S. Standards

The very legal arguments that run amok in the United States (i.e., because celebrities enjoy the public's adoration, they must be exempt from the general protection of the law as they possess enhanced means for setting the record straight and countering false charges) are often rejected throughout Europe. Global incentives have never been higher to address the irrationality of legal interpretations that automatically place every celebrity in the category of all-purpose public figures who retain no rights of privacy. As an analytic construct, the involuntary-role model thesis is ill-conceived. In free societies, role models volunteer for the job rather than being drafted through legal fiat and objectified through artificial media creation.

Expecting and encouraging forbearance of paparazzi interests in a person's chosen profession is far different than upholding legal fictions that convert citizens into "role models" against their will. This is particularly true if we examine the concept. The creators of *rolemodel.net* see their mission as inspiring the next generation toward an outward focus:

> To promote the idea that there is within each of us the ability to inspire those around us by living a life that is more outward focused than inward focused. By being selfless, we can do our part to make the world a better place, spreading love and hope through our daily actions. It is not only by what we say but more importantly by the life that we live out that shows what each of us is made of.[48]

---

48. http://www.rolemodel.net/.

Stalking celebrities to show the world that their private behavior does not "convincingly tally with their public image" is a diversion at best and pernicious at its worst. It also encourages members of the media to ride roughshod over whomever they choose. This is hardly the Fourth Estate envisioned by Burke. This issue was raised by Lord Justice Phillips, and superbly highlighted though imprudently resolved by Baroness Hale in *Campbell v. MGN*:

> If other young women do see [Campbell] as someone to be admired and emulated, then it is all to the good if she is not addicted to narcotic substances. However, it might be questioned why, if a role model has (publicly) adopted a stance which all would agree is beneficial rather than detrimental to society, it is so important to reveal that she has feet of clay.[49]

The answer according to Hale is that possession of illegal drugs is a matter of public concern. Yet outside of a criminal complaint that shows intent to harm others, the public concern is negligible at best. None of the *Mirror's* stories related to criminal investigations or prosecutions, but were instead largely a means of retaliation. The majority of lord justices in the House of Lords concluded that guarantees of freedom for the press is not a declaration of open season but demands respect for individual reputations and privacy. Lord Justice Woolf declared that the fact a person had achieved prominence is not an invitation to the media to lay bare that individual's personal life if the person has not sought the distinction of being a role model.[50] Even a long and symbiotic relationship with the media is irrelevant when it comes to disclosure of confidential information. For those fostering and calling attention to a public image that is false, a public interest may exist, but it is

---

49. Campbell v. MGN Ltd. [2005] UKHL 61, per Lord Phillips at 152.

50. *Id.*, per Lord Woolf.

considerably low on the scale of what the court is interested in protecting.[51] Although recognizing there will always be an interest in public figures whose conduct may inspire emulation by others, European courts reject as fully outside any legally permissible boundaries the tendency of any court to factor into its consideration the prospect of adverse impact on publisher's bottom line. Yet in the United States, some have actually argued that restricting news papers from unauthorized disclosure of private celebrity facts, means that they would experience a decline in circulation and go out of business.[52]

The European Union made significant strides when the head of the Assembly called upon the governments of the Member States to:

(i)   encourage the professional bodies that represent journalists to draw up certain criteria for entry to the profession, as well as standards for self-regulation and a code of journalistic conduct;

(ii)   promote the inclusion in journalism training programmes of a course in law, highlighting the importance of the right to privacy vis-à-vis society as a whole;

(iii) foster the development of media education on a wider scale, as part of education about human rights and responsibilities, in order to raise media users' awareness of what the right to privacy necessarily entails;

(iv)   facilitate access to the courts and simplify the legal procedures relating to press offences, in order to ensure that victims' rights are better protected.[53]

---

51. *A v B Plc*; sub nom *A v B* (A Firm); *B & C v A* [2002] *UKHRR* 457; *see also* Sir MICHAEL TUGENDHAT, THE LAW OF PRIVACY AND THE MEDIA (2nd cum. Supp. 2006).

52. *Conclusions and Recommendations*, ¶ 2.

53. Res. 1165, Art. 16, Council of European Parliamentary Assembly, adopted June 26, 1998; *see also* http://assembly.coe.int/main.asp?Link=/documents/adoptedtext/ta98/eres1165.htm.

Those rights necessarily include the same protections for all citizens. Protections widely available to celebrities in the European Union (which are highlighted throughout Chapter Seven of this book) show that the laws governing defamation and privacy are conceptually similar on both continents, but only meaningfully enforced in the European Union.

NINE

Undue Burdens on Celebrity Speech and Association

As an official celebrity, I know my endorsement has just made up your mind for you.[1]

—Actor Tom Hanks,
endorsing Barrack Obama for President

Although we lack comprehensive data concerning the political impact of celebrity activists, television audiences know the simple act of displaying a pin on a lapel has been known to catapult a star into the lead of an award ceremony review. Recent high profile cases shed light on how the simplest inadvertent expressions (never mind outright political activism) of actors, artists, and musicians affect their professional lives. As actors George Clooney and Brad Pitt made their way through the Washington Beltway to deliver their respective pitches on behalf of the genocide victims in Darfur and those rendered homeless by federal inaction before, during, and after Hurricane Katrina, they were sure to be among the day's top news. Coverage of Oprah Winfrey's official endorsement of Barack Obama was highlighted by the description of her garden party fundraiser as "grand and exclusive on the lawn of her sprawling and gated Montecito estate."

---

1. Posting of Tom Regan to NPR's Blog of the Nation, http://www.npr.org/blogs/talk/2008/05/does_celebrity_activism_make_a.html (May 20, 2008, 13:58 EST).

The official list of "Top-10 Moments of Celebrity Activism in 2008" included Winfrey's garden party, movie producer Norman Lear's getting out the vote, actor George Clooney's hosting of a private dinner party for Obama in Switzerland, comedian Sarah Silverman's sponsoring *The Great Schlep* and *Bubbies for Obama*, and rapper Will.i.am's recording of an inspirational music video featuring Obama's campaign slogan *Yes We Can*. Although not universally recognized as the most powerful or famous celebrities in the world, whatever they lacked in terms of visibility, they more than made up for in conviction. Susan Sarandon has acknowledged that she became an actor because of her very strong imagination and empathy—the exact qualities that make for a strong activist.

These celebrities' collective impact became a steamroller of inspiration. Their shared acceptance of Obama's basic values, belief that the future of the nation was in grave peril, and certainty that their actions could make a difference transformed mere desire for victory into action.[2] The year 2008 was certainly a defining moment in the history of the United States. Well beyond the unprecedented number of conservative Republicans who openly endorsed Barak Obama for the U.S. presidency, even died-in-the-wool conservative pundits who once supported former President George W. Bush came to agree with Bush critics[3] who had long-ago concluded:

Under the corrupt and inept leadership of Bush and Cheney, America has suffered from corporate extortion in the California energy crisis, the worst terrorist attack in America's history on 9/11, unsolved anthrax attacks, an abandoned war in Afghanistan, a failed war in Iraq, a lost American city in New Orleans, the fastest and largest growth in the Federal government ever, a

---

2. Paul C. Stern et al., *A Value-Belief-Norm Theory of Support for Social Movements: The Case of Environmentalism*, 6 HUM. ECOLOGY REV. 81 (1999), *available at* http://www.humanecologyreview.org/pastissues/her62/62sternetal.pdf.

3. *E.g.*, BRUCE BARTLETT, IMPOSTOR: HOW GEORGE W. BUSH BANKRUPTED AMERICA AND BETRAYED THE REAGAN LEGACY (2006).

precipitous decline in national reputation, stagnant middle class wages, rising unemployment rolls, and the most divisive political culture since the 1860s. The Bush administration will go down in history as the most corrupt, least legitimate, most disgraceful administration in American history.[4]

✹ The Fixed Star in Our Constitutional Constellation

There is no debate about the importance of the individual right to free speech in the United States, as it has been the public face of our national identity for the better part of the post-World War II era. Writing for the majority in *West Virginia v. Barnett* in 1943, the late Supreme Court Justice Robert Jackson declared that the fixed star in our constitutional constellation is that "no official, high or petty, can prescribe what shall be orthodox in politics, nationalism, religions or other matters of opinion or force citizens to confess by word or act their faith therein."[5]

Although this is neither the first nor only time that rhetoric has outpaced reality, those caught in the eye of the political storm less than a decade following these famous and oft-quoted words recall a constellation that was pretty grim. For nearly 10 full years, tens of thousands of Americans were accused of being Communists or Communist sympathizers. The accused were subject to aggressive investigations by government and private interests, and the "primary

---

4. *See* J. Timmons Roberts, *What We Feared: A New Geography of Fear in America Post 9-11*, http://jtrobe.people.wm.edu/What_We_Feared_v1.htm (last visited Feb. 23, 2009); Teresa Solkol Thomas, *Study Reveals Impact of Fear, Anger on American* Perceptions of Terrorism, CARNEGIE MELLON NEWS, May 10, 2002, http://www.cmu.edu/cmnews/020510/020510_terrorism.html; Huma Zaidi, *Security Politics*, MSNBC First Read, Nov. 14, 2006, http://firstread.msnbc.msn.com/archive/2006/11/14/14559.aspx (last visited Feb. 23, 2009)

5. 319 U.S. 624 (1943).

targets of such suspicions were government employees, those in the entertainment industry, educators and union activists."[6] The conditions lingered as public media adopted a new defining role, one aptly summarized by Robert Shogan in *No Sense of Decency: The Army-McCarthy Hearings, A Demagogue Falls and Television Takes Charge of American Politics*:[7] "What made the confrontation unprecedented and magnified its impact was its gavel-to-gavel coverage by television. Thirty-six days of hearings transfixed the nation."

The hearings left a major item of unfinished business—the issue of McCarthyism, the strategy based on fear, smear, and guilt by association. But television overlooked this portentous omission, and as it went on to transform American political debate it exhibited the same shortcomings exposed by the hearings: an emphasis on razzle-dazzle and a reluctance to challenge power and authority—traits that persist today.[8]

U.S. scholars devote a lot of energy abroad touting the importance of free speech, mostly by highlighting the many instances of brutal government repression of speech devoted to progressive agendas. However, if the United States is to lay claim to a legacy of freedom, there is still much to account for in both the McCarthy and Bush II eras, where repression and self-censorship loomed large. Coercive destruction of human dignity and free speech alongside government secrecy had begun to take a rising toll on American political participation.

---

6. Wikipedia, *McCarthyism*, http://en.wikipedia.org/wiki/Mccarthy_era (last visited Apr. 5, 2009).

7. ROBERT SHOGAN, NO SENSE OF DECENCY: THE ARMY-McCARTHY HEARINGS, A DEMAGOGUE FALLS AND TELEVISION TAKES CHARGE OF AMERICAN POLITICS (2009).

8. http://search.barnesandnoble.com/No-Sense-of-Decency/Robert-Shogan/e/9781566637701/

⑅ Imposition of Orthodoxy

Artists and musicians have been perpetual targets during periods of repression. Rumors of extended unemployment, lost endorsements, boycotts, reduction of advertising budgets, and elimination of consideration for special honors and awards because of political expression abound. At one end of the spectrum, actor Robert Redford observes: "Anyone with a rational mind and a sense of decency is being positioned as a lefty by the extreme right."[9] At the other end, singer Natalie Maines reported that when she expressed an honest sentiment during a London concert:

> It seemed like traditional values had been temporarily suspended. I didn't recognize this country, we didn't know what year it was and we didn't know what country we were in. The Republicans and right-wing groups were very organized and they knew exactly what they were doing. It seems like our media is dominated by right-wing media moguls like Rupert Murdoch (Fox News). If you don't share their opinions, they label you as a terrorist or a person who doesn't have any family values. Unfortunately, people in the US who don't have the time to seek out the truth through neutral news sources have a real problem.[10]

A similar claim is being leveled by closet conservations in Hollywood. One republican actor reported that he finally understands how it feels to be a racial minority. As there are relatively few closeted minorities, he is either referring to blatant discrimination for his beliefs (as distinguished from self-censorship directed from the bully pulpit) or the reality of living with constant reminders of the low-level contempt with which you are regarded because

---

9. Posting of RM NIXON to Liberty Lounge, http://www.libertylounge.net/forums/8864-robert-redford-almost-admits-hollywood-liberal.html.

10. *Interview with a Dixie Chick*, SPIEGEL ONLINE, July 11, 2006, http://www.spiegel.de/international/spiegel/0,1518,426213,00.html.

your very presence is antithetical to the value-norm of your community. Allegations of backlash against conservative artists seem fraught with strange analogies, faulty syllogism, and other logical fallacies.

Web sites are on the rise that claim to reveal "little known facts" surrounding the impact of liberal bias in what one writer characterized as "our main communication channels today."[11] Highlighting the three main battlegrounds in the lexicon of the information age, a series of articles warn of the destructive effects of liberal bias in mainstream news media, college faculties, and Tinseltown.[12] With specific regard to the entertainment industry:

> Radical environmentalism, animal rights, abortion rights, anti-smoking, gun control, feminism, speaking out against the war in Iraq, and supporting Communist dictators are just some of the favorite pastimes of liberal Hollywood celebrities.[13]

Proof by assertion is a logical fallacy in which a proposition is repeatedly restated regardless of contradiction.[14] An examination of similar campaigns to weed out the so-called radical professors from the halls of academia uncovers a reality that simply does not square with the vitriolic attacks.[15] Scholars are keen to consider probable

---

11. John Eberhard, *Liberal Bias in Hollywood*, INTELLECTUAL CONSERVATIVE.COM, July 6, 2004, http://www.intellectualconservative.com/article3576.html.

12. *Id.*

13. *Id.*

14. http://en.wikipedia.org/wiki/Proof_by_assertion (last visited Apr. 5, 2009).

15. *See generally* Robin Barnes, *Drafting the Priests of Our Democracy to Serve the Diplomatic, Informational, Military & Economic Dimensions of Power*, 27 BUFF. PUB. INT. L.J. (2009) (noting that eight recent studies of faculty politics that alleged disruptive liberal bias were reviewed by experts according to five basic measures of validity in social science research to determine whether they were science or propaganda, and that all came up short in adhering to appropriate research standards.); Robin Barnes, *Natural Legal Guardians of Judicial Independence and Academic Freedom*, 77 FORDHAM L. REV. 1453 (2009).

influences in an underlying sequence of events, but otherwise careful to document specific claims by demonstrating a causal connection. However, studies purporting to prove the existence of a radical agenda in academia were pseudoscientific at best; at worst, they wasted valuable time and seem geared toward the very repositioning that Redford described. Thus, if the right-wing rhetoric were to gain a foothold by infiltrating the more powerful means of influence, it would necessarily target academia, the media, and the entertainment industry.

A new book entitled *Celebutards*, written by *New York Post* columnist Andrea Preyser, claims to expose the "Hollywood Hacks, Limousine Liberals, and Pandering Politicians Who Are Destroying America." With back-flap endorsements from the keepers of the conservative flame, Fox entertainment shock-jocks Bill O'Reilly, Ann Coulter, and Sean Hannity, the book fits nicely with two others: Bernard Goldberg's, *Slobbering Love Affair: The True (and Pathetic) Story of the Torrid Romance between Barack Obama and the Mainstream Media*, and James Delingpole's *Welcome to Obamaland: I Have Seen Your Future and It Doesn't Work*. Conservative comedian Dennis Miller is a regular on the talk show circuit. Former conservative actor Ronald Reagan became governor of California, a position now held by conservative actor Arnold Schwarzenegger. Country music legend Dolly Parton announced in the middle of the 2008 presidential election that she could *relate* to Sarah Palin: "I always say we're very much alike. Both small town girls. Both are Pentecostalists and we both carry an AK-47." Grammy award-winning country singer LeAnne Rimes performed for George and Laura Bush in the East Room of the White House in February 2006.

Moroever, Fox correspondent Greta Van Susteren was quite diligent in covering the controversy over a Halloween display of Sarah Palin hanging in effigy at the home of a California couple.[16] Yet she

---

16. Greta Van Sustern, *Gov. Palin "Effigy" in a Noose: Halloween Fun or Going Too Far?*, gretawire.foxnews.com/2008/10/27/gov-palin-effigy-in-a-noose-halloween-fun-or-going-too-far/ (last visited Apr. 6, 2009).

gave no airtime to the life-sized mannequin found hanging from a tree with a noose around its neck at the University of Kentucky wearing a Barack Obama Halloween mask, suit jacket, sneakers, and sweat pants.[17] Van Sustern's journalistic integrity has also been questioned because of potential conflicts of interests related to her husband's advisory role to Sarah Palin, including the nature of their visits to Palin's Alaskan home.[18] An "exclusive" interview with Palin's teenage daughter following the birth of her son came just before the public learned that Bristol Palin had broken up with the baby's father when son Tripp was only eight weeks old.[19] It might not have been newsworthy except for the ardent claims of Palin staffers—running on a platform that rejects sex education in public schools other than abstinence—that the teens would soon marry.

Van Susteren elicited the following statement from the Alaskan governor relating to her prospects for becoming the top contender on the Republican presidential ticket in 2012:

> Faith is a very big part of my life. And putting my life in my creator's hands—this is what I always do. I'm like, OK, God, if there is an open door for me somewhere, this is what I always pray, I'm like, don't let me miss the open door. Show me where the open door is. Even if it's cracked up a little bit, maybe I'll plow right on through that and maybe prematurely plow through it, but don't let me miss an open door. And if there is an open door in (20)12 or four years later, and if it is something that is going to be good

---

17. Associated Press, *Obama Effigy Found on U. of Kentucky Campus*, MSNBC.COM, Oct. 29, 2008, http://www.msnbc.msn.com/id/27439385/.

18. Geoffrey Dunn, *Palin Pallin' Around with Scientologists: Todd & Sarah & John & Greta*, THE HUFFINGTON POST, MAR. 21, 2009, http://www.huffingtonpost.com/geoffrey-dunn/palin-pallin-around-with_b_177709.html.

19. *Exclusive: A Visit with the Palins*, FOXNEWS.COM, Feb. 18, 2009, http://www.foxnews.com/story/0,2933,494205,00.html.

for my family, for my state, for my nation, an opportunity for me, then I'll plow through that door.[20]

Of course, the professional blogosphere can be counted upon to place all things in proper perspective.[21] *Washington Post* celebrity blogger Liz Kelley featured an interesting exchange with a reader in the District concerning Palin as vice president soon after running mate John McCain made disparaging remarks about the intelligence of starlette Paris Hilton, one of the few celebrities to endorse Sarah Palin:

> *Washington, D.C.*—Love, love, love that Paris Hilton as a "fake President" video. But here's the thing that is troubling me. Paris comes across as so erudite on that vid that I wonder if she has been faking it all these years. Then I remember that she is just reading from a memorized script. But this makes me worried because Sarah Palin is also reading from a memorized script, and isn't nearly as good at it. All of which forces me to the horrible conclusion that maybe Paris would be a better VP than Palin. Oy.
>
> *Liz Kelly*—I'm all for Paris empowerment, but there is a huge-angous difference between a pre-recorded five-minute video piece that has been carefully scripted and practiced and a debate, Katie Couric interview or even a convention speech. So I wouldn't necessarily accuse Sarah Palin of giving bad teleprompter. In fact, she was met with some excitement at the convention when she delivered her original hockey mom speech. It was only when she sat down with Couric and Charlie Gibson—and at the

---

20. *Exclusive—Gov. Palin on 2012:"Don't Let Me Miss an Open Door"*, FOXNEWS. COM, Nov. 11, 2008, http://www.foxnews.com/story/0,2933,449884,00.html.

21. Posting of Liz Kelly to WASHINGTONPOST.COM Celebritology Live, http://www.washingtonpost.com/wp-dyn/content/discussion/2008/10/02/DI2008100203394.html (Oct. 29, 2008, 14:00 EST).

debate—that she started tripping over syntax and talking herself into corners.

Paris, on the other hand, had basically zero pressure on her during these bits and can redo any botched takes. So I wouldn't use these videos as evidence of her faking us all out in some kind of Kaufman-esque scheme to turn celebrity on its head. I think a lot of Paris, but not that much. And if our only choice for VP is Sarah Palin or Paris Hilton, well, that would be a grim day indeed. I mean, it just wouldn't be fair considering the fact that Angelina Jolie knows way more about this stuff than the both of them combined.

✺ High Profile Targets in the Effort to Control Political Debate

In the absence of sociological studies measuring the extent to which celebrity citizens shape civic norms, we have to examine recent cases. How high is the price for speaking out against government policies? Two celebrities (covered in Chapter 10) have exerted a profound influence upon global consciousness. Changes in the law and culture described throughout represent a fierce battleground over control and distribution of their private information that may in fact be related to their influence and has likely exerted a chilling affect on the willingness of many other celebrities to speak out on political issues.

The fundamental premise of the book so far has been that celebrities deserve but fail to receive equal protection of the law. Valid enforcement of constitutional provisions provides every individual with the same opportunities to become *model citizens*—the civic glue that holds free societies together. Now that the media no longer serves its original function, the triple threat of the current assault upon celebrities' personal lives is that it thwarts their free expression, limits public debate, and skews the national dialogue in favor of corporate interests. Pop-country star Natalie Maines is sure of one thing: "We have to create an alternative voice to counter the media concentration of people like Rupert Murdoch."[22]

Is there reason to doubt that celebrities deserve the same opportunities to become model citizens as other individuals in a free society? Model citizens see both themselves and others as free and equal individuals who define themselves beyond the attributes they possess as members of particular ethnic, religious, or class-based communities. Model citizens tend to engage civic culture: they speak up, vote, and take seriously the notion they give consent to those who govern. The dynamic interaction fosters civic culture as well as a desire and capacity for self-governance. Delving into an individual's personal life to disparage their reputation in an effort to discount their political message constitutes bad faith manipulation of public debate. If Caroline von Hannover expressed alarm over spiraling human rights violations and made an international plea for policies that promote peaceful coexistence between and among all people, should that alter her rights as they relate to her private life? Given social and economic globalization, should the answer be different in the United States and European Union.

🎞 America's Poster Girls for Radical Activism

Jane Fonda

The actor reports:

> You know, having become an activist during the Vietnam War and wanting to really understand it, I read the Pentagon papers. And it was an amazing document because what it showed is that five administrations knew they couldn't win in Vietnam,

---

22. *Interview with a Dixie Chick, supra* note 10.

and yet they kept sending men there to die. And the big question for me over the years was why? And as I was writing my book and trying to figure this out, I read a book, "The Secret Papers" by Dan Ellsberg, and then I read Doris Kearns' biography of Lyndon Johnson, and Lyndon Johnson put his finger on it. He said, "If I withdraw, they'll call me an un-manly man." Think about how many Americans have died so our leaders could prove their manhood! This is so deep. And I don't need to say that this culture of toxic masculinity is alive and well right now in this country and it's tragic.[23]

Jane Fonda attended a meeting of the U.N. Panel on Population Control as founder of the Georgia Campaign for Adolescent Pregnancy Prevention. During the meeting she described conditions she had witnessed in northern Georgia (where children were hungry and "living in tar-paper shacks with no indoor plumbing") that reminded her of some developing countries. Governor Zell Miller called her comments "ridiculous and personally offensive," stating "her view from the penthouse is not as clear as it needs to be." Former President Jimmy Carter entered the dialogue to say that her comments were inappropriate and regrettable, but "she is almost certain to continue doing a lot more for Georgia than some of her critics. . . ."

Her protest of the Vietnam War meant that she would be forever dubbed Hanoi Jane. During the 2004 presidential election, conservative Senator Sam Johnson from Texas sought to capitalize on Democratic candidate John Kerry's membership in the group Veterans Against the War in Vietnam by suggesting that they call him "Hanoi John"—it worked so well the first time around. So well, in fact, that Ted Somply, a retired Green Beret who ran a Web site for veterans devoted to defeating Kerry, said he spent months

---

23. Marianne Schnall, *Conversation with Jane Fonda*, FEMINIST.COM, http://www.feminist.com/resources/artspeech/interviews/janefonda.html (last visited Apr. 6, 2009).

looking for a photograph of John Kerry and Jane Fonda together. Miraculously, a message from a stranger arrived telling him exactly where he could find one. He paid $170 and posted it all over the Internet. Why is it that the press only discovered that former President Nixon was escalating the war, rather than pulling out as he had claimed, after Ms. Fonda traveled to Vietnam?

Fonda has recently argued that the military campaign in Iraq will turn people all over the world against America, and that rising hatred abroad will surely result in more terrorist attacks. In July 2005, Fonda said that some of the war veterans she met while on her book tour urged her to speak out against the Iraq War. Others, perhaps stewing in displaced rage over her former acts of protest, branded her as a traitor. A few patriot-zealots continue to post numerous veiled and not-so-veiled threats against the Oscar-winning actor on the Internet.

However, Fonda is heartened by the fact that Cindy Sheehan, whose son Casey died in Iraq in 2004, has stepped up to fill the gap. Fonda recently joined actors Susan Sarandon, Tim Robbins, and Martin Sheen in support of a congressional measure to withdraw U.S. forces from Iraq via a statement published in the *Los Angeles Times* and *New York Times*. On January 28, 2007, the *Boston Globe* reported "Tens of thousands of demonstrators—Iraq veterans, movie stars, and citizens from all walks of life—converged on the National Mall yesterday to demand that Congress act to end the Iraq war, in an event organizers hailed as the largest antiwar protest since the US invasion in 2003."[24] When activist icon Jane Fonda stood before a cheering crowd, she declared: "I haven't spoken at an antiwar rally in 34 years but silence is no longer an option."[25]

---

24. Bryan Bender, *Thousands Rally on National Mall, Protesters Urge Halt to Funding*, THE BOSTON GLOBE, Jan. 28, 2007, http://www.boston.com/news/ nation/washington/articles/2007/01/28/thousands_rally_on_national_mall/.

25. Linton Weeks, *Fonda Reprises a Famous Role at Peace Rally: The Actress Speaks Out against the War in Iraq*, WASH. POST, Jan. 28, 2007, http://www.washingtonpost. com/wp-dyn/content/article/2007/01/27/AR2007012701486_pf.html.

Susan Sarandon

The actor states:

> In the name of fear and fighting terror, we are giving the reins of
> power to oil men looking for distraction from their disastrous
> economic performance, oil men more interested in the financial
> bottom line than a moral bottom line. We here can imagine what
> war will do to human beings whose faces we will never see,
> whose names we will never know, whose numbers we will never
> know, all killed preemptively in our name.

Susan Sarandon is noted for walking her talk. She demonstrated
her active support for racial equality as one of 219 arrested at New
York police headquarters on the 13th day of protests over the police
shooting of unarmed African immigrant Amadou Diallo. A supporter
of gay rights, she was featured in *The Celluloid Closet*, which looked
at how Hollywood films have depicted homosexuality, and *Love is
Love is Love*, a video promoting acceptance of gay, lesbian, bisexual,
and transgender individuals.

Sarandon also works to end hunger at both local and global levels.
She began working with Holy Apostles Soup Kitchen when they "were
one of the few safe havens for people living with AIDS way back when
there was such a stigma with AIDS. They stepped into the breach." In
2005, she hosted a segment of the Live 8 Concert in Edinburgh,
Scotland. Live 8 organizer Bob Geldof expressed confidence that
world leaders would respond to the artists' call for more action to
tackle global poverty, and if the 9.6 million viewing audience was not
enough, they were backed by former-Prime Minister Tony Blair who
characterized the agreement on Aid Africa at the G8 summit a
"mighty achievement" for millions of campaigners worldwide.[26]

---

26. *Live 8 Helped Aid Deal Says Blair*, BBC NEWS, http://newsvote.bbc.co.uk/
    mpapps/pagetools/print/news.bbc.co.uk/2/hi/uk_news/politics/4672797.
    stm (last visited Apr. 6, 2009).

Sarandon spoke at a Mother's Day Vigil for Peace outside the White House on May 14, 2006 with still-grieving peace activist Cindy Sheehan along with many of the 4,580 mothers worldwide of fallen soldiers sent to fight in Iraq. Sarandon declared simply that American mothers "do not want to risk their children or the children of Iraq."[27] She has served as a UNICEF Goodwill Ambassador and was one of eight women selected to carry in the Olympic flag at the opening ceremony of the 2006 Olympic Winter Games in Turin, Italy.

Sarandon has delivered a special message on the dilemma of homelessness:

Seeing people without a home, without their basic needs fulfilled—things that people are entitled to—shelter, safety, food—always really affected me. It's always been very difficult for me to see people on the street. People often burn out on soup kitchen work or humanitarian work like helping the homeless.

It can be discouraging . . . politics [is] frustrating because there are so many lies involved and so much bureaucracy, when you're dealing one on one with people, you meet the most inspiring people . . . [those] who've actually committed themselves— retired schoolteachers, young people who form a community that goes fairly unnoticed until you dive into that pond.

You meet the most extraordinary people who are doing something very empowering, making a difference in another's life, makes a difference in your life to [witness] the power of one.

At a time when everything seems so out of control and the people you've elected are bogus and there's so much random violence and hatred, it fills you with such hope and admiration to

---

27. Phillip Coorey, *Stop This Terrible Waste, Grieving Mothers Tell Bush*, SYDNEY MORNING HERALD, May 16, 2006, *available at* http://www.smh.com.au/news/world/stop-this-terrible-waste-grieving-mothers-tell-bush/2006/05/15/1147545265709.html.

even be part for a short time in a community where people have connected to strangers.

The last time I served down at Holy Apostles, what was really striking to me was how different the group of people were who were coming for food from even a year ago . . . [Now they] have so many people out of work who've had jobs all their lives, young couples that cannot find a way to pay their rent, or an illness. . . . It's so much easier these days to find yourself in a situation where you end up on the street or end up with not enough money to buy your food on a regular basis.

This interviewer asked: "What would a *Susan Sarandon utopia* look like?" The actor returned to the concept of hands-on spirituality, where the plight of the poor, injustice, and all those things that politicize people once they start to open their eyes can be addressed. She also believes closing the huge gap between rich and poor would provide an avenue for peaceful resolutions. As a global priority, she notes that it takes so little effort and money to get rid of malaria, to bring in clean water, or to give people a chance at an education that everyone should have opportunities for education, decent housing, and medical care.

Setting the example with her kids, Sarandon believes that if student leaders from every high school in the United States regularly traveled to other countries, they would be less afraid, more empowered, and more inclined to think twice before they drop bombs from a position of power in adult life. She asks: "If you walk down the street and someone is sleeping in a box, that person is either 'the other' and you're fearful of them, or an extension of your family, how would you respond?"

Sarandon was honored with the Freedom in Film Award for her commitment to free expression and civic activism. On May 29, 2008, she announced to the world that she would move to Canada or Italy if John McCain was elected president of the United States.

Dixie Chicks

I'm not ready to make nice
I'm not ready to back down
I'm still mad as hell and
I don't have time to go round and round and round
It's too late to make it right
I probably wouldn't if I could
Cause I'm mad as hell
Can't bring myself to do what it is you think I should

—Lyrics from "Not Ready to Make Nice"

In the middle of a 10-year career in which they had sold more than 20 million albums, the Dixie Chicks were the most popular female singing group. They were the first to have three albums debut at No. 1, breaking the record they set in 2002 that made them the first female group ever to have two albums debut in the top spot.[28] But heading into a sold-out worldwide tour, on the eve of the U.S. invasion of Iraq, singer Natalie Maines sparked a row in the United States when it hit the international media circuit that in between songs she confided to a concert audience in London: "Just so you know, we're ashamed the President of the United States is from Texas."[29]

Reflecting upon the experience, Maines declared: "It was awesome . . . to be angry, to be sure that you're right and that the things you do matter."[30] She later apologized for "disrespecting the office of

---

28. Editorial, *Taking the Long Way: Dixie Chicks*, AOL INTERNATIONAL MUSIC, Aug. 22,2007,http://www.aol.in/internationalmusic/story/20070425040490190000001/index.html

29. Associated Press, *Dixie Chicks Slammed for Bush Gibe*, CBSNEWS.COM, Mar. 14, 2003, http://www.cbsnews.com/stories/2003/03/15/entertainment/main544132.shtml.

30. *Dixie Chicks Regret Bush Apology*, PEOPLE.COM, May 22, 2006, http://www.people.com/people/article/0,1196749,00.html.

the President," but the backlash was vicious. The group received numerous death threats, and a campaign to boycott their music led to it being banned on country-music radio stations altogether. So much for home girl pride. The Web site for *Entertainment Weekly* displays the following time line:[31]

2003: The Chicks Bare All

MARCH 1 A week after *Home* wins four Grammys, the Chicks break the one-day concert ticket sales record, grossing $49 million.

MARCH 10 Natalie Maines: "'We're ashamed the President of the United States is from Texas,'" she says on stage in London. Also heard: sound of feces hitting fan.

MARCH 14 After CD buyers and radio stations call for a boycott, Maines issues an apology, admitting she was "disrespectful" to Dubya.

APRIL 7 Brett Butler gets loudly booed at the Country Music Television Flameworthy Awards when she attempts to defend the group.

MAY 2 With airplay and sales nose-diving, the Chicks appear nude on EW's cover with painted insults like "'Saddam's Angels,'" "Dixie Sluts,'" and "'Traitors.'" Controversy flames! Again.

One report surmised that "not since Jane Fonda's trip to Hanoi had an entertainer enraged so many people with a political statement." Maines later admitted that she only has one regret: "I apologized for

---

31. Chris Willman, *Pretty, Pissed Off*, ENTERTAINMENT WEEKLY, Apr. 14, 2006, http://www.ew.com/ew/article/0,1181148,00.html.

disrespecting the office of the President. But I don't feel that way anymore. I don't feel he is owed any respect whatsoever. I've said so much worse than that."

Maines, Martie Maguire, and Emily Robison have three husbands and seven kids between then. Their three-year voluntary exile resulted in five of their seven bundles of joy. By the time they released their next album, *Taking the Long Way*, more than 80 percent of citizens worldwide agreed that the war in Iraq was baseless. *Rolling Stone* magazine reported that the 2006 album debuted at No. 1.[32] The very first single released by the labels sums it all up: "Not Ready to Make Nice." The song is powerful and embraces all of the traditional wisdom: *forgive, but don't forget, time heals all wounds, you've made you bed, now lie in it, you have to pay the piper. . . .*

At the time, Chris Willman reported an astounding concensus:

> Many of the nation's country-music radio program directors have heard the upcoming Dixie Chicks album, *Taking the Long Way*. Almost to a person, these programmers agree the May 23 release has "four or five potential smashes'" on it. But even more unanimous is the assessment that "Not Ready to Make Nice" is not one of them.[33]

Maines reported "none of the country radio stations are playing our new single. . . . Instead they asked our label for an alternative single—a request that we, of course, turned down." The United Kingdom's BBC reported "the Dixie Chicks are scheduled to play a sold-out concert at London's Shepherd's Bush Empire. . . . The group's latest album . . . [has] spent the past two weeks at number

32. Charley Rogulewski, *Dixie Chicks Debut at Number One*, ROLLING STONE.COM, May 31, 2006, http://www.rollingstone.com/news/story/10464617/dixie_chicks_debut_at_number_one.

33. *See* Willman, *supra* note 31.

one on the US pop charts, having sold 526,000 copies during its first seven days."[34] Thus, the question arose as to whether the new political consensus meant that people were buying this album to make a political statement against Bush. By 2007, the singers were greeted with standing ovations at the 49th Annual Grammy Awards, topping out in every category for which they were nominated. The Dixie Chicks brought home Record of the Year (for "Not Ready to Make Nice"), Album of the Year (for *Taking the Long Way*), Song of the Year (for "Not Ready to Make Nice"), Best Country Album (for *Taking the Long Way*), and Best Country Performance by a Duo or Group with Vocals (for "Not Ready to Make Nice").[35]

Comedy Central or the South Carolina Legislature?

HOUSE RESOLUTION [H 3818]

South Carolina, USA

TO REQUEST THAT THE DIXIE CHICKS APOLOGIZE TO THE MILITARY FAMILIES IN THE STATE OF SOUTH CAROLINA AND THE UNITED STATES FOR THE UNPATRIOTIC AND UNNECESSARY COMMENTS MADE BY THEIR LEAD SINGER BEFORE THEY BEGIN THEIR UNITED STATES TOURS ON MAY 1, 2003, in GREENVILLE, S.C. AND TO REQUEST THAT THEY PERFORM A FREE CONCERT FOR TROOPS AND MILITARY FAMILIES IN SOUTH CAROLINA AS AN EXPRESSION OF THEIR SINCERITY.

Whereas, the Dixie Chicks are a popular and influential country music group from Texas; and

---

34. *Dixie Chicks Downplay Tour Claims*, BBC NEWS, June 9, 2006, http://news.bbc.co.uk/1/hi/entertainment/5062798.stm.

35. 49th Annual Grammy Awards Winners List, http://www.grammy.com/GRAMMY_Awards/49th_show/list.aspx.

Whereas, before a recent London concert, Natalie Maines, the lead singer of the Dixie Chicks, said that she was ashamed that the President of the United States is from Texas; and

Whereas, members of the United States Armed Forces are outraged at the anti-American sentiment expressed by the Dixie Chicks; and

Whereas, there is a large military presence in the State of South Carolina, whom the Dixie Chicks have offended by their comments; and

Whereas, before the Dixie Chicks kick off their United States tour in Greenville on May 1, 2003, the House of Representatives and the people of South Carolina request that Natalie Maines apologize and that the group perform a free concert for the South Carolina servicemen and women and their families.

There's More

Hurricane Katrina, and the horrific reports coming out of New Orleans:

[Bush Aide Bruce] Bartlett made up a DVD of the newscasts so Bush could see them in their entirety as he flew down to the Gulf Coast the next morning on Air Force One. How this could be—how the president of the United States could have even less "situational awareness," as they say in the military, than the average American about the worst natural disaster in a century—is one of the more perplexing and troubling chapters in a story that, despite moments of heroism and acts of great generosity, ranks as a national disgrace.[36]

In the aftermath of the Hurricane Natalie Maines reported: "We tried to donate 1 million to the Red Cross and they wouldn't take it."

---

36. Evan Thomas, *Katrina: How Bush Blew It*, NEWSWEEK, Sept. 19, 2005, *available at* http://www.msnbc.msn.com/id/9287434/site/newsweek/print/1/displaymode/1098.

The acting president of the United States [Bush II] was the Honorary Chairman of the Red Cross. But not to be outdone by three radicals, a section called "Myths and Legends" on the Red Cross Web site adds more grist to the rumor mill about the donation:

> In 2003, following a political controversy that erupted on a London stage during a live performance, the Dixie Chicks' management approached the American Red Cross and inquired about a promotional partnership for their forthcoming tour. There was no offer for an unrestricted donation to the Red Cross; rather, the "offer" was actually a business proposal. Prior to the controversy, the Chicks' management ignored two successive invitations to join the Red Cross National Celebrity Cabinet. Should the Dixie Chicks ever decide to make an unconditional financial donation to the American Red Cross, we would gladly accept it and put it to work toward our lifesaving mission.

Rosie O'Donnell

Actor-comedian Rosie O'Donnell's criticism of the Bush administration's policies including the war in Iraq and her focus on unanswered questions about the September 11 attacks moved her out of the national limelight. O'Donnell was critical of several Bush policies. One such policy barred coverage of military returning caskets. It was initiated in 1991 by President George H.W. Bush soon after split-screen television coverage by three networks showed the president joking at a news conference opposite images of the first casualties returning to Dover from the 1989 U.S. invasion of Panama.[37] In 2004, an airline contractor in Kuwait photographed

---

37. Connie Schultz, *America's Hidden Caskets*, THE ANNISTON STAR, Feb. 20, 2009, *available at* http://www.annistonstar.com/opinion/2009/as-columns-0220-0-9b19t5409.htm.

about 20 flag-draped coffins being loaded onto an Air Force jet headed for home. When her photo ran in *The Seattle Times*, the contractor was fired.[38]

In August 2008, North Carolina Congressman Walter B. Jones introduced the Fallen Hero Commemoration Act that would permit media coverage of military commemoration ceremonies and memorial services for those who died on active duty and those arriving at military installations. In support of the legislation, the leader of the National Press Photographers Association stated:

> We believe that the Department of Defense ban on media coverage of the return of our fallen heroes, which in turn prevents the public from seeing images of these events, violates the very principles of free speech and free exchange of ideas, for which these very heroes have died.[39]

A *Newsweek* article, "A Matter of Honor" by John Barry provides insight into the practical and privacy implications of the ban.[40] The military operates on a two-day schedule for removal of the bodies and delivery to family members. "If cameras are present to greet the caskets, there will be a great deal of pressure on the families to be there, too—an emotional and financial hardship for many. Some may want a public ceremony; some may want privacy and silence." The question is whether we can effectively honor the fallen, with appropriate regard for undue exposure and hardship of their families, while serving the legitimate public interest in witnessing "the price of war." Barry concludes, "Canada may have an answer":

38. *Id.*

39. Donald R. Winslow, *NPPA Calls on President Obama to Lift Dover Photo Ban*, NPPA.COM, Feb. 10, 2009, http://nppa.org/news_and_events/news/2009/02/dover01.html.

40. John Barry, *A Matter of Honor*, NEWSWEEK, Feb. 14, 2009, http://www.newsweek.com/id/184772.

The more than 100 Canadian soldiers who have fallen in combat in Afghanistan have been flown to Trenton air base, then driven 107 miles to the mortuary in Toronto. A stretch of Canada's Highway 401 has become known as the Highway of Heroes. When the military hearse drives down it, all other traffic is blocked; police and fire trucks, lights flashing, line each overpass, and hundreds of Canadians, flags in hand, wait along the highway. Perhaps fallen American soldiers could arrive at Andrews Air Force Base—with the sort of quiet, dignified ceremony . . . and then be carried by hearse (anonymously; no family need be present) to the mortuary at Dover, 102 miles away by road and highway. The route could pass by the White House.

O'Donnell was known for raising similar questions about military deaths and was often sharply critical of news coverage about the war.[41] In May 2007, O'Donnell rhetorically asked: "655,000 Iraqi civilians dead. Who are the terrorists? . . . if you were in Iraq and another country, the United States, the richest in the world, invaded your country and killed 655,000 of your citizens, what would you call us?" Shortly after, right-wing commentators accused O'Donnell of calling American soldiers terrorists. One week later, a heated discussion ensued between O'Donnell and conservative cohost Elizabeth Hasselbeck on the morning television program *The View*.[42] *ABC News* reported that O'Donnell's arguments with Hasselbeck lifted the show's rankings.[43] O'Donnell noted that whenever they disagreed, conservative talking heads depicted her as attacking the "innocent [Elizabeth Hasselbeck]," while featuring their face-off

---

41. Judy Faber, *Rosie Explains Controversial Photo*, CBSNEWS.COM, June 26, 2007, http://www.cbsnews.com/stories/2007/06/26/entertainment/main2983824.shtml.

42. Brian Orloff, *Elisabeth Hasselbeck, Rosie O'Donnell Square Off*, PEOPLE.COM, May 23, 2007,http://www.people.com/people/article/0,20039945,00.html.

43. Monica Nista, *O'Donnell Leaving "The View"*, ABCNEWS.COM, Apr. 25, 2007, http://abcnews.go.com/Entertainment/Story?id=3077493&page=1.

with a split screen effect showing her and Hasselbeck on each side. To no one's surprise, an agreement to terminate O'Donnell's contract was reached within 48 hours.[44]

Two of the developments in O'Donnell's case resonate with the repositioning that Redford mentioned and repression of peace activists in the 1970s. In October 2006, a few months prior to O'Donnell's departure from *The View*, a British medical journal published the results of a study conducted by Johns Hopkins University's Bloomberg School of Public Health and the Al Mustansiriya University School of Medicine in Baghdad, in cooperation with the Center for International Studies at the Massachusetts Institute of Technology. The study, titled "The Human Cost of the War in Iraq,"[45] was immediately challenged by former President Bush during a White House news conference where he claimed that their methodology has been discredited. Iraqi government spokesman Ali Dabbagh said the "figures contradict the simplest rules of accuracy and investigation." When asked in December 2005 how many Iraqi citizens had died in this war, now-former President Bush replied, "I would say 30,000, more or less, have died as a result of the initial incursion and the ongoing violence against Iraqis."[46] The study's 655,000 figure quoted by O'Donnell, was the midpoint in the estimated range of somewhere between 390,000 and 940,000 deaths in the Bloomberg study.

In the study, 1849 random households surveyed across Iraq provided information about births, deaths, and migration.

---

44. Associated Press, *Rosie O'Donnell Won't Return to "The View"*, MSNBC.COM, May 25, 2007, http://www.msnbc.msn.com/id/18868354/.

45. Gilbert Burnham et al., *The Human Cost of the War in Iraq: A Mortality Study, 2002–2006* (Bloomberg School of Public Health & Al Mustansiriya Univ. School of Medicine); http://i.a.cnn.net/cnn/2006/images/10/11/human.cost.of.war.pdf.

46. Peter Baker, *Bush Estimates 30,000 Iraqis Have Died in War*, THE SEATTLE TIMES, Dec. 13, 2005, *available at* http://seattletimes.nwsource.com/html/nationworld/2002680398_bushiraq13.html.

According to the investigators, the methodology is the same used to survey the rate of major infection (such as HIV) in developing countries. When researchers asked the families for proof in the form of death certificates, those questioned were able to produce them 92 percent of the time.

However we might choose to define matters of public concern, accuracy concerning fallen U.S. soldiers and the number of civilian casualties in a contrived war would be legitimate contenders for the top of the list. Investigative journalists at their best weed out the demonstrably unreliable statistics. News reports tend to mechanically summarize the death toll as falling somewhere between Bush's low of 30,000 and John Hopkins' upper range of 900,000, accompanied by a list of organizations and their sponsors that provided this widely disparate information. CNN went beyond perfunctory reporting by listing congruent data from the study related to Iraqi's death toll: the numbers have risen each year since the invasion; the deceased are largely males aged 15–44; and deaths from coalition forces account for 31 percent. They also interviewed professionals familiar with survey research who confirmed "the survey's methodology is sound."[47]

✐ Fearmongering and the So-Called Liberal Bias

The second development in the O'Donnell story relates to well-known right-wing tactics that played well initially, but ultimately backfired in relation to the Dixie Chicks. The specific instructions for combating the so-called destructive effects of liberal bias in academia offered lessons on strategy that emphasized its unique "subdivisions." Careful observation of the distinctions between

---

47. *Study: War Blamed for 655,000 Iraqi Deaths*, CNN.COM, Oct. 11, 2006, http://edition.cnn.com/2006/WORLD/meast/10/11/iraq.deaths/.

operations and tactics is billed by conservatives as key for success of the "mission." According to one proponent, the grand strategy is a "broad and long-term theme—like containment during the Cold War." Operations and tactics are means for deployment and inculcation.[48] The director of one conservative think tank, Stephen Balch, advocates "a patient siege" and "perpetual attack" on the university's points of maximum vulnerability for purposes of destabilization.[49] In the realm of academic governance, Balch described proposed plans for destabilization as difficult, because academia "if not quite hermetically sealed" has "multiple defensive rings." Balch then prescribes key methods for attacking academic freedom, tenure, and endowment. Similar to the attack on O'Donnell and the Chicks (as they are affectionately described on the Red Cross site), Balch exclaimed that academic freedom can only be "buffeted by scandal or an especially galling ideological outrage," which makes way for an "adventuresome trustee [to] seize [the] occasion for pressing against the perimeters."[50] Training is the first step. Before expecting a trustee to recommend the firing of a tenured professor, they need to be made aware of how to "take advantage of the opportunities before them."[51] Off-the-cuff remarks made during a concert performance and a question presented in the middle of a daily gabfest among four women talking all over each other about politics one day and hair the next represent two recent instances of "seizing the opportunity before them."

Ultimately, we can only hope that blogger Mary Colurso has the final word on the making of heroes and heroines and villains and terrorists. In an article titled "When Celebrities Endorse, Do the

---

48. Lorelei Kelly, *Grand Strategy for Progressives, Democracy Arsenal*, DEMOCRACY ARSENAL, Apr. 6, 2005, http://www.democracyarsenal.org/2005/04/grand_strategy_.html.

49. *Id.*

50. *Id.*

51. *Id.* at 12.

Nation's Voters Listen?" Colurso reminds us: "Politics is just too darn important to base our decisions on sound bites from . . . even the most passionate and articulate stars . . . we must all realize they are just a small part of the national dialogue."[52]

---

52. Mary Colurso, *When Celebrities Endorse, Do the Nation's Voters Listen?*, BIRMINGHAM NEWS, Nov. 7, 2008, http://blog.al.com/mcolurso/2008/11/when_celebrities_endorse_do_na.html.

TEN

John Lennon and Michael Jackson
The Influence of the Superstar

✺ Government Fears and Tactics

Celebrity speech and privacy rights were special targets of the late Wisconsin Senator Joseph A. McCarthy. A corporate giant of the 1950s wrote a letter advising President Eisenhower to deal with McCarthy because many "see in him a potential Hitler . . ." inasmuch as what he had already been allowed to "get away with" in the United States now rendered the very concept of "democratic governments and the rights of individuals" indistinguishable from those allowed by Fascists.[1] The mission of the House Committee on Un-American Activities (HUAC), created in 1938, involved complete eradication of communist thought from American life. Its members launched a strident attack on Hollywood's rank and file by circulating a blacklist identifying those suspected of Communist affiliations. Prominent professional careers were destroyed while personal friends and close relatives were subjected to shame, ridicule, and public embarrassment. Intense fear of being branded a traitor and accused of plotting to overthrow the government permeated all levels of society.

Loyalty to the nation-state demanded that the accused divulge the identities of all known or suspected Communists and their sympathizers. In true political heresy, a group known as the

---

1. http://www.spartacus.schoolnet.co.uk/USAmccarthy.htmPhillip Reed, Letter to President Dwight D. Eisenhower, June 8, 1953.

Hollywood Ten was sentenced to jail for contempt when they refused to cooperate with congressional witch hunts. The blacklist resulted in the widespread use of pseudonyms by a host of actors, writers, and producers. The 50th anniversary of this period presented an occasion for acknowledgement of those victimized by McCarthy and galvanized those committed to restoring "the personal credits of movie workers who had been forced to conceal their identity in order to put bread on the table."[2]

Similar methods were used by the FBI under J. Edgar Hoover during the student-led civil rights and pro-peace movements of the 1960s and 1970s. John Lennon was a natural target, along with actor Jean Seberg for their support of the Black Freedom Movement.[3] Seberg's film career came to a sudden halt; she miscarried a child, and was later found dead with barbiturates near her body.[4] Her decision to raise money for Black organizations led to false media reports that originated with the FBI. Upon discovery of her decomposed body, a series of stunning disclosures were made by her husband during a press conference held shortly before he took his own life.[5] He revealed that when Seberg "read the rumor planted by the [F.B.I.] in Newsweek, she became distraught, went into labor and delivered a premature baby girl who died two days later . . . [afterwards] she tried to commit suicide every year on the anniversary of the baby's death."[6] Following this press conference, then-FBI Director William Webster acknowledged the Bureau planted the story that claimed Seberg was pregnant by a high-ranking member of the Black Panther Party to "cause her embarrassment and serve

---

2. Stephen S. Rosenfeld, *Hollywood Blacklist 50 Years Later: Looking Back on the Blacklisted*, WASH. POST, Nov. 28, 1997, A27.

3. DAVID RICHARDS, THE JEAN SEBERG STORY (1991).

4. *Id.* at 238.

5. Paul Brodeur, *How the F.B.I. Left Jean Seberg Breathless: In the Call for New "Counterintelligence," We Should Remember Some of the Old*, THE NATION, Mar. 25, 1996.

6. *Id.*

to cheapen her image with the general public."[7] Permission to the run the story was granted by Hoover himself with one modification: "It would be better to wait approximately two additional months until Seberg's pregnancy would be obvious to everyone."[8] Webster also offered the following guarantee: "The days when the F.B.I. used derogatory information to combat advocates of unpopular causes have long since passed, we are out of that business forever."[9]

Against this backdrop and the well-documented illegal measures taken to neutralize Lennon's influence, a steady progression of case law and adjudicative procedures imposed significant restrictions on the ability of celebrities to protect their privacy. The misappropriation and/or control of celebrity and fame is of natural interest to governments and their allies, insofar as both are relatively powerless in deploying legal measures to counter the momentum of superstars. The U.S. government's angst regarding the world's two most influential international stars by far, John Lennon and Michael Jackson, presents a fascinating case study that warrants closer scrutiny and investigative research.

Specifically, the nature of fame as a "relational" phenomenon—something conferred by others—is evidenced by the various classifications of stars as A-listers and beyond. According to scholars, natural talent does lead to competency and certain levels of mastery, but not to "fame." Decoupled from questions of merit, fame is "conferred or withheld" on many grounds. Individual efforts to "monitor" and "shape" public image are invariably subject to the substantial role played by the public and media.[10]

---

7. *FBI Admits Spreading Lies about Jean Seburg*, L.A. TIMES, Sept. 14, 1971, A1-A2.

8. *Id.*

9. *Id.*

10. Michael Madow, *Private Ownership of Public Image: Popular Culture and Publicity Rights*, 81 CAL. L. REV. 125, (1993).

Preliminarily, beyond the question of First Amendment rights, a government's deliberate engagement in the process of image making and image breaking seems analogous to the theory used to justify preemptive strike. Thus, attempts to repel celebrity incursions into the realm of political decision making is widely interpreted by media pundits as falling within the bounds of necessity rather than as the unfettered desire of their opponents to gain strategic political or economic advantage. Ongoing threats to individual civil and political rights are dismissed in the *no harm/no foul* parlance of basketball in what have been conveniently and euphemistically dubbed "America's culture wars." Such reasoning is sometimes explicitly though quietly referenced by judges who acknowledge the government's impotence in relation to the potentially unbounded influence of the superstar. Thus, there is little reason to believe that covert government monitoring of rising stars and their political inclinations will diminish. On the contrary, these clandestine operations would have to remain a key tactic in the government's arsenal of weapons used for shaping the tone and tenor of public discourse.

𝕸 Superstardom aka Surrealism 101

Pure psychic automatism, by which one proposes to express functioning of thought in the absence of all control exercised by reason, outside of all aesthetic and moral preoccupation.[11]

John Lennon

The fame secured by John Winston Ono Lennon was if nothing else certainly relational. Lennon, born October 9, 1940, was named after

---

11. http://www.experiencefestival.com/a/Surrealism_-_Philosophy/id/5497659.

a grandfather described as a "happy-go-lucky, musically gifted Irishman."[12] Distraught by the circumstances surrounding the breakup of his parents in 1946, Lennon lived for a brief period with his father whom he would wake at 7:00 a.m. to the tune of Joan Hammond's "One Fine Day."[13] He soon returned to live with his mother, and eventually with his Aunt Mimi, who is reported to have adored him from birth.[14] During his preteen years, Lennon demonstrated a quick wit, sharp tongue, and "total lack of reverence for everything respectable."[15] He went through art school before begging his aunt to buy him a guitar, which he quickly learned to play and which marked the beginning of a story that changed musical and political history.

As part of the legendary pop singing sensation known as the Beatles, Lennon garnered international acclaim.[16] As a solo artist, he was revered, reviled, and martyred for the cause of world peace. Lennon was his own man, intent on changing the world. He rejected the status quo, and above all else, the demand for conformity, as reflected in his number one hit "Watching the Wheels":

People say I'm crazy, doing what I'm doing, Well they give me all kinds of warnings, to save me from ruin, When I say that I'm o.k., well they look at me kind of strange, Surely you're not happy now; you no longer play the game . . .

Lennon's favorite singers, the Shirelles, were a quartet of beautiful black American women—the first girl group to reach No. 1 on

---

12. Pauline Lennon, Daddy Come Home: The True Story of John Lennon and His Father 11 (1990).

13. *Id.* at 70.

14. *Id.* at 72–74.

15. *Id.* at 84.

16. http://www.thebeatles.com/core/home/.

the *Billboard* Hot 100 chart.[17] Lennon's first marriage ended soon after he met the talented Japanese avant-garde artist Yoko Ono, whom he married a short while later.[18] He boldly appeared to the world as a global megastar, part of a highly visible interracial couple who were actively opposed to racial injustice, labor inequality, and war against an Asian enemy. He and Ono continually asked whether it was possible, as indicated in the title of another big hit, to "Give Peace a Chance."

As Britain's most famous son, Lennon was recently named among the top 10 Brits of the 20th century along with Princess Diana of Wales, who just prior to her death was also involved in a highly visible interracial relationship at the height of a brewing cold war that pit Western against Islamic nations.[19] Her partner's father, Mohamed Al Fayed, believes the late Princess Diana was pregnant when she died, and that because the couple had planned to announce their engagement, their deaths were no accident.[20] Similarly, Sean Lennon, the only child of John and Yoko, revealed in an interview with *New Yorker* magazine that he believed that his father was a "counter-cultural revolutionary" who posed a great threat to the American government. According to Sean, "he was dangerous because if he had ever said, 'Bomb the White House tomorrow', there would have been 10,000 people who would have done it. [P]acifist revolutionaries are historically killed by the government."[21] Filmographer Chris Charlesworth concluded that Lennon never realized the strength of the American political establishment and how much power it could exert with regard to

---

17. Jeremy Simmonds, The Encyclopedia of Dead Rock Stars 164 (2008).

18. Anthony Fawcett, John Lennon: One Day at a Time 16–40 (1976).

19. http://news.bbc.co.uk/1/hi/entertainment/tv_and_radio/2341661.stm.

20. *Coroner's Inquest Into Princess Diana's Death Opens*, Associated Press, Oct. 2, 2007.

21. Sean Lennon, quoted by David Sapsted in *Washington Killed Lennon, So Says Son Sean*, The New Yorker, April 20, 1998.

silencing him.[22] If fame is relational, Lennon's undoubtedly was related to his open endorsement of the global peace movement.

The 1984 book *Come Together: John Lennon in His Time* written by history Professor Jon Wiener examines Lennon's beliefs.[23] The U.S. government's efforts to silence the superstar led to revocation of Lennon's immigrant visa. Deportation proceedings against him and Yoko Ono were approved by the Nixon White House chief of staff.[24] Lennon became a target of the Nixon administration because of his popularity with young voters, opposition to the Vietnam War, and advocacy of the view that all power belonged to the people.

The U.S. government justified its 25-year refusal to release Lennon's FBI files by asserting that to do so could "reasonably be expected to . . . lead to foreign diplomatic, economic and military retaliation against the United States."[25] Writer Andrew Gumbel lists all of the "facts about John Lennon [that were] deemed so sensitive to the national security of both Britain and the United States that they have only just been released to the public after 25 years of freedom of information requests and protracted legal battles." [26]

> Lennon has encouraged the belief that he holds revolutionary views, not only by means of his formal interviews with Marxists, but by the content of some of his songs and other publications.
>
> Since 1972, John Lennon has continued from time to time to lend his support to various extremist causes, but does not appear to owe allegiance to any one faction.

---

22. *The U.S. vs. John Lennon* (Lionsgate Films, DVD, 2006). http://www.theusversusjohnlennon.com/.

23. JON WIENER, COME TOGETHER: JOHN LENNON IN HIS TIME (1991).

24. JON WIENER, GIMME SOME TRUTH: THE JOHN LENNON FBI FILES (2000).

25. *Id.*

26. Andrew Gumbel, *The Lennon Files: The FBI and the Beatle*, THE INDEPENDENT, Dec. 21, 2006.

Lennon was a peace activist who opposed the Vietnam War, spoke out against British military intervention in Northern Ireland, met and gave interviews to leading anti-war advocates on both sides of the Atlantic, and was even known, on occasion, to open his cheque book to put his money where his mouth was.

He experimented with illicit drugs, and was busted once for possession of marijuana.

He was hardly a threat to international security.

Lennon also wrote and released *Imagine* in 1971.

> *Imagine there's no Heaven, it's easy if you try,*
> *No hell below us, above us only sky,*
> *Imagine all the people, Living for today*
>
> *Imagine there's no countries, it isn't hard to do,*
> *Nothing to kill or die for, and no religion too,*
> *Imagine all the people, Living life in peace.*
>
> *Imagine no possessions; I wonder if you can,*
> *No need for greed or hunger, a brotherhood of man,*
> *Imagine all the people, sharing all the world.*
> *You may say that I'm a dreamer, but I'm not the only one,*
> *I hope someday you'll join us, and the world will be as one.*

Dating back to its release, *Imagine* is featured "in a broad array of most-influential and greatest-songs-of-all-time lists"[27] in countries throughout the world. They include lists of: the top 100 most-performed songs of the 20th century, best-selling singles in the United Kingdom, 500 Greatest Songs of All Time, greatest song in the past 100 years, Songs of the Century bearing the most historical significance, favorite song, greatest song of all time, and number

---

27. http://en.wikipedia.org/wiki/Imagine_(song).

one in the countdown to the 2008 Beijing Olympics. Former U.S. president Jimmy Carter said, "In many countries around the world—my wife and I have visited about 125 countries—you hear John Lennon's song '*Imagine*' used almost equally with national anthems."[28] The song has been so powerful on the international stage that contemporary songwriter Jim Giatas stated that because "John's song has gone virtually unchallenged for all these years, [I was] compelled to write an answer to it from my own conservative orthodox Christian perspective."[29] Thus, in 2008 he produced the song "I Can Only Imagine" with the following lyrics.

I can only imagine what it will be like
When I walk by your side
I can only imagine what my eyes will see
When your face is before me
I can only imagine
I can only imagine

Surrounded by your glory
What will my heart feel?
Will I dance for you Jesus,
Or in awe of you be still?
Will I stand in your presence,
Or to my knees will I fall?
Will I sing Hallelujah,
Will I be able to speak at all?
I can only imagine
I can only imagine

---

28. http://www.observertoday.com/page/content.detail/id/521866.html?
nav=5070.

29. *Id.*

I can only imagine when that day comes
And I find myself standing in the Son
I can only imagine when all I will do
Is forever, forever worship you
I can only imagine
I can only imagine

On February 25, 2009, the U.S. Supreme Court referenced the lyrics of Lennon's "Imagine" in *Pleasant Grove City v. Summum,* in commentary on monumental messages.[30] The opinion posed the question:

What, for example, is "the message" of the Greco-Roman mosaic of the word "Imagine" that was donated to New York City's Central Park in memory of John Lennon? Some observers may "imagine" the musical contributions that John Lennon would have made if he had not been killed. Others may think of the lyrics of the Lennon song that obviously inspired the mosaic and may "imagine" a world without religion, countries, possessions, greed, or hunger.[31]

Historically, it has always been important to examine critically and redress promptly those illegalities surrounding governmental responses to dissent in constitutional democracies. If the fears of high-ranking officials regarding the potential reach and influence of John Lennon became an ongoing factor in public suspicions about Lennon's assassination, the question automatically arises as to subsequent means for addressing the unprecedented potential for disruption to the status quo posed by an equally powerful superstar: the late Michael Jackson.

---

30. *Pleasant Grove City v. Summun,* 555 U.S. ____ (2009).

31. *Id.* at fn. 2.

Michael Jackson

Michael Joseph Jackson was the consummate superstar: he displayed "extraordinary natural talent augmented by an even more extraordinary perseverance and drive." His musical genius rendered Jackson a force with which to be reckoned. Like Lennon, Jackson began his musical career as the lead singer in a group, the youngest member and star of the Jackson Five. According to *Time*, just one year after they were first featured on national television everyone wanted to know them:

> They are brothers, and taken together they add up to the Jackson Five, a Group that in hardly more than a year-has become the biggest thing to hit Pop Capitalism since the advent of the Beatles. They had four hit singles in 1970, two more already this year, four albums, with all ten releases selling in the millions, and one (I'll Be There) already well over 4,000,000. Teen-age girls besiege their home for autographs and sometimes faint when they sing. They have their own magazine, a quarterly in which fans can revel in a whole issue devoted entirely to the Jackson Five and read things like "Michael's Love Letter to You." Stores now bulge with Jackson Five decals, stickers and sweaters. A Jackson Five hair spray and a Jackson Five watch are planned, as well as a television cartoon about their lives.
>
> Despite this commercial hoopla, the group manages to be one of the best Soul bands in the country. It is also part of the most likable and natural family ever to survive the pressures of teen-age stardom.[32]

Michael Jackson boasted an unprecedented 40-year career at the forefront of contemporary musical innovation that consisted of

---

32. *The Jackson Five at Home*, TIME, June 14, 1971.

album upon album of new material, each outselling the last. Nearly a million tickets to see the London concert scheduled to run from summer 2009 through February 2010 sold in a matter of hours. Apologies rang in from the organizers of the concert tour when their Web site crashed from the sheer number of fans logging on to register for presale tickets.[33]

As noted above, Lennon's "Imagine" holds the world record as the most influential song, with few prospects of fading from mass consciousness. In pure visceral terms, it remains the greatest musical expression of global desire for world peace and unity that we have ever known. Michael Jackson's 1988 hit single "Man in the Mirror" was on a similar trajectory toward inspiring a closer look at the world we have created:

I'm gonna make a change, For once in my life,
It's gonna feel real good, gonna make a difference, gonna make it
right
As I, turn up the collar on my favorite winter coat, this wind is
blowin ' my mind, I see the kids in the street, with not enough to eat,
Who am I, to be blind? Pretending not to see their needs,
I've been a victim of, a Selfish kind of love, its time that I realize,
That there are some with no home, not a nickel to loan,
Could it be, really me, pretending that they're not alone?
I'm starting with the man in the mirror,
I'm asking him to change His ways,
And no message could have been any clearer,
If you wanna make the world a better place,
Take a look at yourself, and make a change!

---

33. http://news.sky.com/skynews/Home/UK-News/Michael-Jackson-Concert-Tickets-Sell-Out-For-Jackos-O2-Residency-In-London-Organisers-AEG-Say/Article/200903215239309?f=rss.

"Man in the Mirror" became a No. 1 hit when released as a single in spring 1988; it was described as "one of Jackson's most critically acclaimed songs."[34] When it was nominated for Record of the Year, Jackson performed a live extended version at the televised Grammy Awards ceremony after it first debuted and then "topped the Billboard Hot 100 chart for two weeks."[35]

Jackson's performance style was said to be one of "whole-hearted sincerity and totally mind-blowing to those fortunate enough to observe him at close quarters."[36] He confessed that he often felt: "touched by something sacred. In those moments I felt my spirit soar and become one with everything that exists."[37]

⅏ Man in the Mirror Video

The impact of his musical genius reached new heights with the advent of music videos. Routine lyrics coupled with footage described as "historic events in escalating intensity of violence and despair, leading up to a nuclear explosion at the key change, followed by footage expressing hope and peace . . . "[38] catapulted the "Man in the Mirror" video to the top of the charts.

The video produced for that song is paradigmatic of the revolutionary nature of the social and political messages featured in both Lennon's and Jackson's music. The song itself inspired awe and reverence, but the video produced for the music put the world on notice. A politically hyperconscious Jackson used footage of:

---

34. http://nl.netlog.com/go/explore/videos/videoid=nl-3252022.

35. *Id.*

36. *Id.*

37. Michael Jackson, *The Dance* of Spirit (2009). http://www.examiner.com/x-13643-Honolulu-Spirituality-Examiner~y2009m7d8-Michael-Jackson-The-dance-of-spirit

38. http://en.wikipedia.org/wiki/Man_in_the_Mirror.

- 1984 famine in Ethiopia with children crying, dying, and near death from starvation;
- Nazi leader Adolf Hitler;
- Operation Crossroads nuclear weapon tests conducted in the Pacific during summer 1946;
- Aerial bombings;
- Ceremony regarding the treaty to eliminate intermediate-range nuclear missiles signed by former Russian President Gorbachev and U.S. President Ronald Reagan in 1987;
- 1986 Chernobyl nuclear reactor spill in the Ukraine;
- Rainbow Warrior and Greenpeace Movements for environmental protection;
- 1978 Camp David Accords, hosted by former U.S. President Jimmy Carter, who brokered a peace agreement between former Egyptian President Anwar Sadat and former Israeli Prime Minister Menachem Begin;
- 1970s global peace movement featuring John Lennon and Yoko Ono;
- Protestors marching through the streets on every continent;
- Iranian hostage crisis when 52 U.S. diplomats were kidnapped and held for 444 days in 1979;
- Anti-American Libyan leader Muammar al-Gaddafi;
- American Nazi leaders;
- Speeches and funerals of President John F. Kennedy, Presidential candidate Robert F. Kennedy, and slain civil rights leader Martin Luther King, Jr.;
- Hooded Klansmen burning a cross;
- Police brutality, including dogs and water hoses deployed during southern resistance to the American civil rights movement;
- 1970 National Guard shooting of student protestors at Kent State University;
- South Africa's march for the release of former president Nelson Mandela who was imprisoned for decades for anti-apartheid demonstrations, along with Desmond Tutu, the South African

Bishop of the Anglican Church and Nobel Prize winner who oversaw the nation's Truth and Reconciliation Commission;

- Mahatma Gandhi, the spiritual leader of India's Independence Movement, who resisted tyranny thru mass civil disobedience;
- Mother Teresa, Nobel Prize winner and Indian human rights advocate on behalf of the sick, poor, and orphaned;
- Lech Walesa, the union organizer and polish solidarity leader who led Poland out of Communism;
- Chinese student protests of 1987–88, leading up to the massacre of 2000–3000 people in Tiananmen Square;
- Worldwide protests;
- Soup lines;
- Unemployment lines;
- Musician Bob Geldof, Live Aid organizer for a series of rock concerts to raise money for famine victims in Ethiopia where nearly a million people died from hunger;
- Country music legend Willie Nelson, organizer of Farm Aid, the 1985 charity concert to raise money for farm families in the United States driven to bankruptcy;
- Homelessness Awareness Month, with footage of people sleeping on the streets under cardboard boxes;
- Efforts to relieve poverty and hunger across the globe.

The video was deemed a masterpiece. But if Jackson's bold political commentary and visual depictions of the horrors of imperialist tendencies signaled a Lennonesque problem for those in power, it would have been dwarfed in scope by the public fervor ready to be unleashed over the nightmare unfolding in New England.

✺ Spiritual Unrest at the Archdiocese of Boston

The Archdiocese of Boston was eventually forced to produce a written policy to control widespread mismanagement of sexual abuse allegations against members of the clergy. The policy was mandated following the October 1993 indictment, guilty plea, and sentencing of New Bedford, Massachusetts priest James Porter on charges of sodomy and assault on hundreds of victims during a 30-year span across numerous states.[39]

Just an hour north of the courthouse by car, jurors heard the final arguments in the rape trial of Hingham, Massachusetts priest John Hanlon.[40] Two hours west, in Springfield, Massachusetts, Father Richard Lavigne plead guilty to child rape, and remains the primary suspect in the 1972 murder of altar boy Danny Croteau.[41]

But having three cases in a single state on the same day was merely the tip of the iceberg. In 1993, attorney Jeffrey Anderson was prosecuting 200 active Catholic clergy sex abuse cases in 27 states.[42] Indictments of Catholic priests came fast and furious from 1992–93. In the book *Lead Us Not Into Temptation: Catholic Priests and the Sexual Abuse of Children*, author Jason Berry estimated that by 1992, American dioceses had paid out at least $500 million in damages, and predicted the eventual cost of compensating victims would exceed $1 billion.[43]

In August 1994 almost three thousand miles away, a confidential case report completed by the Los Angeles Department of Children and Family Services was leaked to *Hard Copy* television tabloid host Diane Diamond.[44] Within hours of receiving the document, the California affiliate of a British news service sold copies to reporters for $750 each.

---

39. Philip F. Lawler, *Suffer the Children*, Oct. 4, 1993. *See also* www.bishop-account-ability.org/resources/resource-files/media/suffer-pf.htm.

40. *The Sexual Abuse of Children in the Roman Catholic Archdiocese of Boston: A Report by the Attorney General*, July 23, 2003, www.ago.state.ma.us/archdiocese.pdf.

41. *Id.*

42. *Id.*

43. JASON BERRY & ANDREW GREELY, LEAD US NOT INTO TEMPTATION: CATHOLIC PRIESTS AND THE SEXUAL ABUSE OF CHILDREN (2000).

44. Mary A. Fisher, *Was Michael Jackson Framed? The Untold Story*, GQ, Oct. 1994. *See also* http://www.usnewslink.com/framedjackson.htm.

The press offered dramatic headlines promising complete details of Michael Jackson's sexual molestation of a 13-year-old boy.[45] While police contemplated filing a criminal complaint, the boy's father filed a $30 million civil claim alleging sexual battery, seduction, intentional infliction of emotional distress, willful misconduct, fraud, and negligence.[46] Jackson's attorney filed a counterclaim against him for extortion. By September 1994, police officials had interviewed more than four hundred witnesses, but following "more than a year of investigation, accompanied by lurid speculation in the press," prosecutors announced on September 22, 1994, that no child molestation charges would be filed, citing the victim's unwillingness to testify.[47] However, a multimillion dollar settlement was paid to the boy's family by insurers on an unspecified standard of negligence. Jackson's defense attorney, Thomas Mesereau, concluded exactly 12 years later that in 1993 Michael Jackson became the victim of very bad advice: "looking backwards—you know, we can all be Monday-morning quarterbacks in life and change things we've done, but I think if Michael could go back, he would never have settled those cases. He would've fought them to the end and the message would have got out, don't make false claims against Michael Jackson or you're going to trial."[48]

Combing through the massive collection of books, articles, and lawsuits involving Michael Jackson is as surreal as travel to Neverland, that mythical dwelling of Peter Pan, Tinker Bell, and lost boys who never age and refuse to grow up. Chronicles of the well-worn methods and madness advanced in hundreds of attempts to extort money from Jackson on an annual basis could fill a library,

---

45. Darren Brooks, Michael Jackson, An Exceptional Journey: The Unauthorized Biography in Words and Pictures (2002).

46. Seth Mydans, *No Charges for Now Against Michael Jackson*, N.Y. Times, Sept. 22, 1994.

47. *Id.*

48. *Larry King Live*: Michael Jackson's Attorney Speaks Out About Trial (CNN June 14, 2005). See transcript at transcripts.cnn.com/TRANSCRIPTS/0506/14/lkl.01.html.

with his reclusiveness and eccentricities making the situation all the more likely. According to Ohio psychiatrist Phillip Resnick, "It was just a matter of time before someone like Jackson became a target: He's rich, bizarre, hangs around with kids and there is fragility to him. The atmosphere is such that an accusation must mean it happened."[49]

The road to perception and identification of Jackson as a cultural enemy began with marginalization: Jackson was framed as being "outside the circle of wholesome mainstream society," followed by objectification or dehumanization (i.e., relentless labeling and references to Wacko Jacko) and finally demonization: Jackson's friendships with teen boys were portrayed as inescapably sinful.[50]

Individuals seeking to capitalize upon public media's obsession with scandal—as news producers battle one another for the interviews, angles, and rewards attendant to their rush to judgment—know that mere accusations can be leveraged to force a legal settlement. American courts have become a vehicle for extortion, driven by a media circus where ratings, lucrative book deals, and photo ops exist for the fomenting of scandal in lieu of investigations of obvious inconsistencies and personal vendettas. Evan Chandler, the father who originally accused Jackson of molestation was found dead by suicide, following a single gunshot wound to the head in November 2009.[51] The creation of media stars such as former prosecutor Nancy Grace who garner ratings by undermining the presumption of innocence and the fairness of the criminal justice system have become the sine qua non of the infotainment networks. Many outside the righteous, ill-educated, and blood-thirsty brand of Court TV consumers agree with the description of Grace's

---

49. Fisher, *supra* note 45.

50. http://www.publiceye.org/tooclose/scapegoating-01.html, citing JAMES A. AHO, THIS THING OF DARKNESS: A SOCIOLOGY OF THE ENEMY 107–21 (1994).

51. http://www.nbcnewyork.com/news/local-beat/NATLFather-of-Michael-Jackson-Accuser-Commited-Suicide-in-NJ-70323882.html,

coverage of the Jackson trial offered by Los Angeles Attorney Thom Mesereau:

> Her coverage of the Jackson case was sub-moronic. She didn't know the facts; she didn't know the evidence. She didn't know the witnesses. She didn't know what was happening in the courtroom. She tried to spin a verdict through a lot of emotional innuendo that was just buffoonery. When humiliated by the acquittals, she lashed out at jurors ... she was a disgrace.[52]

Her rebuttal included assurances that she was an early fan who had enthusiastically danced to Jackson's music, and the real problem was the public's inability to read between the lines. Grace declared: "If you don't have a problem with a 40 year-old-man in his underwear in bed with a non-relative, 7- or 8- or 9-year-old, that's your business. I have a problem with it ... I've tried too many molestation cases not to care."[53] One presumed fact (never established) ... case closed! TV coverage dominated by pundits, new specials, and round-the-clock polling and pre-evidentiary forecasting undermines our values and compromises the criminal justice system.

Former Jackson employees who first testified that they never witnessed anything sexual between Michael and the children who visited his Santa Barbara ranch were known to recant after their extortion attempts failed. More importantly, the fact they were still invited to testify for the prosecution as credible witnesses seemed to escape media notice.

There was, however, a general consensus among serious journalists that the Santa Barbara prosecutor involved in the child molestation cases exploited the tabloid-style reporting of public media.

---

52. Caitlin A. Johnson, "Nancy Grace Stands Behind Jackson Coverage, Court TV Personality Says She Still Believes Michael Jackson Was Guilty of Child Molestation", *CBS Sunday Morning News*, Mar. 7, 2007. *See also* http://www.cbsnews.com/stories/2007/03/07/sunday/main2543490.shtml.

53. *Id.*

Tom Sneddon's announcements of an investigation into the allegations in 1993 and 2003 were predicated upon building a case with smoke and mirrors. Numerous suits against Sneddon for abusing the power of the district attorney have been brought during his time in office. Legal verdicts and settlements on claims of civil rights violations; abuse of prosecutorial discretion; official misconduct; false arrest; false imprisonment; illegal wiretaps; and discriminatory, abusive, and defamatory behavior have reportedly cost Santa Barbara tax payers millions of dollars.

Various conspiracy theories as to why Jackson was charged (though highly entertaining and filled with enough demonstrable claims to insure they would survive for another decade or two) lack irrefutable proof of a conspiracy between California prosecutors and other parties. Descriptions and evidence of the malice and money that motivated individual actors abound, which together created the perfect storm for a public debacle.

Yet to prove and punish an actual conspiracy to imprison Jackson, we would need a smoking gun so hot that actually finding one lies beyond the realm of probability. Although Jackson had not yet become the threat Lennon remained as a revolutionary activist, we would have to concede that stopping his momentum before he gained that level of potency might have been discussed in certain quarters. However, it was the timing alone in terms of pursuing claims against Jackson that suggests an equally plausible reason: the need for a child-molesting poster boy so large that it would effectively divert public attention so that collective anger against the Catholic Church would not insure its ultimate and speedy demise.

Mass social unrest at the unraveling of the façade, of the former glory of the Catholic faith, demanded a target upon which deeply unwanted thoughts and feelings could be unconsciously projected. In psychopathology, projection occurs in an instant. The timing of both sets of allegation and charges against Jackson suggests that beyond his threat to the status quo, he was a handy and convenient target for an establishment in desperate need of a scapegoat to spare the legions of Church leaders, who according to one study for decades "kept horrific tales of abuse out of the public eye through an elaborate culture of secrecy, deception and intimidation. Victims who came forward with abuse claims were ignored or paid off, while accused priests were quietly transferred."[54]

By 2002, the Massachusetts attorney general issued a public statement citing "sufficient evidence of a church cover-up" to proceed with criminal prosecution against the archdiocese under standard doctrines of liability.[55] A number of Catholic bishops were subpoenaed to appear before a state grand jury. "Far from being unaware of abusive behavior, Cardinal Law and his deputies had detailed information on many of the archdiocese's most serious molesters . . . [including] reports of child rape and other criminal behavior by clergymen, [while leaders] made no apparent effort to inform law enforcement authorities.[56] As public furor grew, other dioceses began confronting abusive clergy in their ranks." By the end of 2002, some 1,200 priests had been accused of abuse nationwide. "[R]epeat abusers, including priests who traded drugs for sex with minors, fathered children, and physically assaulted their victims," were known predators that church officials shuffled from parish to another—where they abused again.[57]

2002 was the year for broadcast of the escalating peril to an already weakened Catholic Empire:

As the U.S. Catholic Church battles the most sordid scandal in its history, it is fighting to preserve its moral and spiritual authority as the largest nongovernmental institution in American life. Yet even as it does so, another catastrophe looms—one that is not about sex abuse and priests but about money and management. The fierce scrutiny that is piercing the Church's

---

54. http://www.boston.com/globe/spotlight/abuse/scandal/.

55. http://www.boston.com/globe/spotlight/abuse/investigations/.

56. http://www.boston.com/globe/spotlight/abuse/scandal/.

57. http://www.boston.com/globe/spotlight/abuse/predators/.

veil of secrecy over sex is also beginning to reveal the largely hidden state of its finances.[58]

In the next year, on November 18, 2003, police carried out a pre-dawn search of Michael Jackson's 2,600-acre ranch.[59] Seventy county sheriffs accompanied by members of the district attorney's office presided over a day-long raid. On April 30, 2004, Jackson was charged with 10 felony counts, including child molestation, extortion, child abduction, false imprisonment, and giving a minor an intoxicating agent.

According to *Rolling Stone*, Jackson's trial was nothing less than a zoo and a freak show. "The prosecution's case, seldom satisfactorily explained in the mainstream media, went as follows"[60]:

On February 6th, 2003, the Bashir documentary, in which Jackson is seen admitting that he sleeps in his bedroom with young boys, is shown on British TV. Among the children who appear in the video is his accuser. According to the prosecution, Jackson had not molested the boy at the time the Bashir documentary aired, but he was sufficiently concerned that the boy might make such allegations that he and a band of Neverland courtiers entered into an elaborate conspiracy to "falsely imprison" the boy and his family for nearly five weeks (in luxury hotels, at Neverland ranch and other places), during which time they coerced the family into denying, on camera, that anything untoward had ever happened between Jackson and the boy. None of Jackson's five alleged co-conspirators were ever indicted. It was after the

---

58. William C. Symonds, *The Economic Strain on the Church, Legal Liabilities from the Sex Scandal Threaten a U.S. Catholic Church Already Beset by Systemic Financial Problem*, BUS. WEEK, Apr. 15, 2002.

59. Duncan Campbell, *Police Raid Jackson Ranch Following Fresh Allegations from Boy, 13*, THE GUARDIAN, Nov. 19, 2003.

60. MATT TAIBBI, SMELLS LIKE DEAD ELEPHANTS: DISPATCHES FROM A ROTTING EMPIRE 5 (2007).

filming of this so-called rebuttal video—which, incidentally, Jackson then sold to the Fox Network for $3 million—and after authorities had begun an investigation into Jackson's relationship with the boy, that Jackson allegedly molested the child, in early March. The prosecution's case therefore boils down to this: In a panic over negative publicity, Jackson conspires to kidnap a boy and force him to deny acts of molestation that in fact never happened, and then he gets over his panic just long enough to actually molest the child at the very moment when the whole world is watching.[61]

Prosecutor Thom Sneddon hired a public relations firm, nine fingerprint experts, and a jury consultant; he also developed a Web site at the sheriff's department to collect information on Michael Jackson. According to author A. Jones, the media push for a conviction was fueled by the spiraling expectation of a billion dollar Michael Jackson "Convicted Molester Cottage Industry" in films, prison-reality TV, books, and so forth.[62]

Jackson's political tome "Man in the Mirror", exhorting all to "look at yourself and make a change" was eclipsed in meta search engines by *Man in the Mirror: The Michael Jackson Story*, which first aired in August of 2004. The last scene portrays Jackson exiting the courtroom after his first pretrial hearing on January 16, 2004. The show conveniently aired just as his trial was scheduled to begin. The most objective review of this film states that it:

Tracks Jackson's life from the early days of stardom in the Jackson Five up through the latest allegations of child molestation and scandal—even managing to throw in a Martin Bashir look-alike. Despite claims on the DVD packaging that this film would sidestep (and I quote) ". . . (O)verdone plastic surgery, pet chimps,

---

61. *Id.*

62. Aphrodite Jones, Michael Jackson Conspiracy (2007).

dangling babies, extravagant spending sprees and lurid allegations," it pretty much proceeds to do just that and ignore what is offered up as the film's real raison d'etre: "...(T)rack(ing) Jackson's complicated rise to superstardom—where he came from, how it shaped him, the impact he made on pop culture, and most importantly, who the MAN IN THE MIRROR (emphasis theirs) really is."[63]

✎ Loss of Faith, Accountability, and Responsibility for American Children

As a testament to the morass that is the current state of public discourse, multiple opportunities were lost in the decade of speculation about Jackson, most significantly to discuss the failure of leadership in the Catholic Church and the culpability of their lawyers. "The Shameful Role of Lawyers in the Church Sex Abuse Scandal"[64] is a March 2004 essay by UCLA Professor Stephen Bainbridge wrote a March 2004 essay, titled The Shameful Role of Lawyers in the Church Sex Scandal, for the Mirror of Justice blog that primarily deals with Catholic Legal Theory. His essay notes the grievous errors outlined in the National Review Board report, and describes how "Attorneys used 'tactics' [that] often were inappropriate for the Church, and which tended to compound the effects of the abuse that already had been inflicted."[65] These tactics included defenses that "could be construed as blaming the victim," arguing that priests were "independent contractors," requiring victims to

---

63. Preston Jones, pop music critic for the *Fort Worth Star-Telegram*, http://www. dvdtalk.com/reviews/14653/man-in-the-mirror-the-michael-jackson-story/.

64. *The Shameful Role of Lawyers in the Church Sex Abuse Scandal*, Mar. 13, 2004, http://www.mirrorofjustice.com/mirrorofjustice/2004/03/the_shameful_ro. html.

65. *Id.*

sign confidentiality agreements, and discouraging apologies to victims, thereby undermining "the primary pastoral mission of the bishops, [and leading] to greater legal liability. Misguided perception of the lawyers' loyalty to the Church closed down discussion of a morally superior means of responding to the sex abuse problem. . . . [I]t cannot be gainsaid that, on the whole, the involvement of lawyers made this serious problem a greater disaster."[66] Bainbridge underscores how we missed a profound opportunity we missed for renewed commitment to the greater social good by examining ways to put a permanent end to the exploitation of children everywhere it occurs.

Notably, public media also failed to discuss the long-term ramifications of the crisis of faith experienced by Catholics shocked and stunned all over the world. It failed to educate the public around the prevalence of child sexual abuse in general. It missed a golden opportunity to discuss the plight of child stars. Raised in a large family led by a perfectionist, domineering father and a protective mother who is a devout Jehovah's Witness, Michael Jackson perfectly captured and expressed his life-long dilemma: "My childhood was completely taken away from me. There was no Christmas. There were no birthdays. . . ." [67]

Dr. Jane O'Connor, in her book *Cultural Significance of the Child Star*, explores "the paradoxical status of the child star who is both adored and reviled in contemporary society."[68] O'Connor notes that the concept of transgression in relation to child stars does not typically arise in relation to individual deviant behavior, but rather embodies their special form of social transgression. From a sociological and anthropological perspective, it is the very status of being a child star: "a child who had crossed the fundamental line between childhood and adulthood by working, being economically

---

66. *Id.*

67. http://biography.jrank.org/pages/2808/Jackson-Michael.html.

68. Jane O'Connor, The Cultural Significance of the Child Star (2008).

independent, and having a career without having reached adulthood either chronologically or having passed the liminal stage of adolescence."[69] The boundaries of our social order demand restoration of the balance of power in American society by requiring those who "missed the right of passage to adulthood the first time around to . . . [go] through some kind of identity crisis or publicly shared trauma in later years" before they are accepted as full members of American society.[70]

As a young adult, Jackson transformed himself into a first order world-renowned humanitarian. He created Neverland as a respite where he could experience the joys of his missed childhood when taking a break from the handlers and lawyers who spent most of their time defending him against extortion. He lived there in relative peace until forced to pay the piper as the pressures of political expediency and the need to control his rising political influences burst into a display of multimedia pyrotechnics the world will not soon forget. An American icon: August 28, 1958—June 25, 2009, Michael Jackson will be missed; may he finally rest in peace.

69. *Id.* at 81.

70. *Id.* at 83.

Conclusion

Nascent Influence on Western Democracy

The 20th century has been characterized by three developments of great political importance: The growth of democracy, the growth of corporate power, and the growth of corporate propaganda as a means of protecting corporate power against democracy.[1]

—Alex Carey

ℳ Growth of Democracy

Twenty-first century discourse concerning the rights of all citizens to participate in the political process at all levels of government obscures the long-fought struggle for these rights, neglects the fact they were virtually nonexistent until well into the 20th century, and overlooks the reality that they remain increasingly difficult to fully exercise. Comparative reviews of social and political theories in the West often equate the longest enduring Constitution of the United States with the greatest living democracy. The text and amendments are offered as proof of the extent to which we have formulated laws and legal remedies that remain consistent with our highest ideals of liberty, autonomy, and governance for the general welfare.

---

1. Alex Carey, Taking the Risk Out of Democracy, Corporate Propaganda versus Freedom and Liberty 10 (1997).

The legacy of group rights favoring elite white males at the nation's founding began to give way as the Industrial Revolution altered the political and economic structure in ways that led to demands for change in the existing system of political representation. Significant developments in constitutional doctrine can be traced to meaningful attempts to transform original property rights in the labor of slaves, wives, livestock, and their offspring into short-term contractual, status, or employment relationships that embody fairness and equity—a process that evolved throughout the 20th century. U.S. Supreme Court Justice Stephen Breyer believes that growth of democratic institutions comes with perfecting the practice of interpreting the Constitution as creating: "a coherent framework for a certain kind of government . . . [T]hat government is democratic; it avoids concentration of too much power in too few hands; it protects personal liberty; it insists that the law respect each individual equally; and it acts only upon the basis of law itself."[2]

Individual freedom from unwarranted governmental regulation of the personal and occupational lives of American citizens, as a matter of civil rights, remains at the heart of the struggle. In 1848, suffragist Susan B. Anthony resolved that "in view of this entire disenfranchisement, of one-half the people of this country, their social and religious degradation—in view of the unjust laws mentioned above, and because women do feel themselves aggrieved, oppressed and fraudulently deprived of their most sacred rights, we insist that they have immediate admission to all the rights and privileges which belong to them as citizens of the United States."[3]

The right to vote—originally denied to women despite their status as "citizens"— came in 1920 with the passage of the 19th

---

2. STEPHEN BREYER, ACTIVE LIBERTY: INTERPRETING OUR DEMOCRATIC CONSTITUTIOn (2005).

3. Kristin E. Kandt, *In the Name of God; An American Story of Feminism, Racism, and Religious Intolerance: The Story of Alma Bridwell White*, 8 AM. U. J. GENDER SOC. POL'Y & L. 753 (2000). *See also* http://www.nps.gov/wori/report1.htm.

Amendment, 52 years after Anthony's resolution. Forty-three years following ratification of the Nineteenth Amendment, Martin L. King, Jr. in a famous 1963 address known as "I Have a Dream" stated "the life of the Negro is still sadly crippled by the manacles of segregation and the chains of discrimination. One hundred years later [following emancipation from slavery], the Negro lives on a lonely island of poverty in the midst of a vast ocean of material prosperity."[4] Passage of the 1965 Voting Rights Act fulfilled a promise made but not kept in 1875 with the passage of the Fifteenth Amendment.

The 1965 Act opened the floodgates for federal enforcement of the right to vote for Black America. An April 2009 news report on the oral arguments in a case before the U.S. Supreme Court that involves a southern official's challenge to the Voting Rights Act concedes: "The tenor of the quick-paced argument suggested that there could be a court majority to strike down the provision of the voting rights law that has been the Justice Department's main enforcement tool against discriminatory changes in voting since the law was enacted in 1965. It opened elections to millions of blacks and other minorities."[5]

Formal equality leading to historic elections may yet fail to lead us to historic change. Hence, equitable changes that are sure to last are the only change in which we can believe. This does not reflect upon the wisdom of placing Barack Obama at the helm, but rather raises the question of whether the worldwide sigh of relief over his victory signals misplaced longing for:

[T]he age when Parties stood for defined positions and specific interests within society. It was the child of modernity—the industrial age, which triggered deep and well defined conflicts.

---

4. Martin Luther King, Jr., "I Have a Dream" (Aug. 28, 1963), http://www.usconstitution.net/dream.html.

5. Mark Sherman, *Skepticism at High Court on Voting Rights Measure*, Associated Press, Apr. 29, 2009. *See also* http://www.wtopnews.com/?nid=25&sid=1664270.

Today we have moved into a post-industrial age but political parties still reflect the behavioral patterns of industrial modernity. Political parties play the adversarial game of political contact by exaggerating the most trivial difference into an illusion of grandeur. They grandstand their politics into what is often the theatre of the absurd—absurd because it is not grand, most of the grand ideas have gone. . . .[6]

𝍦 Growth of Corporate Power

In 1997, Jane Wardlow Prettyman published a double review[7] of Ben Bagdikian's book *The Media Monopoly*,[8] along with *Censored 1997*.[9] *Media Monopoly* reported that 14 years prior (in 1983), 50 corporations owned most of the media.[10] Media was then defined largely as TV, radio, print, trade books, and movies. However, by 1997 technological advances and governmental deregulation led to large-scale mergers and acquisitions that brought the number down to 10. In 2009, we appear to be down to 6 traditional mediums, with a host of new digitally driven interactive media accessed through the World Wide Web. Various means and types of organizations through which information and ideas are transmitted to the public have expanded well beyond the traditional realms of publication upon which much of the current legal doctrine is based. Books, magazines, journals, newspapers, private or commercially owned television and radio broadcasters (whether via cable or satellite),

---

6. Francis Sealey, *Our Sorry Democracy*, SOC. ENTERPRISE, Nov. 8, 2008. *See also* http://www.justmeans.com/editorials/socialenterprise/329.html.

7. Jane Wardlow Prettyman, *Some Things Considered*, THE AM. REPORTER, Sept. 14, 1997. *See also* http://www.americanreview.us/bagrevu.htm.

8. BEN H. BAGDIKIAN, THE MEDIA MONOPOLY (1997).

9. PETER PHILLIPS & PROJECT CENSORED. CENSORED 1997: THE NEWS THAT DIDN'T MAKE THE NEWS (1997).

10. BAGDIKIAN, *supra* note 8.

and nearly all types of theater, movies, film, and video provide avenues for publication.

In 2010, personal identifiers of nearly every user of the Internet for information and services is locked in a data web from which it is impossible to escape. As the ability to track our pathways meets the incentive to do so, the increased monitoring of all communication devices coupled with revolutionary methods for recording, tracking, processing and storage of data, has changed the world as we know it.[11] The sheer volume of consumer information and preferences, including photographs on social networking sites alone have increased the demand for system changes. Despite assurances concerning privacy, Facebook (in competition with Twitter) has information programs "that will allow third-party developers to create applications that pull in Facebook 'streams'—the current of status updates, photos and links that members see."[12] This would allow ordinary monitoring of the "stream of information from [individuals'] Facebook friends, and contribut[ion] to it, without ever visiting Facebook.com."[13]

Thus, the expansion of media platforms along with the concentration of ownership makes Prettyman's review of the second book all the more relevant. She describes *Project Censored* at Sonoma State University that began in 1976 as "an annual review of the systemic withholding of public access to important news facts by the mainstream media."[14]

In 1997, an analytic team of professors and students, including novice researchers and veteran analysts, selected the top 25 most important undercovered news stories from hundreds of

---

11. Julie E. Cohen, *Privacy, Ideology, and Technology: A Response to Jeffrey Rosen*, 89 GEO. L.J. 2029 (2001).

12. Brad Stone, *Facebook Lets Others Tap Its Information Stream*, N.Y. TIMES, Apr. 27, 2009. *See also* http://bits.blogs.nytimes.com/2009/04/27/facebook-lets-others-tap-its-information-stream/.

13. *Id.*

14. Jane Wardlow Prettyman, *Some Things Considered*, THE AM. REP., Sept. 14, 1997.

nominations and found that the under reported stories "upset corporate interests," shed light on ultra-conservative and militia activities, involved racism, and included suppression of human rights."[15]

In 2008, four Global Research Writers received the Project Censored Award: Constance Fogal, Stephen Lendman, Michel Chossudovsky, and William Engdahl.[16] A common thread in the unreported stories in 2008 was the media's routine coverage of terrorist attacks without discussing how public "fear of attacks is used to manipulate the public and set policy."[17] Seven Stories Press publishes a yearly analysis of mainstream media's suppression of topics that fly under the radar. In 2008, war and civil liberties stood out. The top picks were the stories reporting:

1.   Federal funding for the study of radicalism that led to the quiet expansion of the North American Free Trade Agreement [NAFTA];

2.   U.S. refusal to keep count of the number of Iraqi civilians killed in the war;

3.   Widespread use of fearmongering to silence individuals and expand power;

4.   Expansion of InfraGard, consisting of some 23,000 members of the business community that "tip off the feds in exchange for preferential treatment in the event of a crisis."[18] "Eighty-six chapters coordinate with 56 FBI field offices nationwide";

5.   ILEA: Training for counterinsurgency death squad leaders. The school opened in June 2005 (before Salvadoran government approval) with "$3.6 million from the U.S.

---

15. *Id.*

16. *The 10 Big News Stories the Mainstream Media IGNORED*, Syracuse News Times, Oct. 1, 2008. *See also* http://www.globalresearch.ca/index.php?context=va&aid=10411.

17. *Id.*

18. *Id.*

Treasury and staffed with instructors from the DEA, Immigration and Customs Enforcement, and the FBI, and tasked with annually training 1,500 police officers, judges, prosecutors and other law enforcement agents in counter-terrorism techniques." "Critics point out that Salvadoran police, who account for 25 percent of the graduates, have become more violent." Furthermore, "a May 2007 report by Tutela Legal implicated Salvadoran National Police officers in eight death squad-style assassinations in 2006";

6. A 2007 Executive Order allowing immediate seizure of assets of anyone who "directly or indirectly" poses a risk to the war in Iraq. "Critics say the orders bypass the right to due process and the vague language makes manipulation and abuse possible. Protesting the war could be perceived as undermining or threatening U.S. efforts in Iraq";

7. An October 2007, congressional appropriation of $22 million to establish a 10-member National Commission on the Prevention of Violent Radicalization and Homegrown Terrorism, as well as a university-based Center of Excellence "to examine the social, criminal, political, psychological and economic roots of domestic terrorism." The policy "redefines civil disobedience as terrorism;"

8. H-2 visas in the guest worker program that resemble slavery and "modern-day indentured servitude." A report released in March 2007 concludes that "guest workers do not enjoy the most fundamental protection of a competitive labor market—the ability to change jobs if they are mistreated. Instead, they are bound to the employers who 'import' them. If guest workers complain about abuses, they face deportation, blacklisting or other retaliation." In 2005, the program included 32,000 agricultural and 89,000 nonagricultural workers;

9. Media failure to adequately cover the Silver Spring, Maryland, Winter Soldier hearings, "where 300 veterans from the wars in Iraq and Afghanistan convened for four days of

public testimony. Their testimony was entered into the congressional record and filmed and shown at the Cannes Film Festival." Instead, many major news outlets managed to send staff to cover New York City's Fashion Week;

10. American Psychological Association approval of psychologists helping the CIA with "interrogation and torture of Guantanamo detainees . . . in spite of objections from many of its 148,000 members";

11. Pundits being paid to push No Child Left Behind to the detriment of the nation's children;

12. The way we lost track of billions of dollars in Iraq;

13. New hazards associated with nuclear waste disposal;

14. Worldwide slavery;

15. Cruelty and death in juvenile detention centers;

16. Japanese officials' suspicions about the official account of 9/11 and the Global War on Terror; and

17. Removal of N.Y. Governor Eliot Spitzer from office, after he became increasingly vocal about the need for legislative penalties for mortgage fraud and . . . predatory lending. Spitzer warned:

When history tells the story of the sub-prime lending crisis and recounts its devastating effects on the lives of so many innocent homeowners, the Bush administration will not be judged favorably . . . it will be judged as a willing accomplice to the lenders who went to any lengths in their quest for profits. The administration was so willing, in fact, that it used the power of the federal government in an unprecedented assault on state legislatures, as well as on state attorneys general and anyone else on the side of consumers.[19]

---

19. Eliot Spitzer, *Predatory Lenders' Partner in Crime: How the Bush Administration Stopped the States from Stepping In to Help Consumers*, THE WASH. POST, Feb. 14, 2008, A25.

𝘔 Growth of Corporate Propaganda

According to Glenn Greenwald, the misappropriation of concepts related to pragmatism and the exhortation to remain "realistic" keeps the average individual in a state of endless speculation about what others find acceptable or which stimuli are likely to produce a desired response, both of which tend to overshadow the desire for mutual problem solving.[20]

Edward Bernays stated the obvious when he remarked:

> If we understand the mechanism and motives of the group mind, it is now possible to control and regiment the masses according to our will, without their knowing it. In almost every act of our daily lives within the sphere of politics or business, in our social conduct or our ethical thinking, we are dominated by the relatively small number of persons who understand the mental processes and social patterns of the masses.[21]

Our freedom depends on an independent media and its ability to report news rather than opinion—as much as justice depends upon an independent judiciary with loyalty to the public above political factions. News from as wide a range of sources as possible is the only contemporary method to avoid falling victim to endless repetition. Propaganda has been defined by Randall Bytwerk as "the art of very nearly deceiving one's friends while not quite convincing one's enemies."[22] Lately in the United States, it appears to take the form of encouraging the masses to turn a collective

---

20. Jay Rosen, *Audience Atomization Overcome: Why the Internet Weakens the Authority of the Press*, PRESS THINK, Jan. 12, 2009. *See also* http://journalism. nyu.edu/pubzone/weblogs/pressthink/2009/01/12/atomization.html.

21. EDWARD BERNAYS, PROPAGANDA 71 (2004).

22. RANDALL L. BENDING SPINES: THE PROPAGANDAS OF NAZI GERMANY AND THE GERMAN DEMOCRATIC REPUBLIC BYTWERK, 2 (2004).

blind eye to social phenomena that converge with such great distraction as to destroy the anticipated relationship among democracy, justice, and legitimacy in the media. An article written for the *Journal of Comparative Economics* discusses various approaches to political economy and the strong empirical evidence for the argument that "inefficient policies and institutions are prevalent, and that they are chosen because they serve the interest of politicians or social groups holding power, at the expense of the society at large."[23]

The lack of public debate about the manipulation of public discourse, especially concerning the shrinking number of corporate owners of media—alongside the great-give away—is astounding. Consumer activist Ralph Nader and others have lamented the fact that in 1996, "Congress quietly handed over to existing broadcasters the rights to broadcast digital television on the public airwaves [free of charge]—a conveyance worth $70 billion."[24] John Stauber believes that U.S. journalism is in vast demise: "There's been tremendous downsizing, tremendous conglomeration; journalism is in demise, and its collapse is opening ever more opportunities for PR (public relations) practitioners to increase their influence in the newsroom."[25]

Given the psychology of media control and the sociology of media power, how can we continue with the mergers and deregulation that draw us closer to the black hole of public dialogue. Widespread violations of privacy and decency standards have become full-blown impediments to full and free democratic debate. Commercialized interests now control the media and specialize in producing commodities for sale, while predatory lenders ran amok and the lives of celebrities are served up at the tabloid-style buffet.

23. Daron Acemoglu, *Why Not a Political Case Theorem? Social Conflict, Commitment, and Politics*, 31 J. COMP. ECON. 620–52 (2003).

24. http://www.issues2000.org/Ralph_Nader_Technology.htm.

25. John Stauber, *Corporate PR: A Threat to Journalism*, http://www.abc.net.au/rn/talks/bbing/stories/s10602.htm.

Artificial linkages equating celebrity morals and lifestyles to legitimate public discovery of and opinion regarding the ideas and attitudes of political leaders have lulled a nation to sleep and failed to promote honest political debate.[26]

Privately owned media in Europe are bound to observe rights confirmed by the European Human Rights Convention because they perform a public function. Advancing the cause of open debate in a democracy brings us back to questions of public ownership and regulation. If the press is to serve the primary watchdog function with a particular view toward monitoring the hefty alliances between government and big business, then forcing media to rely upon the goodwill and clear conscious of either the government or corporations for monetary support bodes poorly for protection of the public interest.

Having relied upon corporate sponsors during the past 30 years, the print media is now threatened with its complete demise. It is widely claimed that people stopped paying for news when it became free on the Internet. That explanation dominates the echo chamber. But the truth may be that people stopped buying papers when they found them less than newsworthy and of limited practical value, in comparison to saving trees or packing with bubble wrap in a highly mobile society, or because wood stoves, charcoal grills, and fireplaces went out of fashion with the advent of central heat and air conditioning and easy-to-clean propane-powered BBQ grills. Whatever the cause, the social impact of the decreased number of owners, cross-media ownership, and monopolies by major corporations has all but escaped public debate.

When press freedom was expanded throughout the 20th century in the United States, professional journalists—hired for their instincts concerning the news and their years of experience with investigative journalism—were in complete control of the content of the news as an editorial board charged with the responsibility of informing the public. Those decisions were not designed to protect

---

26. Lingens v Austria, 8 EHRR 407 (1986).

the profit margins, shareholders and directors of multinational corporations. As the mergers severely narrowed the field of competition, scholar Howard Davis observed that there was little reason to think that a free, competitive market will necessarily produce plural and critical press presenting the full range of reasonable ideas about the world to the reading public rather than a preponderance of broadly right-wing, non socialist, views which will not seek to undermine either the predilections of press barons or the needs of media corporations to promote consumer capitalism."[27]

Our current circumstances provide the clearest evidence. No one is suggesting that all programming be government-run; however, developing a mechanism for weeding out grossly unfair and hateful propaganda is not just a matter of decency, but necessary for the survival of democracy. The number of Americans who are lately discovering that cable programming is filled with talking heads without formal training in journalism or many of the other areas in which they claim expertise, demonstrates the tremendous toll this has taken on the quality of public discourse. Two incidents demonstrate just how much ground we have lost and where we are headed as a nation.

✐ May They Rest in Peace

As President Obama said at his commencement address to Notre Dame University on May 17, 2009: "As citizens of a vibrant and varied democracy, how do we engage in vigorous debate? How does each of us remain firm in our principles and fight for what we consider right without demonizing those with just as strongly held convictions on the other side?"

---

27. HOWARD DAVIS, HUMAN RIGHTS AND CIVIL LIBERTIES 186 (2003).

News Report

Dr. George Tiller, an outspoken advocate for abortion rights and one of the few late-term abortion providers in the country, was shot dead in church yesterday morning in Wichita, Kansas.[28]

Author Cristina Page notes that in March 1993, three months into Bill Clinton's administration, "Abortion provider Dr. David Gunn was murdered in Pensacola, Florida, [representing] the beginning of what would become a five-fold increase in violence against abortion providers throughout the Clinton years;[29] [the May 31, 2009] assassination of Dr. George Tiller comes 5 months" into Obama's term. This is far from a statistical anomaly, as there were no murders, attempted murders, and only one clinic bombing during the entire Bush administration, but during Clinton's administration there were 6 murders of abortion providers and clinic staff, 17 attempted murders, and 12 bombings or arsons. "One can only conclude that like terrorist sleeper cells, these extremists have now been set in motion. Indeed the evidence is already there. The chatter, the threats, the hate-filled rhetoric are abundant." She continues, "The recent execution of Tiller, 67, is not only tragic but ominous. He was born into an era when being an abortion provider meant saving women's lives."[30]

Where should we lay blame? According to one blogger, it would be Fox News pundit Bill O'Reilly: "No other person bears as much responsibility for the characterization of Tiller as a savage on the loose, killing babies":

---

28. Peter Rothberg, *George Tiller's Assassination*, THE NATION, June 1, 2009, http://www.thenation.com/blogs/actnow/439831/george_tiller_s_assassination.

29. Christina Page, *The Murder of Dr. Tiller, a Foreshadowing*, DEMOCRATIC UNDERGROUND, May 31, 2009. *See also* http://www.democraticunderground.com/discuss/duboard.php?az=view_all&address=103x452894.

30. *Id.*

Tiller's name first appeared on "The Factor" on Feb. 25, 2005. Since then, O'Reilly and his guest hosts have brought up the doctor on 28 more episodes, including April 27 of this year. Almost invariably, he is described as "Tiller the Baby Killer, [who] destroys fetuses for just about any reason right up until the birth date for $5,000." He's guilty of "Nazi stuff," (June 8, 2005); a moral equivalent to NAMBLA and al-Qaida (March 15, 2006). "Mao's China, Hitler's Germany, Stalin's Soviet Union," (Nov. 9, 2006). O'Reilly has also frequently linked Tiller to his longtime obsession, child molestation and rape. Because a young teenager who received an abortion could have been a victim of statutory rape, O'Reilly frequently suggested that the clinic was covering up for child rapists (rather than teenage boyfriends) by refusing to release records on the abortions performed.

A Gentle Soul

While attending the University of Wyoming, 21-year-old Matthew Shepard was tortured and murdered near Laramie on October 6–7, 1998. The perpetrators, Aaron McKinney and Russell Henderson, offered Shepard a ride in their car, then robbed, pistol-whipped, and tortured him before tying him to a fence in a remote rural area where he was left to die. Shepard was discovered 18 hours later, then still alive but in a coma.[31]

Fred Phelps, leader of the Westboro Baptist Church of Topeka, Kansas, picketed Shepard's funeral displaying signs with the following slogans: "Matt Shepard rots in Hell", "AIDS Kills Fags Dead," and "God Hates Fags." Shepard's father was forced to wear a bulletproof vest under his suit when he spoke at his son's funeral service.[32]

---

31. http://www.geocities.com/corkymcg/crime/proj005.html.

32. http://www.onphilanthropy.com/site/News2?page=NewsArticle&id=6871.

After the Wyoming Supreme Court ruled that it was legal to display religious messages on city property (in a case involving the Ten Commandments), Phelps attempted and failed to gain city permits in Cheyenne and Casper to build a monument. He proposed a 6-foot marble or granite monument with a bronze plaque bearing a picture of Shepard next to the words: "MATTHEW SHEPARD, Entered Hell October 12, 1998, in Defiance of God's Warning: 'Thou shalt not lie with mankind as with womankind; it is abomination.' Leviticus 18:22."[33]

According to one writer, our interconnected world has led to circumstances where the U.S. Supreme Court now grapples with how to view foreign legal precedent. As we discuss these and other cases in Advanced Constitutional law classes, students question how we might regulate this type of behavior. There are countless ways and means that have been undertaken abroad with great success. The one question that needs answering before we can move toward meaningful resolution is as follows: if O'Reilly's level of incitement, and Phelps so-called protest and free speech could not lawfully occur in our neighboring country of Canada, or in our friendly allied nations in Europe, as keepers of the Western democratic flame why is it possible here? Whose interest does it serve, and where is it leading? It is time to look in the mirror, and if our collective goal is to make the world a better place, then the time has come for meaningful change.

---

33. http://en.wikipedia.org/wiki/Matthew_Shepard.

Index